M106

THE TRUCKER'S WORLD

" Is,

Our journey!
Our destination!
Our love.

Traffic Safety Series

Published in Cooperation with
The Insurance Corporation of British Columbia

J. Peter Rothe, *The Trucker's World*. 1991. ISBN: 1-56000-551-3.

J. Peter Rothe, ed., *Challenging the Old Order: Towards New Directions in Traffic Safety Theory*. 1990. ISBN: 0-88738-828-0.

J. Peter Rothe, ed., *Rethinking Young Drivers*. 1989. ISBN: 0-88738-785-3.

J. Peter Rothe, *The Safety of Elderly Drivers: Yesterday's Young in Today's Traffic*. 1989. ISBN: 0-88738-728-4.

J. Peter Rothe and Peter J. Cooper, *Never Say Always: Perspectives on Seatbelt Use*. 1989. ISBN: 0-88738-775-6.

J. Peter Rothe and Peter J. Cooper, eds., *Motorcyclists: Image and Reality*. 1989. ISBN: 0-88738-784-5.

THE TRUCKER'S WORLD

Risk, Safety and Mobility

J. Peter Rothe

Transaction Publishers
New Brunswick (U.S.A.) and London (U.K.)

Library of Congress Catalog Number: 90-28971
ISBN: 1-56000-551-3 (paper); 1-56000-023-6 (cloth)
Printed in the United States of America

Library of Congress Cataloging-in-Publication Data

Rothe, John Peter, 1948–
     The trucker's world: risk, safety, and mobility / by J. Peter Rothe.
     p.   cm. – (Traffic safety series)
     A project of the Insurance Corporation of British Columbia.
     ISBN: 1-56000-551-3 (paper); 1-56000-023-6 (cloth)
     1. Truck driving. 2. Traffic safety. I. Insurance Corporation of British Columbia. II. Title. III. Series.
TL230.3.R78   1991
363.12'59–dc20   90–28971
                                                               CIP

*To Nicco, Blaise and Barb
whose love reminds me daily that
my project is worthwhile.*

Contents

Preface

In Canada and the United States, the topic of truck driver risk and safety and its consequences burst upon the consciousness of safety agencies and government policy developers in the late 1970s. Unfortunately, the upsurge of interest has been a fragmented one where hot safety issues such as driver fatigue, inadequate vehicle maintenance or use of illicit drugs have been studied in isolation from the truckers' broader socioeconomic environment.

Most often truckers are requested to complete structured questionnaires at roadside stops upon which researchers establish safety related trends. Accident data bases consisting of messy statistics are continuously being analyzed and causes of fault in crashes are determined with uncanny regularity. Policy makers pounce on these data to define truck driver risk-taking and to develop regulatory policies intended to solve the safety problems.

Invariably research into the larger social, political and economic forces that effect the production of truckers' safety problems has been scarce. Yet, I believe it is the socioeconomic environment in which truck driving occurs that has profound implications on driver decision-making and behavior. For example, a trucker who operates a rig while fatigued usually does so to fulfill the everyday needs and expectations demanded by the company dispatcher. To maximize the profits of a carrier, the dispatcher may pressure the driver to undertake driving challenges that are considered high risk and illegal. It is this influence of which we know virtually nothing. Yet it is vital for earnestly developing comprehensive policies.

In this book I have come to terms with the socioeconomic environment that pronouncedly affects the breakdown in trucker safety. Rather than magnify the structure of the trucking industry and statistics on such economic features as operating expenses, profitability, fleet size or commodity movement, I chronicle the life and times of truckers as they try to make ends meet. The drivers, who carry the weight of the trucking industry, are discussed in detail. With a set of broad lenses, I analyze driver risk, by exploring the reasons for it, reactions to it and the consequences of it.

I began the task with the research question, Why is the average trucker continuously placed in conditions that, according to the truckers, demand risky driving? Observation of driving practices, in-depth accounts offered by truckers and other relevant persons, and a review of available research literature provided me some answers. While I sifted through the reams of data, I made a conscientious effort to retain the reality of driving as it is and not pick and choose the data that Gusfield (1981) described as having been scrubbed, polished, selectively highlighted and offered as discoveries in the context of the particular and practical considerations of the researchers.

By experiencing trucking, I noted the breadth and depth of interpretations truckers, industry officials and other relevant parties assigned to such features as driver risk, driving safety, vehicle maintenance, owner operator, company driver, making a living, policing, home life, drugs and alcohol, government regulations and hours of service. These are essential factors nested in the socioeconomic reality and the culture of truck driving.

It became clear to me that truck drivers behave to gain autonomy over their work, freedom from control of others and assurance of a reasonable life-style. In order to maintain a sufficient income in the transportation market, even the most serious truckers perform tasks that often impinge on legality and safety. They break laws, stretch safety regulations, engage in unsafe driving practises and negotiate risky driving behaviors not as blatant radicals fighting the system but as persons responding to the fear that they may lose their livelihood in trucking. It is here, I believe, the crux of the problem lies.

Up to now, the thrust in trucker safety has followed a victimization philosophy whereby emphasis on interventions has been aimed directly at truckers. Few researchers have addressed the more immediate question of why so many truckers willingly engage in risky driving in the first place. To gain information on this topic, I believe we need to swim upstream rather than solely concentrate on downstream efforts, by stressing forces within the trucking environment that influence, motivate or encourage truckers to take chances on the road. By expanding our vision, we move towards far-reaching consequences safety has for truckers, other road users, policy makers and traffic safety educators.

"Nature will have its course," said Cervantes, "every production must resemble its author . . ." (Leonard, 1943; vii). Conversely, if we are to find the meaning of trucking, the reasons for its peculiar risks and safety, we must look to the truckers themselves. That is why I have tried to describe truckers – to sketch their behaviors and personalities, historical backgrounds and the events which shape their thoughts and actions on the road. Each trucker and other interviewees' described and quoted in the text have been assigned a pseudonym to defend their confidentiality and anonymity. At times I have included minutiae to bring to the foreground the intensity of the moment when risks are taken, to detail the vignettes of real life drama.

References

Gusfield, J.R. 1981. **The Culture of Public Problems.** Chicago: University of Chicago Press.
Leonard, R.A. 1943. **The Stream of Music.** Garden City, N.Y.: Doubleday, Doran and Co.

Acknowledgments

The Insurance Corporation of British Columbia is a provincial Crown Corporation created in 1973 with authority to provide and administer a universal, compulsory automobile insurance fund for the motorists of British Columbia. The Corporation's mission is to provide protection from motor vehicle-related loss to B.C. citizens, and an important component of that mission is the commitment to undertake research which will contribute to the development of programs aimed at reducing traffic accidents and injuries.

At the time of writing, Peter Rothe was the Manager of Research and Evaluation in the Traffic Safety Research Department of the Insurance Corporation. He has been active in the traffic safety research field since 1982 and is the author of numerous papers and publications.

This project arose from the Insurance Corporation of British Columbia's support for traffic safety research. It is another example of the Corporation's desire to publicize important issues on highway safety.

I should like to thank the many truckers and related members of the trucking industry for generously sharing their time, experience and insight with me. Unfortunately, I cannot name the companies, government officials and drivers for the sake of anonymity.

The logistics involved in organizing such a project is mind boggling. The leader for much of the behind-the-scenes planning for the road research, interviews, and questionnaire surveys was Fergus Savage, Manager of Fleet Safety, Insurance Corporation of British Columbia. His breadth of information and inside knowledge of trucking is so extensive that it provided me with many useful leads, ideas and opportunities.

Specialized knowledge was retrieved from John Pullyblank whose expertise in statistics provided me with insight on the use and misuse of numbers for this book. Actual number crunching was done by Mario Pineli.

Transcribing the interview tapes taken within the noisy grinding chambers of semi-trailer tractors was no easy task. In fact it was horrendous. Still, members of the production team prevailed. A special thank you is extended to Corinne Bauder and Flo Reusch, two word processing operators who offered their quality of hearing and sanity for a professional transcription job and later, a terrific word processing job. Sue Anderson, Jo-Ann

Ljubinkovic, Dorothy Smith and Pat Welford also contributed immensely in the technical production of this book. To all, a special thank you.

I am deeply indebted to Irving Louis Horowitz for his rigorous critiques of earlier drafts. His energetic reviews and commitment to perfection forced me to re-evaluate not only original concepts, analyses and text, but also my writing style.

1

INTRODUCTION

This book is about truck drivers' lives, risks and views on safety. As a group, truckers represent a significant population of road users whose high exposure driving creates a major challenge for safety. With tractors pulling loads upwards of eighty thousand pounds, truckers routinely cover one hundred thousand to one hundred and fifty thousand miles per year, running a gamut of terrain, traffic and weather conditions. From the desert to the mountains, from the coast to the prairies, from falling snow to beating sun, from the open freeways to the congested city intersections, truckers ply their trade, exposing themselves to a wide gamut of risks.

To help assure that truckers maintain a wary approach to driving, federal and regional jurisdictions in Canada and the United States enforce regulations, policies and laws such as maximum hours on duty, vehicle maintenance and use of illegal substances. The extent to which truckers obey these regulations is a reflection of the circumstances they experience in daily driving. Yet it is common knowledge in the trucking industry that for drivers to earn sufficient money for a decent living, they must routinely challenge the laws. As one trucker told me, "We'll do anything to make a buck. If that means we have to screw the regs, so be it. Everyone knows that."

Screwing the regulations means cutting corners in vehicle maintenance, disobeying traffic laws, shirking general safe driving behaviors and taking illicit drugs. Although truckers routinely break laws and regulations, the drivers do not believe that these actions make them unsafe drivers. They believe that their superior operating skills, extensive trucking experience and quick reflexes compensate for breaking laws which many truckers write off as being punitive anyway.

While they are on the road truckers worry little about getting into accidents. Their main concerns are to deliver the loads on time and to avoid being caught by the police. When truckers fail to deliver loads on time or get caught by the police, a large dent is made in the truck drivers' pocket books. That is the predominant theme for truckers' versions of risk taking. It is a matter of how much the consequences of problems with the loads and/or police will cost them in terms of money and time.

The Research and Design of Book

The focus for the book is the meanings truckers assign to various facets of their driving lives, their regard for risk and safety and their observable behaviors on the road. To arrive at the focus, I established a series of ideal-type truckers developed from my research. The ideal types reflect Weber's (1949) definition of concrete individual phenomena. Each trucker described in this book represents an analytic construct that emphasizes a clear, understandable expression of trucking. By combining the ideal-type truckers into a comprehensive whole, I hoped to produce a realistic portrayal of trucker and safety.

The ideal types were rationalized from in-depth involvement with the ongoing interactions and events of fifteen truckers, and with interviews of fifty more truckers at truck stops and truck yards, ten dispatchers, three fleet managers, ten police officers and scores of individuals such as waitresses, weigh scale attendants, motel managers, driving school instructors and newspaper reporters.

Most of my observation and interview scheduling was planned through trucking associations, fleets and the Teamsters. The selection of specific drivers and situations was undirected, depending on the circumstances at any particular time. During the observations I sometimes became the objective interviewer directing questions like an investigative journalist. At other times I became a confidant with whom truckers shared emotional insights.

Intensive ten to twenty hour interviews per trucker could only be done with audio recordings and field notes. Before going to bed each night I noted in as much detail as possible unrecorded conversation with people that I met and other relevant information such as observable habits and strategic behaviors. Later all the recorded interviews were transcribed. For a detailed description on methodology see Appendix A.

The ideal-type truckers that evolved from the observations and interviews accentuate the discrete factors evident in trucking. However, because this manuscript focuses on risk and safety, I have included important quantitative research findings that address particular issues resulting from my observations and lengthy interviews. Survey data gathered in Washington State and British Columbia, closely monitored experiments on braking undertaken at the Pacific Training and Education Centre in British Columbia, analysis of truck-related accident data in British Columbia and a thorough review of relevant literature were undertaken. Finally, I investigated hundreds of trucker magazines to establish the driver's reality as represented in the trucker media.

Because trucking is rich in myth, romance, exaggeration and conflict, it is impossible to capture all the safety themes a prudent reader may believe is worthy of print. To maintain control of the manuscript and to retain a consistent focus on the topic of trucker life-style, risk, safety and behavior, I imposed certain limits on the book's organization. The most important one is the way I linked the chapters to portray the every day exigencies of a truck trip and to illustrate the ideal-type drivers who comprise the world of trucking.

So that I would not deviate from the truckers' everyday world, I presented the quantitative data in the Notes section at the end of each chapter and in Appendices B and C. When combined, these sections represent a story within a story, an ongoing discussion on the statistical, deductive nature of trucker safety within the description of the everydayness of truckers-in-action.

A second restriction in this book is geography. The truckers involved in the study operated in western Canada and/or the western United States. Whereas driving in central and eastern North America may have built up my sample of subjects, I do not believe it would have significantly altered the presentation of drivers' frustrations, tensions, rationalizations and concerns. Presumably trucking is a national/international event, one that blurs any dominant and idiosyncratic points of view reflecting unique locations. In any case, the featured drivers live in all parts of the United States and Canada.

By articulating the truckers' world in an ethnographic style with demonstrations of statistical evidence, a description is provided that I believe is not only intellectually alive and provocative but that captures Horowitz's expectations of sociology:

> Sociology must be practical. It must understand the difference between tough-minded scholarship and tenderhearted sentiment. It must offer useful consultations to useful businessmen. It must make recommendations to policy-makers and it must provide a service to industry worth the cost. The notion of impersonal and abstract research must give way to, or at least share the wealth with, the "scholarly confrontation" – which of course is personal and highly concrete. (1970: pg. 280)

As the readers peruse the manuscript they will note a number of phrases in italics. This was done to indicate verbatim talk by the trucker with whom I was conversing. The procedure is purely stylistic to escape the boredom brought on by repeatedly invoking "the trucker said," or similar phrases whenever a noteworthy quote, a provocative description or unique concept was offered by an interviewee. Each trucker described has been assigned a false name to protect the individual's anonymity.

References

Agar, M.H. 1986. **Independents Declared**. Washington, DC: Smithsonian Institute Press.

Berger, Peter, and Berger, Brigitte. 1972. **Sociology: A Biographical Approach**. New York: Baric Books.

Horowitz, I. 1970. "Sociology for Sale." In L. Reynolds and J.M. Reynolds (Eds.) **The Sociology of Sociology**. New York: David McKay Co. Inc.

Thomas, J.H. 1979. **The Long Haul**. Memphis: Memphis State University Press.

2

CROSSING THE CANADA–UNITED STATES BORDER

Truckers exist on roadways running north to south, east to west, shared by hustling men and women, whatever their nationality, culture or color. Within the context of North America, truckers migrate daily from Canada to the United States and vice versa. They cross near Houlton, Maine; Champlain and Buffalo, New York; Sault Ste. Marie, Ontario; Emerson, Manitoba; and Blaine, Washington. Although truckers are guided by different laws when they cross the 49th parallel, they do retain their fashions, habits, beliefs, perspectives, their sense of "every trucker knows . . . ."

We can register the ongoing commerce in fresh produce, meat, newsprint and lumber crossing the border, north to south, south to north on any day at the Canada – United States border near Blaine. Although North America is fast becoming homogeneous, integrated and interdependent in transportation, each country has retained its own institutionalized trucking priorities. This became obvious when I experienced a border-crossing trip in a semitrailer truck.

Crossing the border does not represent a change in the truckers' mind sets. Although there are some economic differences, a driver hauling goods from Vancouver to Montreal requires the same skills and has similar interests as a trucker operating between Seattle and New York. They experience familiar pressures, feelings, perspections and road conditions. The major difference is institutional, where Canada's rules and regulations are dissimilar to those of the United States. To portray the Canada – United States differences an attempt is made to describe macro factors as they arise through discussion with a trucker named Vic.

From Vancouver To Blaine

Mayfair Industrial Park, located under the Port Mann Bridge in Coquitlam, British Columbia is a piece of real estate where much of British Columbia's warehousing and trucking is located. I began my journey here on Tuesday, four p.m. With the help of the Insurance Corporation of British

Columbia's fleet safety manager, Fergus Savage, arrangements were made with Z Transport for me to ride along with a United States bound trucker named Vic.

Vic, hauling rolls of newsprint for the Los Angeles market, was originally scheduled to depart at noon. However, mechanical problems with his tractor postponed his departure to four p.m. As the second driver for an owner operator who runs two trucks, Vic's responsibility not only includes driving but also tractor maintenance such as washing the vehicle, undertaking minor repairs, making brake adjustments and recognizing potential major repairs. On this particular day Vic was a little late because he had a mechanic oversee suspicious sounds in the clutch.

Around quarter to four Vic was becoming antsy about being delayed by the dispatcher. Any additional waiting time would seriously alter his driving itinerary, such as where he eats and rests and when he arrives in the Los Angeles traffic. Because of his delay in Vancouver, he may get caught in Los Angeles morning rush hour, further extending his driving time.

While waiting for the dispatcher to complete some last minute paper work, Vic was giving the windshield and headlights a last minute touch-up cleaning, although he had already washed the tractor and vacuumed the cab. When I introduced myself to Vic, he welcomed me, suggesting that my company would erase the boredom he usually experiences on this trip.

At four p.m. Vic was motioned to visit the dipatcher's office and pick up his bills of lading. We were ready to leave. A blast on the air horn signified "take care guys, bon voyage."

After a short chat, Vic offered a few precautions. He advised me that once we arrive in Blaine, Washington, I should be prepared to declare my electronic equipment, answer politely any questions border personnel may have about me entering the United States and to show the agents my prescription for the back pain killers I was carrying. Attention to these matters would assure smooth administrative processing.

As a regular traveler to the United States, Vic is accustomed to the border crossing demands. Several times in his career border crossings were problematic when agents spot checked his unit for contraband. Based on tip offs from various sources or random searches, American and/or Canadian border guards often do comprehensive searches of trucks. Whenever this happens truckers must "swallow their pride and wait it out." Most times, however, the border crossing is part of Vic's trucking routine, an integral part of north to south freight hauling. It takes on a series of activities or guidelines with which truckers are well acquainted.

Upon arrival at the border, Vic stopped his unit in a parking facility at the Canadian side of the border. With briefcase under arm Vic walked to the Canadian customs office presenting an officer with bills of lading and an export declaration. He assured the agent that he was not carrying any expensive personal equipment, such as a mini computer or a portable television. The officer treated Vic's explanation in a routine manner, as he casually flipped through the documents.

While Vic tended to his legal obligations I approached another officer to declare my research equipment. The Canadian representative informed me that this was unnecessary, because it is assumed that researchers carry electronic equipment, such as micro cassette recorders. He did not envision any problems on my return into Canada four weeks later.

The next step consisted of retrieving the export declaration documents from the broker's office. Before Vic arrived his dispatcher already notified the broker about the nature and value of the load, its destination point and the anticipated time of the driver's arrival at the border. When we entered the broker's office a secretary requested Vic's bills of lading and asked him to wait for ten minutes. To ease the wait, the broker offered us free coffee.

A secretary's hand gesture and a smile symbolized that all was in order. Vic retrieved his papers at the counter and walked briskly to the United States customs office where four officers were positioned to offer assistance. The declaration forms were given to an American official, whose nod of approval signalled us to continue our trip without Vic having to present his cargo for inspection or us having to wait for the results of a police records enquiry. We were permitted to proceed.

The border crossing scenario took forty-five minutes. It was a smooth crossing at a time of day when truck traffic was moderate. On weekends or high traffic volume times of the year truckers may lose upwards to four or five hours waiting to cross the border. Such delays are resented by drivers because they cut directly into driving time and scheduling. For the trucker the wait translates into lost revenue.

During our walk back to the parking lot Vic suggested that "you don't screw with the customs." The officials have unlimited power to search "anything anywhere." Still, things are better today than they were several years ago. Up to the late 1970s Canadian truckers wishing to enter the United States required a NON RESIDENT ALIEN CANADIAN BORDER CROSSING CARD that included a photo, full name, address, date of birth, place of examination and date of card distribution. The card is no longer necessary.

Vic slowly drove out of the parking lot and entered the Interstate Five freeway. Rather than the fifty-five mph speed limit allowed in Canada, he now drove the sixty-five mph speed limit legislated in the United States. Vic favored the higher speed limit and he appreciated the uniformity rule whereby truck drivers and four wheelers (car drivers) obeyed the same speed limit. For Vic it is symbolic, a feeling of equality, a personal sense that truckers are equal to others. The fact that increased speed contributes to a higher probability of accident was not an issue or a point of discussion. The dignity of truckers was Vic's only interest. As Vic began to pick up speed he emphasized that Washington's Bow Hill Inspection Facility was just a few miles away. The center represented an essential facet of trucking, one which he was obliged to obey.

Vehicle Inspection Centers/Weigh Scales

Every state in the United States and province in Canada has points of entry which range from full truck inspection facilities to weigh scale stations. In the United States they are usually administered by the state's Public Utility Commission, which is the administrative arm of the state police patrol. In Canada, these facilities fall under the jurisdiction of the provincial Departments of Highways. An attending police officer, weigh master or other official, federal, state or provincial, may examine the vehicle, load, freight bills, the authority, the lease, the driver's license, physical exam certificate, vehicle registration or driver's log book (Agar, 1986; pg. 129).

About a mile from the Washington Point of Entry, Vic discussed the power of enforcement assigned to officers or weigh scale attendants. Recently he "flew right by a weigh scale" because he was daydreaming. As he passed by the facility he recognized his error. He stopped his vehicle and walked back up the hill to the weigh scale and told the attendant, "I missed your scale by accident." The attendant's response was "Pal, get your truck, go around and come back." Without dispute Vic drove his truck to the first exit ramp, went north and returned southward on Interstate Five. When he returned Vic asked the officer, "What's going to happen?" The patrolman answered, "Nothing, as long as you realized, (your mistake) stopped and reported it. If you had kept going we'd have chased after you, and it would have cost you at least $95.00."

According to Vic "most guys are scared of scales." Truckers do not talk back to the officials. As Vic indicated, if a trucker does:

They'll come out and find something wrong with your truck. They can ticket you - the tickets can pile up to $500.00.

Some truckers travel at night or arrange their trips for late night travel to intentionally miss scales. They radio oncoming truckers to find out if the "scales are open up ahead," hoping that they are closed. This tactic is usually practiced when truckers are operating in a province or state for which they do not have proper permits or their load weight exceeds state regulations. Some companies negate their responsibilities by not acquiring or renewing permits for the truckers to operate in certain states or provinces. They expect drivers to run assigned loads illegally in these jurisdictions. Vic provided a personal experience:

> I worked for X Trucking in Richmond. He (the dispatcher) just got a permit a month at a time and the month would roll around, and the permit would run out. You'd be on a trip, but the permit is no good. Just before you'd come to the scale, you'd phone and say, "You better get a hold of the permit office and get a permit." "Go around it." "Why should I go around it, you know." I mean speed is a fact, and you try to ask these owners, "Okay, I'm going to go through it but if I get stopped, you gonna pay the ticket?" They won't ever give you an answer, because they don't want to pay the ticket.

On his previous job Vic was expected to travel from Vancouver to Calgary, although the carrier did not have authority to operate in Alberta. Needing the job, Vic consented to driving on Highway 1A to enter Calgary, instead of the Trans Canada Highway which has a weigh scale. According to Vic:

> If they stopped you, they'd throw you in jail. It's obvious what you're doing – they know what you're doing, you are going around (the scale). So I just told this guy, "I'm not going to do this. I'm not going to run your scales for you. It's my license – I do it for a living, if I get caught I lose my license." So I just quit. But there's a lot of them kind of operators.

To run a scale was not an occasional event. Rather, the owner-manager of the Vancouver – Calgary Freightlines expected Vic to run the scales as a customary practise. Witness Vic's remarks:

> The boss didn't like the scales. He always wanted you to run around scales and stuff like that. I don't go for that stuff. I am just a driver, I am not getting caught for someone else.

The impact weigh scales have on truckers was a recurring theme expressed by every trucker I met. To portray it's significance, I have included the topic whenever it arose with drivers. Truckers are fully aware about the legal authority behind the scales.[1] Consequently most truckers are cautious, if not apprehensive, whenever they approach one. The predominant rule is "don't look conspicuous." To "stand out" increases the trucker's chances of being stopped and harassed. According to Vic, unkempt driver appearance, dirty windshields and/or tractors and poorly loaded cargo are visible factors that may encourage an attendant to "stake out" a truck and initiate a thorough examination of the vehicle, load and documents, and driver. The investigation results in delays and almost certainly fines.

Some truckers define scale operators as "uncanny people" who can tell just by looking at a trucker how long "it's been since he's gone to bed and done any sleeping." They "harass" truckers on the job and even off the job. Hank, a trucker I met in Norwalk pinpoints California as being especially bad:

> California is real bad, they'll leave that "Open" sign on the scale, nobody in the scale house whatsoever. They're just harassing the drivers, making them pull across the road and run across their stupid scale. As far as I'm concerned that should be a felony on the police department because that's just wasting your time – it costs fifteen minutes out of your driving day, every time you stop at a scale. People don't realize that. Say you're coming to a scale and you know it's open and you start your stop watch at the mile mark before the scale and kick it again at the mile mark after the scale. Then when you're running down the highway, run another mile on your stop watch and see how much time you lost. You lose a whole bunch of time.

The trucker reminded me that just visiting weigh scales without legal delays impacts drivers economically. To enter and exit a weigh scale takes about fifteen minutes. When we multiply this time by the number of scales a trucker enters before he arrives at his destination, total time lost becomes noticeable.

Vic echoed the driver's explanations that the rigor of enforcement at weigh scales differs between provinces and states. Tim, who drives between New Mexico, Colorado and Texas told me that on Sunday afternoons Arizona's Interstate 40 is packed with trucks heading from Texas to California. Because the point of entry has "trucks backed up for miles," most trucks are not weighed, and truckers are not queried for papers. Instead, the attendant "stands on a little balcony and the trucker hands her a credit card (government identity card)." She "runs it through the machine," and the trucker continues. According to Tim, some states do not properly maintain weigh scales:

> . . . they don't even know what a set of scales are in Texas; I bet you they have three for the whole state, and the ones that they do have in Texas they don't use. Colorado will weigh you if they're gonna check your permits. Back East is where they're pretty picky . . .

Trucks in Canada are expected to display "P" plates, recognized by scale operators as official permits to operate in particular provinces. If truckers do not possess these permits they must purchase one at the point of entry.

Each province has jurisdiction over the operation of its weigh scales. How provinces operate their scales is dependent on manpower and funding. Because there is a shortage of both, weigh scales are often closed for specific periods of times, making it easier for truckers to avoid them.

Our weigh-in at Washington's Bow Hill Point of Entry went smoothly. But Vic had little reason to worry, because he takes extensive precautions to enhance problem-free runs. For example, before he departs on a trip, he pre-checks the vehicle and inspects the load. He weighs the load's gross vehicle weight and its weight by axle unit, to assure proper distribution of weight. If there is a problem of load placement Vic readjusts the weight "a little from here or there."

By operating a washed truck and by being clean shaven and respectably dressed, Vic further limits his chances of being stopped. When it comes to appearance and personal grooming Vic prefers to be conservative. It is his best insurance against possible weigh scale troubles. On this day his strategy was successful. Our actual stopping time was only five minutes.

While we exited from the weigh scale it began to pour rain. The clouds hung low, visibility at times was limited because of the fog. The windshield wipers pounded continuously. These weather conditions did not faze Vic. For him heavy rain was an inconvenience that necessitates slower speed, but it was not a major problem. After thirty years of driving, Vic's only worry is snow and ice conditions in the mountains. They reduce his ability to brake, making driving more dangerous. According to Vic, the braking problem does not exist during heavy rainfall because the sheer weight of the truck compensates for the slick pavement.

About ten miles south of Bellingham, we noticed two long truck skid marks on the pavement that veered across both traffic lanes ending in the ditch. "No front axle brakes," explained Vic. He believed that the form of the skid marks suggests that a trucker probably disconnected the front axle brakes and lost control, a tactic still used by many truckers.

Front Axle Brakes: The Canadian And American Scene

Vic disagreed with truckers dismantling their front axle brakes on the basis of better stopping control. Such truckers are, according to Vic "old knights of the road who live by some old beliefs, not common sense."

Whereas it is illegal to operate a truck without front axle brakes in the United States[2], at present Canada does not have a parallel law. Front axle brakes, proven effective in numerous experiments, are not compulsory on Canadian roads – except on the West Coast.

British Columbia legislators, desiring to be in-synch with the rest of Canada, yet mandate front axle brakes, stipulated that all three-axle tractors on provincial highways produce a brake efficiency of 43.5 percent, at a speed of twenty miles per hour (thirty-two kilometers per hour) on a dry level road. Anyone in the trucking world knows that this requirement cannot be met without properly operating front axle brakes.

Major truck manufacturers such as Peterbilt, Kenworth, Freightliner, Mack, Volvo/White, International or Ford, have installed front axle brakes since 1980. This does not, however, assure compliance on the part of drivers. As Vic outlined, some old truckers disconnect the brakes believing that they lead to accidents. They assume that front axle brakes lessen the driver's ability to control a vehicle on ice or rainy road because all of the truck's weight is in the back, giving front axle brakes little grabbing power.

In the United States truckers are restricted from tampering with front axle brakes. The Federal Safety Regulations state that "Every commercial motor vehicle shall be equipped with brakes required on all wheels." (American Trucking Association, 1989, p. 179). The issue of front axle brakes is fully discussed in Chapter Twelve.

Operators' Licenses

In North America changes in trucking regulations are occuring at a rapid pace. This is evident in the United States licensing procedures. To illustrate the changes in the American driver license rules, I first describe a typical traditional Canadian system.

As a Canadian trucker, Vic received his class one operator's license from the British Columbia government. He passed a series of examinations to operate combination unit multiple axle vehicles. He cleared his medical test, which every class one license candidate in British Columbia must do within forty-five days of application. While the medical clearance is processed by a physician, the trucker-to-be completes a learner's permit. To obtain one a candidate writes a twenty item multiple choice test, on which he is not allowed more than four errors. Also, a knowledge test on road signs and traffic lights must be passed as must be a vision test – whereby the applicant must have binocular vision, 20/30 eyesight in the better eye, and 20/50 eyesight in the poorer eye.

Any trucker wishing to drive Vic's cab over Freightliner, must also possess an air endorsement ticket. Since most three-axle tractors have air brakes, and British Columbia stipulates that operators of such vehicles be qualified users, candidates must become certified for this equipment.

Two avenues for air brake certification are possible. The first is a sixteen hour driving school theory class. A candidate completes the course, passes a written test, and demonstrates hands-on ability at the beginning of a Motor Vehicle Department administered road test. The second opportunity is a twenty-four hour certification course, where some driving schools or community colleges provide instruction, test the student's knowledge of theory, and rate the practicum. Upon successful completion, the institution presents the student a certificate of achievement, endorsed by the British Columbia Motor Vehicle Department.

Vic never attended formal air brake classes. Like many older Canadian drivers, Vic learned about air brakes from his father. Later, when the government demanded formal certification, Vic passed the provincial tests. Reviewing or "brushing up" on the air brake manual helped him succeed.

For driving evaluations, examiners expect candidates to engage in rigorous pre-trip inspections and complete road tests. If the exams are passed, the future truckers receive a temporary license followed by a permanent license, mailed to them shortly thereafter.

While awaiting his permanent license, the Motor Vehicle Department may decide to review an applicant's record for driving violations and criminal charges. The agency extracts files from the Interprovincial Record Exchange, a computer base shared by all Canadian provinces and territories. Assuming that the candidate's record is clean, he is permitted to drive in all Canadian provinces because of the "Reciprocal Agreement," whereby all the provinces agree on acceptable testing standards.

Commercial vehicle operators are not allowed to possess more than one driver's license in Canada. The law holds true for the United States. However, the rules, regulations and procedures for obtaining the equivalent of a Canadian class one license in the United States differs significantly.

Earning a Class 1 Equivalent License In the United States

The year 1986 represents a bell weather year in American trucking because of the federal proclamation of the Commercial Motor Vehicle Safety Act. Its aim was to ensure national standards for the Commercial Driver License (CDL). Effective April 1, 1992, no persons are allowed to operate trucks unless they have passed written and driving tests that meet federal standards.

To obtain a CDL the candidate must "possess and demonstrate basic motor vehicle control skills," safe driving skills for their vehicle group (e.g., double/triple trailers, passenger, tank or hazardous materials), air brake skills, pre-inspection skills and on-road driving skills. The air brake endorsement would be a first for the majority of states, unlike the regulations enforced in Canadian provinces. Testing procedures are undertaken by each state.

To illustrate the scope of these changes, let us briefly review present day procedures. Each state has authority to implement its own criteria of licensing. A road test can be managed by a motor carrier or an appointed representative, whose only qualification is sufficient competence to evaluate and determine how well a candidate can operate the equipment he is expected to run after examination. This process is open for abuse. Some truckers confided that in some states like Texas, New Mexico and Oklahoma, receiving a license is not based on objective testing. Instead road tests change according to the whim of the tester and the candidates' driving performances are judged with bias. Licenses are often granted to candidates by word of mouth. The applicant may convince a driver examiner about his abilities without actually taking a road test, then present witnesses with truck drivers' licenses to speak on his behalf. The exchange of money to pay for the license may be all that is necessary to obtain a license.

As in Canada, candidates for the CDL must have a medical examiner's certificate that proves they are physically qualified to drive trucks. The list of features to be assessed includes general appearance and development, eyes (Snellen chart), physical ear and hearing, throat, thorax-heart, blood pressure, lungs, gastrointestinal system, abdomen, abnormal masses, tenderness, genito-urinary, neurological, extremities, spine and recto-genital areas. Added to this list is evidence resulting from diabetes tests, controlled substance tests, and urinalysis for such diseases as latent syphilis. Further studies can be undertaken on the advice of an attending physician. The testing procedures for health and driving skills is undertaken by each state upon a series of regulations defined by the Federal Motor Carrier Safety Administration.[3]

The gap between safety in the United States and Canada is rapidly closing. In Canada the National Safety Code established by the Canadian Council of Motor Transport Administrators (CCMTA) is placing trucking under the influence of a national umbrella as is the United States Federal Highway Administration with its Commercial Driver License. Free Trade between the two countries promises to usher in further uniformity of standards.

National Uniformity

The Canadian Council of Motor Transport Administrators presented a draft safety code intended to curtail the traffic infractions among truckers. A major cornerstone of the National Safety Code is the compliance system, adopted by all provinces. Offenses that truckers receive anywhere in Canada will be logged in a central computer data bank, retrievable by any province.

After a year-long national debate over hours of service the Canadian Commercial Vehicles Drivers' Hours of Service Regulations were officially proclaimed in 1989. In short, truckers are allowed to drive for thirteen hours in a twenty-four hour period for interprovincial driving. Furthermore, truckers are restricted to being on duty no more than fifteen hours a day or sixty hours during a seven day week period or seventy hours during eight consecutive days (Independent Trucker, 1989, p. 8).[4] Log book maintenance is required and will be strictly enforced by provincial authorities.

[margin note: American vs Canada rules]

Once the trucker hits the United States the rules change.[5] Truckers are not permitted to drive more than ten hours following eight consecutive hours off duty or more than sixty hours in a period of seven continuous days. Any law officer can review a trucker's log book to check the official hours on duty.

Vic was aware of the American laws, but like so many of his colleagues he seriously questioned how the regulators arrived at the ten hour driving rule. He, as did many other drivers, suspect that the Teamster Union lobbied the carriers and government officials for the ten hour driving limit. Vic believed that the union wanted to restrict owner operators, most of whom are non-union, from earning more money than union drivers. Although the suspected union strategy still upsets Vic, at his age it's all "water down his back." According to the trucker, "young guys like his son" will have to challenge the rule, because they have a stake in the future. Vic is quite content to skirt the law by running two log books. It was his way of fighting the system.

Drug Testing

Drug use by truckers is **the** major challenge faced in the Canadian and United States transportation industry. Articles abound in trucker magazines that outline the pros and cons of drug testing. The issue of drugs and drug testing turns Vic off. He does not use drugs nor does he like it being used in trucking. He refuses to worry about it because, "sure as hell I can't do anything about it, and you can't let everything worry you."

In 1988 the United States Federal Highway Administration established procedures for administering five drug tests: pre-employment, post-accident, periodic and random testing along with testing for "reasonable cause" (Independent Trucker, 1987). The rules require that urine specimens be taken at designated "collection sites" at specific times and under rigorous control to ensure accuracy, honesty and confidentiality of information. A medical doctor is in charge of testing and interpretation.

The imposition of mandatory drug testing resulted in a lawsuit filed by the OOIDA (Owner-Operators Independent Drivers Association of America) in the U.S. District Court for the Northern District of California.

As of the time of this writing, the court has imposed a preliminary injunction against random and post-accident testing provisions contained in the regulations (Johnson, 1989).

Based on intensive lobbying efforts by the motor carrier industry, post accident testing is no longer required after every Department of Transport reportable accident, and a drug test taken within six months by a previous carrier can be used for a driver's pre-employment test in a new company (Safety Focus, February, 1990). Regardless of the regulations Vic would "be glad to pee in a bottle."

Nevertheless he resented the idea that his constitutional rights are violated. According to Vic why, after a truck crash, should the trucker be the only person tested? Shouldn't the other "assholes" be checked? They drive like maniacs, causing accidents, taking drugs and plugging up truck lanes. Yet "the cops do nothing." For Vic the rule is blatantly biased. He considered himself fortunate to be Canadian. Then he smilingly suggested that the regulation may lead to a new industry, selling viles of "clean piss" at truck stops. As long as the trucker can urinate in privacy, he has the opportunity to exchange samples. For truckers who may question the purity of their urine, or who wish to make a statement of defiance, exchanging urine is a reasonable strategy.

In Canada there are no formal drug testing regulations. Some motor carriers have a voluntary employment urine testing program or "spot checks" which are not governed by federal jurisdiction. The future, however, may hinge on American initiative. United States legislators may demand greater efforts to gain Canadian compliance, under guise of trucking deregulation and free trade. Furthermore drug testing in Canada may receive serious consideration once the OOIDA lawsuit in California passes through the court systems. (For an in-depth discussion on drug use and research see Chapter Six.)

As we were approaching Seattle Vic hit the rush hour traffic. It is during such times that the trucker quality, "lots of patience," is needed. Vic believed that he acquired it from having his pilot's license. According to Vic, whenever he flies he "has to be calm and observant." In heavy traffic, Vic believed that "you might as well stay in your lane and take your time. There's no use cursing and swearing."

Consistent to his pronouncements Vic stayed in the middle lane until conditions changed. A half-ton truck in front of us was driving forty m.p.h. Vic decided to pass him despite the poor visibility created by the fog and rain. Vic checked his rear view mirror and saw a sedan moving up. After passing the half ton Vic wanted to maneuver back into the middle lane. Unfortunately the car behind us "shot the gap" between us and the small truck, blocking Vic's attempt to re-enter the middle lane. Vic was stranded in the left hand lane. The car driver laid on her horn as if, according to Vic, she was "never going to stop." Vic was becoming "really embarrassed because people were starting to look at us." Rather than become impatient and chance an unsafe return to the right lane in heavy traffic, Vic continued to drive in the passing lane throughout the Seattle area, hoping that we do not meet a police officer and end up with a charge of driving in a non-trucking lane.

We made it through the Seattle corridor without meeting a police officer and with no further problems. Our average speed ranged from ten to thirty m.p.h. on a sixty mph freeway. Rush hour traffic seriously hampered Vic's movements. However, as we pulled out of Seattle, the freeway opened up. We could now drive sixty to sixty-five m.p.h., destination, Portland, Oregon.

Notes

1. The weigh scales in British Columbia are mandated to enforce the following regulations:

15. (1) No person shall, without a permit issued or authorized given under this Act, operate on a highway a commercial vehicle if
    (a) the gross vehicle weight of the commercial vehicle exceeds its licensed gross vehicle weight,
    (b) the weight on an axle, group of axles or axle unit exceeds the weight permitted by the regulations,
    (c) the dimensions of the commercial vehicle do not conform to the regulations
       (i) with load included, and
       (ii) without load, or
    (d) the distances between axles, group of axles or axle units do not conform with the regulations.
    (2) A person who contravenes this section commits an offence, and is liable, on conviction
    (a) for a contravention of subsection(1)(c) or (d), to a fine of not more than $500; and
    (b) for a contravention of subsection (1)(a) or (b), to a fine of not less than the amount prescribed by the regulations but not exceeding $500 and, in addition, to a penalty of not less than the amount prescribed by the regulations but not exceeding $6 for every 45 kg of overload,
    (3) A person contravening any other provision of this Act or the regulations is liable, on conviction, to a fine of not more than $500.
    (4) No person shall be acquitted of an offence under subsection (1)(a) or (b) on the defence of due diligence in respect of the loading of a commercial vehicle unless that person establishes

that on completion of the loading of the commercial vehicle it was weighed on a properly functioning scale and was not overloaded. (Ministry of Transportation and Highways; 1978, pp. 6 – 7.)

2. The United States Federal Safety Regulations on front axle brakes state:

393.42 Brakes required on all wheels.
(a) Every commercial motor vehicle shall be equipped with brakes acting on all wheels.
(b) Exception.
  (1) Trucks or truck tractors having three or more axles –
    (i) Need not have brakes on the front wheels if the vehicle was manufactured before July 25, 1980; or
    (ii) Manufactured between July 24, 1980, and October 27, 1986, must be retrofitted to meet the requirements of this section within one year from February 26, 1987, if the brake components have been removed.
  (2) Any motor vehicle being towed in a driveway – towaway operation must have operative brakes as may be necessary to ensure compliance with the performance requirement of 393.52. This paragraph is not applicable to any motor vehicle towed by means of a tow-bar when any vehicle is full-mounted on such motor vehicle or any combination of motor vehicles utilizing three saddle-mounts. (See 393.7(a)(3).)
  (3) Any full trailer, any semitrailer, or any pole trailer having a GVW of 3,000 pounds or less must be equipped with brakes if the weight of the towed vehicle resting on the towing vehicle exceeds 40 percent of the GVW of the towing vehicle. (American Trucking Association, 1989; pp. 179-180).

Other than the grandfather clause to July 25, 1980, all American tractors with three or more axles must have brakes on "all wheels."

3. The Federal Motor Carrier Safety Regulations define state run test procedures accordingly:

Examiner procedures. A State shall provide to test examiners details on testing and any other State-imposed requirements in the examiner's manual, and shall ensure that examiners are qualified to administer tests on the basis of training and/or other experience, States shall provide standardized scoring sheets for the skills tests, as well as standardized driving instructions for the applicants. Such examiners' manuals shall contain the following;

(1) Information on driver application procedures contained in 383.71, State procedures described in 383.73, and other appropriated driver information contained in Subpart E of this part;
(2) Details on information which must be given to the applicant;
(3) Details on how to conduct the tests;
(4) Scoring procedures and minimum passing scores;
(5) Information for selecting driving test routes;
(6) List of the skills to be tested;
(7) Instructions on where and how the skills will be tested;
(8) How performance of the skills will be scored; and
(9) Causes for automatic failure of skills tests.

383.133 Testing methods.

(a) All tests shall be constructed in such a way as to determine if the applicant possesses the required knowledge and skills contained in Subpart G of this part for the type of motor vehicle or endorsement the applicant wishes to obtain.
(b) States shall develop their own specifications for the tests for each vehicle group and endorsement which must be at least as stringent as the Federal standards.
(c) States shall determine specific methods for scoring the knowledge and skills tests.
(d) Passing scores must meet those standards contained in 383.135.
(e) Knowledge and skills tests shall be based solely on the information contained in the driver manuals . . .
(f) Each knowledge test shall be valid and reliable so as to assure that driver applicants possess the knowledge required under 383.111.
(g) Each basic knowledge test, i.e., the test shall contain at least 30 items, exclusive of the number of items testing air brake knowledge. Each endorsement knowledge test, and the air brake component of the basic knowledge test . . . shall contain a number of questions that is sufficient to test the driver applicant's knowledge of the required subject matter with validity and reliability.
(h) The skills tests shall have administrative procedures, designed to achieve interexaminer reliability, that are sufficient to ensure fairness of pass/fail rates. (1984; pp. 42-44)

4. Canada's hours of driving rules are:

13 hours driving in a 15-hour work shift, or 16 hours driving in a 24-hour period for interprovincial driving. The trucker is also restricted to no more than 60 hours behind the wheel or in onduty time during a seven-day work period, 70 hours of onduty time in eight consecutive days. Cumulative hour restrictions include no more than 120 hours in 14

consecutive days, with a minimum of 24 consecutive hours of offduty time before completing 75 hours of onduty or driving time.

Provincial and territorial directors of safety – administers of the federal rules in each jurisdiction – may issue exemptions to these rules under certain specified conditions, provided safety and the health of the driver or public is not jeopardized. (Independent Trucker, 1989, pg. 8)

5. The Federal Motor Carrier Safety Regulations on maximum driving and on-duty time are:

   Maximum driving and on-duty time.
   (a) Except as provided in paragraphs (c) and (e) of this section and in 395.10, no motor carrier shall permit or require any driver used by it to drive nor shall any such driver drive:
       (1) More than 10 hours following 8 consecutive hours off duty; or
       (2) For any period after having been on duty 15 hours following 8 consecutive hours off duty.
       (3) Exemption: Drivers using sleeper-berth equipment as defined in 395.2(f), or who are off duty at a natural gas oil well location, may cumulate the required 8 consecutive hours off duty resting in a sleeper berth in two separate periods totaling 8 hours, neither period to be less than 2 hours, or resting while off duty in other sleeping accommodations at a natural gas or oil well location.
   (b) No motor carrier shall permit or require a driver of a commercial motor vehicle, regardless of the number of motor carriers using the driver's services, to drive for any period after –
       (1) Having been on duty 60 hours in any 7 consecutive days if the employing motor carrier does not operate every day in the week; or
       (2) Having been on duty 70 hours in any period of 8 consecutive days if the employing motor carrier operates motor vehicles every day of the week.
       (3) Exception: This paragraph shall not apply to any driver driving a motor vehicle in the State of Alaska, as provided in paragraph (e) of this section, or to any driver-salesperson whose total driving time does not exceed 40 hours in any period of 7 consecutive days. (1989, pg. 111)

References

American Trucking Association. 1989. **Federated Motor Carrier Safety Regulations**. Alexandria, VA: American Trucking Associates.
1990 "Drug Testing Update." The Safety Focus, February.
CCJ Washington Bureau. 1987. "Random Drug Testing of Truck Drivers Is A Step Closer." **Commercial Carrier Journal**, July.

Homes, B. 1988. "Truckers Protest New Regs At Nippon." **Motor Truck**, May, pp. 28-31.

Independent Trucker. 1989. "Hours of Service Law." July/August, pg. 8.

Johnson, Jim. 1989. "DOT Rules Violate Driver Rights." **Transport Topics,** January 23, pg. 7.

Motor Truck. 1989. "U.S. Message To Canadian Truckers Is Loud and Clear." April, pp. 26-28.

Pollock, James. 1989. "New Drug Testing in U.S. Will This Happen In Canada?" **Independent Trucker,** April, pg. 15.

Transport Topics. 1989. "California Driver Gets 1st CDL." January 2, pg. 19.

3

THE CULTURE OF COMMUNICATION

The weather was deteriorating – fog, rain, slippery roads, windshield wipers steadily slapping away the wetness. For Vic it was like another "day in the office," one of many in which he drives over twelve thousand miles a month. Dreary weather was just another part of a working day.

Visibility was worsening. A few miles from Tacoma a tanker truck passed us preparing to move back into our lane. Vic "gave him the lights," flicking his bright lights on and off. It was the trucker's way of signaling safe re-entry for the bulk carrier, especially in bad weather.

Inter-Trucker Communication: Flicking Lights

A rule followed by truckers is to flick their lights for safety. Whenever trucks pass one another, the passing driver must make accurate judgments on length of his trailer, his speed and available space before re-entering the lane. The trucker being passed helps out with a quick flick of the headlights, a signal that all is clear. He communicates that there is enough distance between trucks for the passer to re-enter the lane safely, or as Vic indicated, "go ahead pull in and just say thank you."

Flicking lights for a passing truck constitutes a routine or norm understood, accepted and practised by truckers. It happens on all roadways, whether it is on Interstate freeways or secondary highways.

As in any communication an initial signal or gesture of friendliness requires a return gesture. Passing drivers who have received clearance from truckers passed will flick their trailer lights showing appreciation or as Vic suggested, "saying thank you." A communication exchange is completed. An unspoken, yet visible understanding between two truckers occurred.

Flicking lights for safe passage between two truckers represents the bottom line of consideration, empathy and colleagiality amongst truckers. Failing to participate in the ritual is like a rupture in the truckers' code of expectations. It demands an explanation! For example, Vic passed an unmarked bobcat pulling a pup trailer. Despite the terrible rain and poor visibility the driver failed to provide the re-entry signal, whereupon Vic looked at me and asked, "You see who's driving?" I described the driver as being East Indian. Vic's response was that immigrant drivers like him did not know any better, or they don't "give a damn" about other truckers. As a result Vic tries to "keep a big distance between him and ethnic drivers."

Non truckers are not offered the same communication privileges. "Four wheelers" represent the unacquainted, outsiders to the truckers' world. Vic goes so far as to collectively call them "the enemy." According to Vic, some drivers "don't respect truckers at all. Shit, anyone can drive a truck is what they think." People may believe this because many of them drive Recreational Vehicles (RV's), thinking that it is the same as driving a truck. In fact, Vic and other truckers I met shared a common concern about RV drivers. Large Winnebago's are like small trucks. Yet the drivers, usually "older guys" or "their wives" drive them like their cars. Vic explains:

. . . they don't have to take courses for driving . . . They'll come up and all of a sudden they'll decide to come into this lane. You've got to be watching because if you don't pull over and put your brakes on, they hit you.

Other drivers try to get in front of him and give him the finger. There will be a car "poking along," Vic goes out to pass and the other driver "steps on it." It does not matter how much Vic "pushes out," other drivers "just keep stepping on it." They don't want to be behind a large truck.

For Vic, to flick his lights for such drivers is out of the question, unless there is an emergency, then a different set of rules prevail. Saving the other driver from possible disaster is the only concern, regardless of the driver's culture or type of vehicle driven.

The Wave Of The Hand

When we wave to our neighbor over the backyard fence we achieve a silent greeting. Similarly, in trucking, drivers wave to one another to acknowledge each other's presence. But, for some drivers waving carries some social restrictions. Vic explained that, "in Canada if you haul flat deck, most of them don't wave to tankers, and they don't wave back." The tankers will wave to each other.

Guys driving for well known big companies may just wave to other fleet drivers. Some company drivers have the reputation of prima donnas. For example, a large British Columbia supermarket carrier was highlighted by several truckers I met as having drivers who are "stuck up" and refuse to wave to anyone except other truckers "running for prestigious outfits." Consequently, drivers like Vic do not wave to these drivers.

While discussing hand waves with Vic I related a story told to me by a Canadian trucker named Slim in Lytton, British Columbia. As a company driver, he refused to wave to owner operators, viewing them with suspicion because they are out to get his job. "Why be friendly to these guys looking to do you in?" reasoned Slim.

Vic shook his head and smiled in disbelief. He was aware of the owner operator – company driver dispute, but he could not envision how a driver could translate such personal feelings on the highway. It is nearly impossible to identify some owner operators from company drivers because their leased trucks are painted company colors. Vic stuck to the general hierarchy theme. If he feels friendly and if he is not driving on a four lane highway he will wave to nearly all drivers, except tankers (high prestige) and livestock carriers (low prestige).

The social determinators of trucker greeting is not only restricted to truck type, or company affiliation, but it also includes sex factors. As a rule male drivers do not wave to their female counterparts. If they do signal a hello, they are likely to have their greetings rejected. Women drivers tend to translate men's hand waves and their desire for eye to eye contact as a search for "bedding down." According to Vic, for men, the wave is a ritual, a big part of being a trucker. Women drivers see it differently!

Jan, a driver I met in Redding, California sees every male trucker as trying to "hit on her." She believed that there is little neutral ground for colleagiality. When she first became a trucker she made the mistake of waving to men, followed by exchanges on the CB. The results were always the same, male truckers making crude remarks. Now she refuses to exchange courtesies that may lead to further interaction. When guys initiate an exchange by waving, she looks straight ahead until the male driver has passed. Tim, my New Mexico driver, provided this distinct illustration between male and female drivers:

> They (women drivers) don't wave. There is one that I meet all the time going to Reno. I've run in and around her all the time for about three or four years and it wasn't up until the last year before she waved when I went by. Yeah, and then she wouldn't even talk to me on the radio . . . But I guess they just don't want to lead any trucker on or something . . .

Although women drivers are cautious about waving to and exchanging glances with men drivers, they do flash their lights for truckers wishing to re-enter the lane. Their anonymity is retained because of the distance and obstructed vision between drivers. The male – female driver interactions is more fully explained in Chapter Eight.

The CB

We were passing Tacoma, Washington when Vic decided to turn on his CB. Channel seven was loaded with chatter. We listened for twenty minutes before Vic decided to shut it off. The talk was vulgar. For example, one user asked, "Any nigger drivers out there today, any watermelon runners around?" whereupon another speaker answered, "Why, you horny fucker!" This tenor continued during the time the CB was operating.

Vic suggested that the rough language on the CB usually happens around western cities like Seattle, San Francisco, Phoenix and Los Angeles. He placed the responsibility on CB enthusiasts around town and a handful of bad mannered truckers in the vicinity. The drivers were most likely delivery or short distance operators who get their jollies "crapping on people."

Vic is not impressed with people using vulgarity over the air waves to escape their boredom, especially when it impacts him directly. For example, Vic described a time when he was driving around Phoenix and a trucker pulled out of a parking lot and cut him off. The other driver hit the CB and said, "Ah these goddamn (Z Company) drivers." Vic asked what the other guy's problem was, since he had the right of way. The other trucker responded, "Oh, you fucking Canadian drivers." Vic shut off his CB and kept on driving, knowing that the other driver will likely continue to abuse him.

I must have looked surprised because Vic continued to provide further description on "bluffs" over the CB between truckers that go on "every night."

> One gets on a dare, maybe it's a lot of time over girls. A woman driver will come on and she'll be talking to some guy, it's just their goddamn conversation . . . Some guy, just because it's a woman, gets on there and says, "Oh, I would like to fuck," and all this stuff. I mean they are terrible down here. And so the other guy gets mad and then you hear "Oh, you fucking faggot" and this goes on back and forth until one of them says, "Why don't you just meet me up the road and we'll see how big you are," and all this shit. They never stop, they are all mouth, eh. Most of the guys, they don't listen to that, they just, they turn their radios down. They get fed up with it.

Being fed up with garbage on the CB was a quality that was shared by every trucker I met. They were especially down on the "CB enthusiasts," persons who use their sets at home, and who likely belong to radio clubs (Kerbo et al., 1978). Line drivers like Vic questioned the devotees' rights to plug the channel with swearing and bitching for no "other purpose than to get attention." Repeatedly, over-the-road drivers spoke of how the "garbage" on the CB made them "feel cheap." That is not to say that the drivers with whom I spoke were prissy or prudish. They knew that they also swear, but they did so within topical conversation to emphasize points, a form of talk well accepted in trucking. To swear for swearing sake over the CB was generally frowned upon. Whenever a line driver decided to intervene and stop the profanity, he will likely be told to "mind his own fucking business."

Lisa, the trucker I met in Los Angeles believed that such operators are cowards or "chicken" operating behind anonymity, so they can talk dirty. Vic presented a similar line of reasoning indicating that, "at least it keeps this kind of a person off the street and keeps him from doing some real damage."

I asked Vic about the legality of using the CB for chatter, racial slurs and on-going swearing. He was sure it was not legal, suggesting that I ask the police for a definite answer. I followed up Vic's recommendation, querying police officers in Canada and the United States. The police in both countries concurred that chatter and profanity over the CB is in violation of the communications law in Canada and the United States. Unfortunately, it was nearly impossible to enforce unlawful chatter or "profane/obscene talk" on a citizen band radio because CB operators, although obligated to use their call letters, fail to do so. Since most of the discourse is technically illegal, obviously operators would not give call letters that would be self-incriminating. Instead they use handles like Night Rider, Dusty Toad, Galloping Gourmet or Tricky Dick to maintain anonymity, yet keep a distinct identity. As a result the requirement is virtually unenforceable (Dannefer and Poushinsky, 1977).

The CB For Illicit Business

Vic explained that at times the CB facilitates the negotiation of an illegal sales contract between a prostitute and trucker. A typical scenario is when a vehicle, likely to be a RV or Winnebago pulls up beside Vic. A woman inside begins to strip or pose in erotic positions, followed by a hand signal for the trucker to pick up his CB. When he does, the trucker is asked to change the frequency from channel 17 to the last two numbers on the RV's license plate. This strategy reduces the chance of detection because it is nearly impossible for the police to trace the transaction on a channel whose numbers are known only to the seller and buyer.

If the trucker is agreeable, a price, location and extent of services is negotiated. Whenever Vic talks to the prostitutes or, as they are often referred to, lot lizards and commercial beavers, he tells them that he is married. There may be some persistence by the ladies, but usually they stop. The large number of truckers on the highways guarantees that customers for the sexual marketplace are always available.

Vic lets it be known that he "sticks to trucking and that's it." He is happily married and sees no reason why he should entertain commercial beavers. However he acknowledged that there are many drivers who engage prostitutes for services. For him it is a trucker's preference if he wants to "get laid or not." Although negotiation through the CB is a dominant strategy, it is not the only one. Face-to-face encounters between prostitutes and drivers at truck stops is another procedure typically used by women or by pimps proposing sexual services from their women.

Drug sales may follow a similar design. The commodity, price and pickup spot are arranged over the CB. The latter is usually a truck stop. A deal goes down. The police may try to monitor the sale events but, like the prostitution dealings, members find it almost impossible because of the channel shift and short term nature of the negotiation.

More recently, the CB has become the focal point for selling illicit truck parts. Because truck parts are becoming increasingly expensive and because of the long downtime a trucker may experience waiting for certain parts to arrive, "chop shops" have become dominant underground facilities. A truck is stolen, driven to a "chop shop" and stripped in about four hours. The parts are advertised over the CB. Like the sex and drug trade, arrangements are made for a pick-up spot over the CB. The seller makes excessive profits. Although the truckers pay premium prices for the parts, often two to three times the price of new parts, they avoid the heavy expense of downtime.

The CB For Thwarting Justice

While Vic and I discussed police use of radar traps Vic declared that whenever the opportunity arises he will use his CB to warn other truckers of a speed trap. He feels that this is his duty as a "professional," as it is the police officer's job to catch him.

Truckers going in different directions are warned of speed traps, passing police cars, roadside checks or any other enforcement activities occurring on the highway. As illustrated by Vic, using the CB for warning is more than just a generous move, it is an expectation, an obligation for every trucker. It is more personal than some motorists flashing their lights to warn oncoming traffic about police radar speed traps.

Often, when a trucker warns another that "there's a bear on his tail," the officer listens, tries to pinpoint the source, and takes action. Vic described a situation that happened to him a few days ago. He was driving southbound on the I-5. Going north was a truck being followed by a police cruiser. Vic got on the CB and said, "Northbound, there's a smokey right behind you." Both truck and police car passed him. Vic then received a message from a truck following him, "The smokey going northbound, is now behind you southbound." Apparently the police officer, after overhearing Vic's warning, hit the ditch and turned around, intent on catching Vic. But Vic was on to him. He stuck strictly to the speed limit. Even a few miles per hour over the speed limit would have given the "cop" enough reason to stop him. According to Vic this scenario "goes on all the time."

Unusual events at weigh scales, inspection centers, or the roadside become grist for the CB mill, as truckers inform others, who warn others still, forming a complex network. The CB grapevine becomes very active whenever state highway patrols establish spot checks at select weigh scales. In minutes truckers are aware of the police activities. The result may be quick updating of log books, fast assembly of relevant papers or, in extreme cases, search for a detour or a wait at the side of the road, the latter of which I observed with logging trucks in British Columbia.

I learned of a drug bust in Arizona that was aborted because the truckers used scanners to tap police talk. Information about the sting operation was radioed to truckers near and far. As a result the police were forced to use hand held telephones to continue their bust. Officers considered the exercise a failure because of the energetic communication amongst truckers.

The CB For Safety

As we approached the Oregon border, a car suddenly pulled out to pass at the same time Vic initiated a lane change. In an instant Vic steered the rig back into the right hand lane. A close call! But for Vic this was an everyday occurrence which he expects of four wheelers and one with which he can easily deal.

If a traffic situation becomes too dangerous Vic may radio the police on channel 9, monitored by the police for emergency and assistance calls. Vic explained that one night not too long ago, there were two trucks and a car in front of him. One trucker pulled out to pass the other one. As they were side by side the car driver "zipped over on the shoulder beside the truck" to pass both of them. Fortunately the trucker saw the car and compensated accordingly. If he had not, the trucker may have hit the car.

One of the truckers "tried to get hold of a smokey." Vic overheard the driver's request. It was not too long before a police cruiser came on the spot to investigate the situation.

"Smokies," are obstacles in the trucker's minds. Drivers work hard at thwarting the police whenever they can. However, sometimes the conditions are such that truckers and smokies align themselves to stop a dangerous four wheeler. The shifting alliances between truckers and the police are more fully described in Chapter Nine.

My time on the road provided several examples of truckers using the radio not only to call the police but also to warn other truckers about hazardous roadway conditions. A car stalled around the bend near Shasta Mountain was the reason Simon, the driver with whom I was traveling at the time, received a warning call from a northbound trucker. He slowed down, noticed the broken-down vehicle, then related the message to other truckers.

A dramatic use of the CB in an emergency appeared in Motor Truck Magazine (April 1989, pg. 70). A trucker loaded with thirty-six pallets of bricks was in fifth gear as he rolled down a four mile slope towards the Horseshoe Bay Ferry. In the trucker's own words:

> "Well, we started rolling down and I got on the radio. There were a lot of trucks down there. I said listen fellas, I got a 10-33 (disaster) here, so get the hell outa the way 'cause I don't know where she'll stop."

> "We busted through the ferry gate at 70 to 80 miles an hour. There were some cars there, so I swerved but a load of bricks fell off and totalled the cars. I told the swamper when we go airborne, you jump out and we're gonna go for a swim."

The trucker finally stopped against a cement barrier about fifty feet from the end of the dock. His warning calls over the CB helped a bad situation from becoming worse.

Nearly all truckers use the CB to stay up-to-date on road and weather conditions. It is a vital asset for a successful trip, especially when they drive through rough terrain in inclement weather.

Sometimes the CB becomes the intermediary where two distant truckers become co-pilots. A trucker may encounter another driver who is tired. The former may carry on a conversation over the radio with the latter to alert him, or talk him down the road for a distance. The strategy is for the awake driver to keep asking the tired driver questions, forcing the fatigued operator to think and thereby stay alert.

To suggest that truckers are continuous users of the CB exaggerates the point. Most truckers use it intermittently for information about law enforcement activities, road and weather conditions, assistance to troubled drivers, and for breaking personal boredom. Some truckers, especially line drivers who know local drivers and their schedules, use the CB to greet each other "good buddy," and wish each other "a good day." Others employ it for conducting illicit business. Vic did not speak on the radio for sociability reasons. He used it only for specific information or for an immediate purpose such as advising other truckers about roadside or weigh scale police action.

At Truck Stops

Truck stops are central locations for trucker interactions, built for the convenience and needs of drivers. This became obvious not only when Vic and I pulled into the Unocal 76 Truck Stop for dinner, but also from the many hours I spent at these facilities. Although a detailed description of the social organization of a truck stop would be interesting, for my purpose I shall limit the description to trucker communication.

As we sat in the booth Vic and I ordered dinner. Located around the perimeter of the restaurant was a row of booths with telephones for the convenience of truckers. Drivers use them primarily to inform dispatchers of their trips, or to call home. Throughout our time at the restaurant truckers wandered in, sat down, telephoned, the walked out, without ordering food or drink. Waitresses did not bother these drivers because, according to Vic, free use of the telephone is a trucker's privilege not shared by other road users. Motorists are not allowed to sit at the telephone tables. The latter are restricted for the privileged clientele, truckers.

Nearly all big-rig operators I observed and whom I met at truck stops were solo drivers. They entered alone, sat down, ate and left. I noticed little interaction amongst truckers taking place. Occasionally truckers met friends whom they had not seen for a while but who were in the vicinity for a short visit over lunch. Whenever possible, Vic will organize a social lunch with his son or friend who he knows will be heading north when Vic travels south. However, most of the time he enters truck stop restaurants alone and minds his own business.

Truckers with a little extra relaxation time may loaf about in the parts shop or general store located in the truck stop compound. Pick-up-talk ensues. Groups of two, three or four truckers meet and talk about their trucks, mechanics, freight, or specific components of the tractor such as tires, engines or fuel filters. The conversations are proximate. Each time I observed or participated in these chance conversations I was left with the impression that the truckers were lonely people sharing a few moments about common interests, only to again leave as lonely individuals.

Truck stops are not universal in design and meaning. For example, Canadian truck stops are smaller, designed to encourage truck driver communication and collegiality. Many locations have tables arranged to encourage drivers to sit and be sociable. They are called relaxation tables. A late arriving trucker can sit with truckers already there and engage in conversation without apology or conventional request for the right to enter their social turf. When Canadian drivers stop at truck stops in the United States competition rather than collegiality often becomes the operative rule. According to Vic, many American truckers believe Canadian truckers are "screwing up the rates and taking away their work." As a result they refuse to talk to Canadian drivers. Some won't give Canadians "the time of day."

The competitive aspect of trucking is also evident in terms of age. Some older drivers will not speak with younger drivers, thinking that the latter will do them out of business. In Vic's own words, "everybody seems to forget how they got started and nobody is out there making it any easier for anybody." Things change once truckers see each other as equals. Then they may sit around at truck stop restaurants "giving advice . . . most of which is bullshit."

Whether a driver is an owner operator or a company driver also makes a difference at truck stops in the United States. Company drivers are usually members of the Teamsters Union. Many have a loyalty to this organization that exceeds any commitment to a company. Their motto is "Real truckers are Teamsters." So, real tuckers who wish to talk about issues with equals will not discuss them with owner operators, the majority of whom are non union drivers. The reverse is also true. Many owner operators consider themselves to be the backbone of American transportation, hitting the road without depending on other people. For them, the Teamster drivers hide behind the union and company skirts. If given a choice, most owner operators would not choose company union drivers as dinner guests.

The lines of competition for truck comradery is not as solidified in Canada. The long established tradition or mythology surrounding the American owner operator is not as evident. There are fewer owner operators proportional to company drivers in Canada than in the United States. Finally, the truck stops in Canada are not designed as large anonymous neon light truck complexes found in the United States. For example, some truck stops I visited in California were sprawling centres that included restaurants, motels, television rooms, cinemas, pharmacies, barber shops, souvenir shops, clothing shops, lounges and vehicle-related facilities such as gas pumps, parts shops, repair stations, truck wash sites, and huge parking lots. Whereas the shopping center style of truck stop is a growing trend in the United States, in western Canada the facilities are still more intimate, generally consisting of a gas bar, parking lot, repair station and restaurant, the latter of which is smaller, more casual and friendly. If given a choice Vic prefers the Canadian style of truck stop. He likes the "gentle" atmosphere. Vic believes that the Canadian drivers are friendlier in Canada. Witness:

> . . . I could sit there (truck stop) and talk to the drivers. It doesn't matter who you work for where you come from or what you drive.

Based on conversations with many truckers, I would say that most of them do not spend excessive time at truck stops. The need for food, sleep, shower, fuel, or truck maintenance are major reasons for stopping. Once their needs have been fulfilled truckers move on. Although many truck stops are modernized scaled-down versions of shopping centers, they still are considered by many truckers as undesirable places where "misfits" hang out, food is "greasy and expensive," showers are "filthy," and truck maintenance costs are "jacked up." So drivers quickly fuel up, wash their windows, update their log books, telephone their dispatchers, eat, have a smoke, rest for a few moments and head out on their trip. If Vic did not have to stop at the Portland truck stop to let me off, he would have trucked on until late at night. He would have then slept in his truck "somewhere," find a truck stop restaurant to have a shower and breakfast and drive on.

Vic's Departure

As we ate dinner Vic talked about the feeling of trucking that makes it all worthwhile. His earnings are $600.00 a week net, an income that does not keep Vic committed to trucking. Although the economics are tough and the regulations are getting tighter, still Vic "loves driving." He explains:

> I like the mountains, going up the mountains in low gear, going slow, you get time to look around, look down where the train tracks are. Everything is just beautiful. Yeah, I love that.

An hour later Vic said goodbye. He was destined for Redding, California. I rented a room at the truck stop complex. From here I was destined for California with a driver I had yet to meet.

References

Dannefer, Dale, and Kasen, Jill. 1981. "Anonymous Exchanges: CB and the Emergence of Sex Typing." **Urban Life**, Vol. 10, No. 3, October, pp. 265-286.

Dannefer, Dale, and Poushinsky, Nicholas. 1977. "Language and Community" **Journal of Communication**, 27 Summer, pp. 122-126.

Keller, Suzanne. 1981. "The Telephone in New (and Old) Communities." In Lthiel de Sola Pool (ed.) **The Social Impact of the Telephone**. Cambridge, MA: The MIT Press.

Kerbo, Harold; Marshall, Karrie; and Halley, Phillip. 1978. "Establishing Gemeinschaft? An Examination of the CB Radio Fad." **Urban Life**, Vol. 7, No. 3, October, pp. 337-358.

Motor Truck. 1989. "CB Radio Users Are An Extinct Breed." April, pg. 70.

Motor Truck. 1989. "Good Lord Helps Halt Runaway Rig." April, pg. 70.

Stern, J. 1975. **Trucker: A Portrait of the Last American Cowboy**. NY: McGraw-Hill.

Watzlawick, Paul; Bavelar, J. Beavir; and Jackson, Dan. 1967. **Pragmatics of Human Communication**. New York: Norton.

4

DRIVING BY THE LIGHT
OF THE MOON

The trip out of Portland, Oregon was scheduled for seven o'clock in the morning. I telephoned the company dispatcher at six a.m. to receive directions on how to continue my trip. I was told to be patient. A driver would arrive around noon.

I sat in the restaurant interviewing truckers and waitresses. After a two hour wait I became impatient and walked around the large parking lot searching for a semi trailer truck with blue markings around the trailer. It became a long search, one that ended around half past twelve when Dale arrived in a maroon colored tractor, Number 549.

Dale identified himself as a risk taker, a cowboy on wheels. Before deciding to become a trucker, Dale was a professional Brahma bull riding competitor with the North American rodeo circuit. He did not earn a great amount of money, but his prize money was enough to keep him in "beer and bread."

Once Dale got married, he and his wife opened a small restaurant near Shue, Oregon. Suddenly, as he described it, he was "bitten by the trucking bug" to "groove with a load." Shortly after, he was hauling firewood into Reno for a "local guy with a truck." This led to "hauling flatdecks," cattle, gasoline and anything that came along.

Dale always wanted to buy his own truck and become an owner operator. As he saw it, a trucker can make more money per mile because "its like two people working, except one of them is a truck." Two weeks before I met him, Dale reached his goal by purchasing a 1981 Kenworth cab-over for $17,000. Although the truck had already logged one million miles, Dale believed that "the old truck's got over a million miles on her yet." The truck he drove previously for hauling firewood had nearly three million miles on her and she was running smooth except one night while driving down the road the truck started shaking and:

two wheels off the drive axle came off and rolled out in the fields. One of them cut across this guy's yard . . . that wheel went right into his pump house.

The wheel knocked off the plywood on the pump house and fell inside where Dale found it the next morning. Did the resident sue Dale? He answered, "No, I had a couple of pieces of plywood on my truck so I just gave him that to fix his place up."

Dale didn't believe that the same thing would happen to his newly-owned truck. If it dies, he is in serious trouble. He owes the bank the full price of the truck plus interest. To help secure his financial future, Dale signed a lease-on agreement with M Transport, assuring him of constant loads. He receives 42 cents a mile of which he pays his truck 21 cents. Dale reasoned that if he can run 100,000 miles trouble free at 21 cents a mile, he can take some of the money to rebuild the engine. Furthermore, he said, "If I get a third of it (taxes paid) back, all I got to worry about is driving for the next three to four months to pay off the truck."

Dale's presentation of his financial position appeared a little simplistic. Other drivers I asked disagreed with Dale's equation that an owner operator with a family could live on twenty-one cents a mile for the driver and an equal amount for the truck. The cost of fuel, oil, rubber and general maintenance eats up the truck's twenty-one cents. If a little is left over, the cost of insurance and acquisition of state transportation authorizations takes up the rest. Finally, the trucker's personal costs on a trip must be met. Once these expenses are factored in, there is little extra money to save for a rebuilt engine.

As we were cruising south on Interstate Five, Dale mentioned that he had not showered or shaved for three days. He was not apologetic about it. For him, as for other truckers that I met, it was a case of the "it can't be helped" rule. If a driver is expected to run a load for fifteen hours, sleep for a few hours in his bunk, then back haul another load for sixteen hours without access to shower facilities, "it can't be helped" that the driver is dirty. However, Dale believed that truckers should make every attempt to be washed and clean shaven. According to Dale, "to be clean helps drivers' morale."

Dale's Truck

To the right of the freeway was a sign that read "Stage Coach Pass." We raced by it. Dale had his "pedal to the metal" to make it up the oncoming mountain pass. About a half a minute up the pass we slowed down considerably. Interstate Five had a wide shoulder for the uphill traffic. At times three trucks side by side were inching their way up. Dale was one of the passers, traveling 20 miles per hour in the fast lane, overtaking a SWIFT truck which was passing a CF set of doubles driving on the shoulder. Dale felt confident that he could overtake other rigs because of the powerful 400 CAT engine under the hood.

A glance around the inside of Dale's cab showed signs of wear and tear. The windshield was plastered with bugs. Two large yellow blobs made it difficult to see through the lower part of the windshield. The dashboard was dusty. The door handle on the passenger side was inoperable because of a broken crank and a missing knob. The passenger side window was cracked. The sleeper was disheveled and the CB was out of commission. But I soon discovered, the worst was yet to come. To retain the driving context of those difficulties I describe the worst later in the chapter.

The problems made little difference to Dale. As long as the engine and drive train held up, he was satisfied. Dale suggested that although the truck is "running good enough," the engine is using "a little bit of oil every fifteen hundred to sixteen hundred miles." He will likely have the engine rebuilt within the next six weeks at a cost of approximately five thousand dollars. If he was to tear up his engine and buy a new one, the cost would jump to fourteen thousand dollars. If this were the case, Dale would be bankrupt. Witness:

> I couldn't do that, it'd break me. Of course, I was broke when I started. It's just what it is, I'm just playing the chances. When I looked at the truck it was mechanically sound enough, so I think it'll run for at least another 15,000 miles.

But then again, the truck's engine could blow tomorrow! After all, it had a million miles on it. Dale knew he was gambling. He bought the truck on impulse, checked it out and drove it home. Later, he told me that he was not a mechanic, but he knew enough maintenance tidbits to get by. On this basis he concluded that the truck will likely operate trouble free for at least six weeks.

As we drove down the freeway, Dale kept pointing to nice looking rigs, often comparing them to his truck. To improve his truck's looks, Dale discussed his desire to install fibreglass fairings for the roof and the sides of the tractor. Although the changes would increase the weight of the unit, still the aerodynamics would improve fuel consumption.

Buying a new truck was beyond Dale's reach. His theory was that owner operators bought new trucks for economic advantages rather than need based on mechanical failure or wear and tear. According to Dale, an owner operator can use his new truck as a tax write-off for three years, after which, the write-off expires. So, Dale reasoned, truckers buy a new unit to maximize depreciation write-off. They keep their tractor for three years, maintain it, then sell or trade it.

If Dale could afford a new truck he would purchase a Peterbilt, the Mercedes of the trucking world. According to Dale, the "Pete" is the envy of truckers – a luxurious, expensive machine. But, the reliable working machines are the Freightliners or the Kenworths. If he ever found the cash he would buy one of these new machines.

According to Dale, a driver's prestige hinges on two important points: the make of truck and the condition in which a driver keeps his truck. A new Kenworth or "Pete" has a good image because it has style, performance and ride. The machines are awesome in power, and magnificent in looks. A trucker who does not own one of these new machines may still have prestige by having an old one fixed up so that heads turn when he drives by. Chrome stacks and bumpers, extra lights, fairings and unique paint jobs are extras Dale considers to be image makers. More commonplace, yet highly relevant to a truckers esteem, is keeping his tractor washed. On this particular run, Dale was unable to clean his truck because there was no provision for it at the yard. He did not feel like driving two hours to the nearest truck stop for a wash. So he drove a dirty truck, knowing that his image for a time may suffer.

For Dale, his truck has special meaning. It is a partner or a co-driver. In Dale's words, "I got to treat her right and she's gonna treat me right. You go to abusing her, she's gonna cost you a lot of money." She is paying him money of which Dale said he will take a third and "go fishing out on the ocean."

Near Springfield, Oregon, Dale decided to visit a bank and withdraw some money needed for his trip to San Jose. He was aware that the bank was located in the center of the city and that semi trailer trucks were restricted from entering the area. Dale felt that businesses like banks should cater more to truckers so a "guy can get off his truck and get right in there." Because truckers must have cash on hand and their time to bank depends on their random yet long driving hours, truckers break city bylaws to get to banking facilities. In Dale's case, "Often," he said, "I've turned off the road and got myself in a bad jackpot and didn't know what I was getting into. I couldn't turn around, I couldn't go anywhere."

Business owners have come up to Dale to tell him, "I don't want that truck in my parking lot," to which Dale responds, "Well, okay, I'm gettin' out of here as quick as I can. I didn't deliberately come over here and cause you a problem, sir." Dale's point was that since there was no sign stating that trucks were disallowed, more sensitivity should be shown to truckers who are unaware of the no parking rule.

We turned off Interstate Five onto some narrow streets, made a tight left-hand turn at a downtown intersection and maneuvered through to the Springfield Shopping Center parking lot. Dale requested that I stay beside the parked truck while he walked to the bank. He wanted someone to watch the vehicle in case the police arrived or vandals tried to loot his tractor.

My fifteen minute wait was uneventful. Dale returned to the truck with a smile on his face. He withdrew thirty dollars to cover his subsistence to San Jose. Several tight turns later, one in which Dale had trouble getting the truck into gear, and we were back on Interstate Five. Other than backing up some traffic at the lights, Dale managed to drive his vehicle on restricted streets without being noticed by the police. He anticipated no further delays.

The Load

Dale was hauling eighty thousand pounds of flour to a San Jose pizza company. His task consisted of driving eight hundred miles in twenty hours, from Elkhead, Oregon, to San Jose, California. The day before he hauled a load of coffee from San Jose to Seattle. Between trips he rested "for a couple of hours."

In the early days, Dale loaded all of his cargo. Every day he filled a semi trailer full of firewood by hand, throwing it in the back and stacking it to the top. Then he drove to Reno, slept for a few hours and unloaded the wood. His return trip to Seattle was usually a dead head run, unless he could get a hot load for a few dollars "under the table."

At M Transport, Dale usually observes helpers loading his trailer. Although he does not get involved in the physical labor, he must attend to keep count and to make sure that he is not overweight. Dale uses the eighty thousand pound rule to clear all the scales and to allow him to drive without excessive burden on his equipment.

On this particular trip, Dale exceeded eighty thousand pounds. He was worried about the weigh scales because he fuelled his truck after the flour was loaded and weighed. In Dale's own words, "I'm runnin' close, real close." He anticipated burning several hundred pounds of diesel before we passed through the California weigh scales. If he could not do this he expected to get fined by the authorities.

Not long ago, Dale was eighteen hundred pounds overweight in California where his weight for the size and make of trailer exceeded the "bridge law." Yet when he weighed his load in Oregon, he was legal. He paid a $250 fine, whereupon he was free to leave. The inconsistent weight laws in states was a major point of contention with Dale and other drivers I met. Their concern is reflected in the facts. The American federal government's bridge formula is eighty thousand pounds gross, thirty-four thousand pounds on a tandem axle and twenty thousand pounds on a single axle. As of 1986, twelve states exceed the twenty thousand pound single axle limit; thirteen, the thirty-four thousand tandem axle limit; and four, the eighty thousand pound gross vehicle weight limit (Eicher, 1986). The answer for Dale is to stick as close as possible to the federal guidelines.

In his short trucking career, Dale has hauled different loads from high combustible fuels in old "wrecked-up beaters" to cattle in "pig pen" trucks. He does not let a load affect his driving because, according to Dale, "If its bothering you, you're not gonna drive very good." However when you drive a tanker you are in "a bomb," not wanting to "add weight to it, or overload it" because it increases the chance of "blowing a tire of having a wreck." To illustrate the drama of an accident with a tanker, Dale described:

> I seen guys going down the road throwing cigarettes out the window. Now, would that be sensible throwing a cigarette out the window and a tanker behind me. That's gas, that's bad stuff. I'll guarantee you that stuff'll go up so fast. If that tanker went up, we probably wouldn't make it. We'd be toast, just like a couple slices of toast . . . The fire will be hot, and you're not even gonna know it.

Regardless of the danger, Dale was prepared to haul any cargo. For example, he would transport atomic waste without much thought. If everything was set up safely like it was when he worked for a brief period at the Weyerhauser radioactive tanks, Dale could see little reason why he should not haul radioactive waste. At Weyerhauser, Dale worked with a sixty-year-old colleague who, Dale said, after having worked there all his life, "was eating and smoking without washing his hands. He was with it."

The difference between industrial loads such as fuel, oil, pipe and lumber and commercial cargo, such as flour, coffee or vegetables is a trade-off. Whereas commercial cargo is safer than certain industrial commodities, it is more difficult to get it to its final destination. When Dale hauls commercial goods like flour, he must reach warehouses that are usually located in the old, narrow-laned, hidden sections of San Francisco. It is difficult for a trucker driving a conventional type tractor pulling a forty-five foot trailer to squeeze around traffic in tight spots with parked cars on both sides. It is not unusual for Dale to "nick" a parked car or to hit a traffic sign. Whenever either one happens, Dale continues on his way, believing that nothing worth worrying about occurred.

Industrial loads are more dangerous, but they are also more convenient. They are usually designed for easily accessible industrial plants situated on the outskirts of cities. Dale provided the following example to illustrate the ease that may come with an industrial load:

> The other night I was just whipping along there, and all of a sudden I saw an exit, then I wondered . . . do I turn off on this one or the next one? I turned off, pulled off and parked and I was only a block away. And then the other night again, I did the same thing. One night I thought I was lost – I was driving along, and I thought, 'Here's a good wide spot, I'll just pull and sleep and find out where I am in the morning.' I was sitting right in the yard where I was

supposed to unload. And I didn't even know it. I woke up the next morning and I thought, 'Look at this, there's telephone poles laying all around here.' Sure enough, that's where we unload them.

On Risk and Safety

As we approached the California border, Medford, Oregon, came into view. In the distance lay Mount Shasta, lording over all the other mountains, fully dressed in snow. Dale had the truck chugging like a locomotive. He was traveling full out between sixty and sixty-five miles per hour.

As we passed the small city we encountered a section of highway that included long, steep mountain passes, some of which extended for seven miles at six degrees incline. The driving was slow-going, about twenty to thirty mph, six trucks back-to-back forming an unplanned convoy. Dale described this stretch of highway as being "polluted with trucks trying to reach California."

For Dale, the bottom line of being a "real good trucker" is that "you're responsible for yourself." When truckers leave home in the morning they go out there to make a living. According to Dale, "Its just like skin divers, they know when they dive there is a certain amount of risk involved." Whenever Dale begins a trip, he is playing the odds. The best he can do is recognize this and act accordingly. It is not much different from the risks he took riding bulls for fifteen years. According to Dale, a cowboy knows the odds when he starts and does his best to avoid serious injury.

To further illustrate his version of risk, Dale spoke about his hobby of racing Baja cars, or going "Bajaing." Jumping brush, roaring up to a hundred and thirty miles per hour in a "beefed up" Thunderbird is a good time for Dale. He likes to drive erratically. However, he knows that square turning on a dime is dangerous and could cause him to flip and roll. Still he does it for the thrill:

> We run dirt roads and stuff like that in ditches. I've been out there just spinning, sliding it, run down the road 70 mph and lock it and see what it will do. I've done that lots of times on snow or ice – try and run 100 then lock it. I've taken chances.

One of the precautions Dale takes racing Baja cars is to wear a seat belt because "all the way around the top of the car there ain't much protection when you roll over." Yet in the truck, Dale has never worn a seat belt in his life because when driving a rig he is "just cruising the freeway." Because he has avoided many accidents that could have cost him his life, Dale considers himself adept at preventing possible injury-producing accidents.

I repeatedly observed discrepancies between truckers stating their positions on wearing seat belts in cars and actually wearing them in trucks. Truckers are more likely to strap on seat belts in private cars than they are in trucks. After repeated interviewing, I came to the conclusion that the discrepancy in seat belt wearing behavior was based on factors such as control, confidence, size of vehicle and role.

Not wearing safety belts reflects the truckers' views of controlling destiny. They believe that in eighty thousand pound machines there is a limited chance of them getting hurt. Typically, in collisions it is the other drivers who suffer injuries. Truckers sit high, well protected by steel. If or when close calls happen, truckers believe that they have enough natural driving skill to escape getting into a crash. They consider themselves to be professionals able to control their vehicles. Although many trucks do crash, few drivers see themselves as victims. Chapter Fourteen discusses the statistical side of truck crashes.

It is when they perceive lack of control because they no longer have a metal shield around them that truckers become more conscious of their mortality. For example, in a family sedan they feel as vulnerable as every other driver. Some truckers are more wary around trucks than they are around any other roadway features, fully appreciating that many things could go wrong as, for example, a flat tire, loss of brakes, or a jackknifed rig. To protect themselves and their family from possible death and injury, they demand that all members of their family wear seat belts. In a truck they are the "lone rangers," who are only concerned about themselves. In a family vehicle they become husbands and dads trying to protect the family. Confidence in their own ability to escape close calls is overruled by the threat of being victimized by another driver's actions.

Dale and other truckers' views reminded me of a motorcyclist I met a year previously (Rothe, 1988). He was riding with his five-year-old son. Although the biker refused to wear a helmet, he forced his son to strap on a hockey helmet. When I confronted him about the possible contradiction, he answered assuredly that he did not need to wear one because he was in full control of the bike. His son was not. Should the unforeseen happen, his son's head would be protected. Because of his ability to anticipate danger, the biker believed he could jump off the bike with a few bruises. Similarly, truckers also believe that they can control destiny in their trucks. Increased vulnerability in cars encourages them to take less risks and to take precautions against members of their families who have little control of the car.

Farther up the highway I asked Dale why his truck did not have a trip recorder or tachograph. Dale became emotional, responding angrily that if a company mandated or forced him to install a tachograph in his tractor he would "quit running for that outfit." Dale's reason was simple, but important. "Company snooping" is how he termed his concern. As an American owner operator, a trucker has the right to privacy and to drive according to his abilities. Dale does not want to be questioned, if, for example, he stops at a bank to withdraw money and the trip recorder showed downtime.

Furthermore, the Oregon and California highways are mountainous. To make it up one side of the mountain you have to "slap the truck into Oklahoma Overdrive" coming down the other side. That means the trucker while going downhill shifts the gears into neutral to gain maximum speed. At the proper moment, he revs the engine and shifts the truck back into gear. Dale takes this action to save time. A fact in a driver's life! By showing excessive speed, the tachograph may penalize him for something truckers consider to be normal driving; short distance downhill speeding for long distance hill climbs.

Over the last two years Dale experienced three truck crashes, none of which he judged to be his fault. Icy roads, mechanical breakdown and other drivers were assigned blame for the accidents. Dale claimed that he has never "caused a wreck"; he was only a victim of circumstances.

Dale's self-promotion as a safe driver was not restricted to a rationale of non-involvement in "preventable accidents" but included other safety factors. Dale suggested that he does not accept loads if he feels tired. He refuses trips if his equipment needs repairs and he never accepts hauls if he feels ill or weak. Furthermore, Dale proposed that he never intentionally misses weigh scales and he does not possess more than one log book. Dale did admit, however, about cheating on the entries in the log. His explanations provided me with the moral grounds upon which he conducts himself as a safe driver. His announcements were like guides for me to interpret his driving behavior as safe and admirable.

Throughout our discussion, Dale kept reaffirming that he was a safe driver. He spoke eloquently about why he would never agree to a trip if he was tired or if his equipment was not "up to snuff." If, on a haul, he becomes fatigued, he will always pull off the road and take a nap. According to Dale, he never speeds, except to make up lost time in mountainous terrain.

While Dale was defining himself as a safe driver, I introduced the topic of daytime running lights, trying to uncover the reasons for him not using them. Dale's primary reason for not engaging his headlights during the day was that, "when you get tired you pull over and go to sleep for a few hours. When you wake up, your battery's dead." Turning off his headlights when the engine is shut down is not yet Dale's habit.

When I explained that truckers can buy a switch that automatically turns off the lights whenever the motor is shut off, Dale changed his reasoning.

If everyone began to drive with headlights turned on, he said, "pretty soon there'll be other drivers looking at them just like you don't have them on at all." As the novelty wears off, drivers will take them for granted, negating any safety effects. Whether you use daytime running lights or not, or whether you "take all kinds of precautions," the sheer fact that Dale drives six thousand miles a week places him in a position where:

> Your chances are coming closer, your number is coming closer . . . There's going to be accidents.

Dale's argument on daytime running lights symbolized an absolutist position shared by other truckers. During my trip in Canada and the United States I witnessed few trucks with daytime running lights. The prevailing thinking amongst truckers is that using lights during the day drains the battery, has limited or no proven effectiveness and leads to "headlight burnout." Also, they questioned whether lights on during the day lessen the risk of accidents. [1]

In response to Dale and the other truckers' suspicions, I searched through the research literature to establish whether daytime running lights are proven effective. The analyses are included at the back of this chapter. In the sections entitled "Notes," it is shown that in experiments carried out in the United States, Sweden, and Finland, daytime running lights have reduced the number of accidents from seven to thirty-eight percent. They help drivers estimate more conservatively the distance of another vehicle. Attwood (1981) concluded that as the headlight intensity on a vehicle increases, the driver's estimate of distance to that vehicle decreases. Whenever two cars are at the same distance from a person, the lit car is usually judged to be closer than the unlit one. From the point of view of safety, the discrepancy in judgment contributes to greater awareness and driver response time. [2]

Driving With Lights

It was eight o'clock in the evening. We were about two hundred miles from Redding, California. Dusk was creeping up. In the distance larch trees were forming dark statues against the horizon.

We crept up a mountain grade, a vertical climb seven miles long at a speed of twenty miles per hour.. We gained on two trucks that had previously passed us. This was a recurring theme on the trip, being overtaken by trucks that we had already passed, only to again pass them later on.

The time approached eight thirty. Oncoming vehicles already had their headlights on. Dale had not yet flicked on his headlights. I became curious and asked him about it. The driver responded that if I wanted lights at dusk I should turn on the floodlight in the upper right-hand corner of the window. My attempts met without success. Also the floodlight at the upper left-hand side of the window did not function. Dale shrugged his shoulder, responding, "Big deal."

After a few minutes of weighted silence, Dale explained his circumstances. He originally experienced problems with headlights two days ago. To avoid losing time on that trip for repairs he guided his truck behind other trucks that were lit up. So that he could see the shoulder markings, he placed a large flashlight on the dashboard, directing the ray to the side of the road. These improvised tactics helped him arrive safely in San Francisco. The next morning Dale, with limited mechanical skills and experience, thought that the problem was a loose wire. By tightening it, he considered the problem solved. He had once again escaped the cost of major repairs.

I had difficulty understanding how Dale, as a self-proclaimed safe driver with limited mechanical knowledge, would trust solving a vital safety problem like the electrical system. When I probed further, Dale responded that it was not the case of feeling confident in his mechanical abilities, rather, he had trouble finding mechanics to work on his truck. According to Dale, owner operators have such a poor reputation for paying their bills, few mechanics want to work on their trucks. As a result, he is forced to solve minor mechanical problems without placing the truck out of commission for several days. Too much money would be lost! So Dale defines truck maintenance as a day by day issue. It is another chance he is prepared to take in his driving career.

Up to now Dale considered the headlight issue as little more than an inconvenience because a good trucker like him can compensate by driving safely in moonlight. Dale saw little reason for me to worry because "all systems are go," the headlights are repaired. He gave me a smug smile, pointed to the light switch and mumbled, "mmm?" The headlight-turn-on event was about to be celebrated.

Dale flicked the switch. The headlights responded. He glanced at me, asking, "There you go, so what's the problem?" I saw none. I felt relieved that the lighting issue was resolved, because we were now cutting through total darkness.

Dale's confidence in having fully operational headlights soon shattered when, after two minutes of illumination, the lights went out. Dale's diagnosis was that the lights were heating up creating a short circuit. He shrugged it off as "no big deal." He denied the seriousness of the event by generalizing it as something that "happens to every trucker." "Besides," Dale said, "we're safe, there's a moon rising."

During this time we were driving through mountain passes, steep grades, and sharp turns, in total darkness with no illumination to guide us.

At nine thirty p.m. we approached Anderson Peak. Oncoming truckers continued to flash their lights, signaling Dale to turn his on. Dale couldn't. As on his previous trip, he placed his commercial flashlight on the dashboard, aiming it at the roadway's shoulder markings with his right hand while steering the truck with his left hand. Whenever Dale shifted gears, he let the flashlight sit while attending to the transmission and steering wheel with both hands.

The unfolding drama took on new meaning with each passing moment. Whereas ten minutes ago Dale de-emphasized, even trivialized the event, now as we headed toward Anderson Peak, Dale showed signs of concern by invoking the rule of "backup" safety. He assured me that although the headlights failed, the tractor and trailer had enough back-up lights to help other drivers see us. According to Dale, being seen reduced the chance of being hit. Dale's difficulty of seeing where he was going was considered to be less serious because the full moon overhead was thought to provide sufficient light.

Around ten p.m. we reached Anderson Peak, where Dale stopped at the road side brake check to survey the damage. While he wiggled the headlights, I walked around the trailer and discovered that not one light on the entire unit worked. Simply speaking, the rig was blacked out. This news forced Dale to do his own check. No lights! He was puzzled, believing that the fault "must be somewhere in the trailer system," not the truck headlights.[3] Realizing that he could not repair the damage at this time, Dale planned to take the system apart "at the next stop." Because he believed he had little option but to "carry on," we jumped back into the cab to continue the trip. According to Dale, "It'll be hell driving on the other side to California."

Our first challenge leaving Anderson Peak was to drive down a steep grade full of "S" turns. Typically, truckers use their engine brakes for such driving situations. Dale couldn't because he said his engine brake left him two weeks ago. They were not repaired because Dale considered these brakes to be unnecessary, or as he stated, "Just another extra which a trucker can live without." Like the headlights, braking problems "just happen." You "can't do nothing about it."

Going down the steep mountain pass became a memorable experience. Fifty miles per hour (eighty km/hr) in an eighty thousand pound rig without lights or engine brakes! I offered to hold the flashlight on top of the dash so that Dale could steer with both hands. On our way down two trucks passed us, traveling well over sixty miles per hour (ninety-six km/hr). Ahead were some very tight turns, that could prove fatal. As Dale said, any kind of trouble around those bends and the trucker would be forced to "ditch it."

Dale remained calm, taking the problem in stride. As the smell of burning brakes filled the cab, Dale casually informed me that he intended to drive without headlights until two o'clock in the morning. His real problem was how to make it through the California Inspection Center two miles ahead. We were less than a mile from the facility when Dale flicked the switch. The lights responded. As we entered the compound Dale again turned off the lights to avoid them heating up. His move was well thought out. It paralleled the facility's policy which states that to avoid glare at night, approaching drivers extinguish their lights. Following two trucks, Dale looked nervously about while we moved slowly under the large compound floodlights. The inspector looked, but did not notice our problem. He waved us through. To assure he would not be caught, Dale turned on his lights as we began to exit. They worked long enough for a successful escape. Within two minutes they went out. Back came the flashlight. I held, Dale drove!

During this phase of the trip Dale began to redefine the issues. In a serious tone he reported that because of the truck's mechanical failures he did not originally intend to take this trip to San Jose. But he reconsidered his options because:

> . . . if you don't put the loads on when the dispatcher wants, he's not gonna give you any loads tomorrow.

Dale could ill afford to lose loads due to truck malfunctions. He made a calculated decision to withhold vital information about the lights and brakes from the dispatcher. When I asked him how this decision reflected safety, Dale answered that there are times when a trucker's best intentions are overruled by necessity. This was one of those times.

As we approached Vista Point I advised Dale that I must soon depart. The dangerous driving circumstances and insurance company expectations that I take precautions for safety on this research trip did not allow me to drive with him through the night to Redding, California. Dale responded with a questioning look, "Why, what for? It isn't that dangerous you know. I mean it isn't like it's totally dark. The moon is partially out."

We stopped at a roadside inn in Yreka, California. A small truck stop was located two blocks away. I offered to provide Dale sleeping accommodations at the motel if he decided to repair his vehicle in the morning. Dale declined the offer. He stopped in a small shopping mall parking lot, wiggled the lights, shook his head in disgruntlement, jumped in his cab, turned his lights back on and drove off. In the distance I saw him leave with lights turned on. Then sudden darkness! Dale had to keep moving because the flour had to arrive in San Jose by eleven a.m. next morning, even if it meant risking a heavy fine from the California Highway Patrol. When will the lights be repaired? In Dale's own words, "Sometime soon, real soon."

Notes to Chapter 4

1. The May 1989 volume of **Truck World** included a special front page article entitled "Daytime Lights Are Safer, But How Much Is It Going To Cost?" Vehicle fade-out is a major factor leading to truck crashes. Drivers do not see or comprehend another vehicle or they misjudge its speed. According to the author, multi-vehicle accidents could be avoided if the beams were on. In short, the author wrote:

> Translation: 120 deaths, 11,000 injuries, 38,000 accidents and over $200-million in straight material and medical costs. And that's before the lawyers get involved. (Leidl, 1989; pg. 1)

According to Leidl, if a trucker uses all existing lights it draws about two hundred and sixty watts. At full burn, full time, the low beam halogen lamp will blow in about thirty-two days. This translates into twelve extra replacements of headlamps over the life of the tractor. Further problems may arise at the one thousand, five hundred to two thousand hour mark. At that point "secondary instrument, clearance ID and other bulbs will blow." Overall, Leidl costed it out as:

> Fuel costs: full intensity low beams and related glassware burn an extra 0.597 litres per 100 kilometers (0.254 gal/100 miles). At 160,000 km per year, an extra 955 litres or about $315 more per year. Add another $260 for lights.
>
> If you go the reduced intensity route, it's easy to retro-fit the units yourself. Automatic two headlamp CSA-approved switching kits take about 30 minutes to fit, and cost between $20 and $40. (1989; pg. 7)

Other options are reduced intensity headlamps, reduced intensity high beams, reduced intensity low beams, and turn signals, fog lamps or separate DRL lamps. The costs vary from thirty-seven dollars (diesel cost per year) for reduced intensity high beams to one hundred and sixteen dollars (diesel cost per year plus $70.00 bulb) for reduced intensity low beams.

Some common rationalities concerning mass use of daytime running lights are:

> Most motorcycles run with DRLs; the fear here is that they'll now be "masked" by a virtual forest of four-wheel vehicle DRLs. And what you can't see, you can still hit – or get hit yourself.
>
> While Mike Boyd says DRLs are a good idea ("I drive with mine on"), the Volvo sales engineer wonders if he'll get lost in the common glare: "If

everybody has them on, does it counteract the whole fact that you don't stand out anymore?"

"That's the argument I've heard from a lot of people. If they're all on, then you notice the ones that haven't got them on better."

Others say the worry is groundless. "You may see a lot of cars with headlights, but you're still going to see them," says Freightliner Canada's Wayne Brock.

Transport Canada expert Jim White agrees. He likens DRLs to traffic lights: they might get as common as road citations, but they sure are conspicuous.

"People notice them, and traffic lights have certainly been around a long time." (Leidl, 1984; pg. 7)

2. It is impossible to write about lights without describing daytime running lights. Experiments on daytime running lights were undertaken by Greyhound Bus Lines (Allen and Clark, 1964, Attwood, 1981) A T and T Lines (Diesel Equipment Superintendent Journal, 1973) and Checker Cabs (Allen, 1979). Based on survey results each company experienced reductions in accidents during the time of experiment. For example, Greyhound Bus Lines noted a twelve percent reduction in accidents, A T and T Long Lines, thirty-two percent overall and Checker Cabs found that it had seven percent fewer collisions.

In naturalistic and controlled experiments daytime running lights were proven to be effective in reducing the number of fleet collisions.

In Sweden a daytime running light law was legislated on October 1, 1977. As a result, the use level by all motorists was raised from fifty percent to ninety-five percent. According to Andersson and Nilsson (undated), the estimates of resulting accident reductions vary from six to thirteen percent, for mishaps that involve two or more vehicles. Similarly, Rumar (1981) reported that crash reductions varied from five to fifteen percent.

Charles Kaehn (1981) recorded a six-year experiment in Finland. He established that for the winter months there was a twenty-one percent reduction in collisions overall and a twenty-eight percent reduction in crashes involving vehicles traveling toward each other. The daytime running light law, implemented in November 1972, initially applied only for urban areas during the winter months.

The effects of daytime running lights on distance judgment was tested by Horberg (1977). A group of subjects, within a given time of several seconds, were instructed to compare the distances between themselves and two stationary vehicles sitting in adjacent lanes between 820 and 1,510 feet (250 and 460 meters) away. One of the cars had its lights turned on at different intensities while another had its lights off. Subjects were asked to assess whether one vehicle was closer; if so, which one, or whether they were both the same distance away.

The conclusion reached was that as a vehicle's headlight intensity increases, the judged distance to that vehicle decreases. Although both vehicles in the experiment were the same distance from the subjects, the lit vehicle was judged to be closer than the unlit one (Attwood, 1981).

Earlier, Attwood (1981) designed an experiment with moving vehicles where subject drivers followed a lead car while monitoring the location of the oncoming vehicle.

The results from this study again showed increased awareness of distance when lights are on. The safety gap accepted during a passing task varied with both headlight intensity and the daylight level. When an approaching vehicle was unlit, drivers tended to overestimate the distance to it. Attwood reasoned:

> . . . practical terms, the SG data indicate that many more risky passes would occur at low daylight levels when the approaching vehicle is unlit than when it is equipped with either full or reduced-intensity, low beam headlights. (1981; pg. 6)

Although the research undertaken in the Nordic countries and in laboratory-like conditions in the United States illustrated major safety-related benefits to daytime running lights, the findings may be questioned when applied to North America. The light conditions are different between the Nordic countries and the southern United States. In fact, they are different between northern Canada and the United States. In a series of safety recommendations arising from the National Transportation Safety Board and presented to the National Safety Council the chairman wrote:

> But the very reasons that prompted these Nordic countries to lead the way in daytime running light use also limit the applicability of their research to the United States. The light conditions are very different. During the long winter in high northern latitudes, ambient light is low throughout most of the day, with lengthy periods of twilight. And with the sun frequently low in the sky, glare is common. These are the kinds of conditions in which daytime running lights are thought to be most effective, but such conditions are not found with comparable frequency throughout the United States.

> There are differences as well in climate and road conditions. However, there have been studies in this country that suggest that daytime running lights would be effective, to some extent, in cutting the toll from highway accidents. (1985; pp. 3-4)

3. To experience electrical problems in truck trailers is commonplace (Leugner, 1989). The key causes are "less-than-acceptable preventive maintenance" and severe weather conditions. Electrical failures like the one experienced by Dale can result from "undersized or poorly designed original wiring, road vibration, corrosion and chafing, poor ground circuits or connections and a lack of preventive maintenance inspections." Such inspections must make sure:

that all wiring is 14 gauge
that all wiring is copper and not aluminum
that the wiring circuit conforms to the SAE Color Code
that lamp units are shock mounted
that the trailer has a special common ground for the trailer
that connections are soldered and taped with water resistant tapes
that the alternator does not overcharge the bulb.
(Leugner, 1989; 35)

References

Allen, M.J., and Clark, J.R. 1964. "Automobile Running Lights – A Research Report." **American Journal of Optometrics**, 41 (5), pp. 293-315.

Anderson, K., and Nilsson, G. (no date) **The Effects on Accidents of Compulsory Use of Running Lights During Daylight in Sweden**. Linkoping, Sweden: Swedish National Road and Traffic Research Institute S-581 01.

Anderson, K.; Nilsson, G.; and Salusjarui, M. 1976. "The Effect of Recommended and Compulsory Use of Vehicle Lighting on Road Accidents in Finland." Swedish Road and Traffic Research Institute, Report No. 102.

Attwood, Dennis. 1981. "The Potential of Daytime Running Lights as a Vehicle Collision Countermeasure." SAE Technical Paper Series, 810190.

Bentham, J. 1948. **The Principals of Morals and Legislation**. New York: Macmillan Co.

Bobell Transport **Drivers Manual**.

Bok, S. 1978. **Lying: Moral Choice In Public And Private Life**. New York: Vintage Press.

Croffman, I. 1967. **Interaction Ritual**. Garden City, NY: Anchor Books.

Eicher, J.P. 1986. "Important United States Issues or Truck Weights and Dimensions" In **Proceedings: International Symposium on Heavy Vehicle Weights and Dimensions**. June 8-13, Kelowna, B.C.

Henderson, Robert L.; Ziedman, Kenneth; Burger, William J.; and Cavey, Kevin E. 1983. Motor Vehicle Conspicuity. SAE Technical Paper No. 830566.

Horberg, U. 1977. "Running Light-Twilight Conspicuity and Distance Judgment." University of Uppsala, Department of Psychology, Report No. 215.

Kaehn, C. 1981. "A Cost/Benefit Study of a Potential Automotive Safety Program on Daylight Running Lights." NHTTSA, April.

Leidl, D. 1989. "Daytime Lights are Safer, But How Much Is It Going To Cost?" **Truck World**, Vol. 6, No. 5, May.

Leugner, L. 1989. "Trailer Electrics." **Independent Trucker**, October.

National Transportation Safety Board. 1985. "Safety Recommendations." Washington, DC, November 5.

Public Information, Insurance Corporation of British Columbia, News Release, June 4, 1984.

Rumar, K. "Daytime Running Lights in Sweden – Pre-Studies and Experiences." SAE Technical Paper Series, 810191.

Stamler, P. (ed.). 1989. "South Carolina Becomes 34th State To Enact Belt Use Law." Highway and Vehicle Safety Report, June 19.

Stein, Howard. 1985. "Fleet Experience with Daytime Running Lights in the United States, Insurance Institute for Highway Safety." May.

5

OWNER OPERATOR VS. COMPANY DRIVERS

At six in the morning, I telephoned the president of M Transport at his residence to report my predicament. He was not thrilled that one of his owner operators drove without headlights but he did not appear overly concerned either. "These things happen," he told me. If there was a full moon, it was not all that bad. The president's administrative assistant telephoned me at nine a.m. and informed me that another company truck was in the vicinity and would pick me up later in the morning.

Around eleven a trucker named Simon pulled up to the motel and invited me to hop aboard. He wondered aloud why the company management selected him among the many other drivers nearby to retrieve a stranded researcher. He considered his assignment to be a privilege.

Simon opened the conversation by detailing his driving biography that began thirty-five years ago. When he was six years old, Simon was driving on his "dad's big dairy farm and fuel business." As Simon described it:

> I was six years old and naturally too young to drive. My brother, he's a year older, would stand on the seat. I'd be on the floor boards working the pedals.

When the hay was loaded, the hired people would holler for young Simon, crouched on the floor, to push in the clutch and brake with his hands while his brother steered. When Simon reached twelve he was driving alone around the farm. At sixteen, he was driving commercially for his father hauling wood and coal.

Although Simon had ample childhood experiences driving trucks, he did not make trucking his first choice for a career. He always wanted to be a lawyer. To pursue his goal, he attended a college in Washington, hoping to earn high enough grades for entry to the University of Washington law school. However, while playing football for the college team he was seriously injured on the "next to last game." In the words of Simon, "I got my head split wide open. I was six months in the hospital . . . I didn't finish my schooling." To this day, he believes that had he not been injured he would have become an attorney.

Over his long trucking career Simon has driven with different companies. Just before he signed on with M Transport, Simon was hauling chips for a company that went bankrupt in 1980. According to Simon, "That's the only reason I changed jobs. It was not my doing, just something that happened."

Entering Interstate Five, Simon shifted the truck smoothly into ninth gear. The inside of his Freightliner was clean and orderly. The windows were washed and the bunk was made. On top of the engine case or "doghouse," between the driver and passenger seats, sat a cooler filled with vegetables, sandwich meat, bread and soft drinks. I accepted his offer of a drink and indulged in a cola.

After a few miles down the freeway Mount Shasta came into full view. Simon volunteered to stop the truck so that I could take a proper snapshot of the scenery. Part of the offer was that I also take a picture of him standing beside the truck.

When we began to roll again, Simon described what trucking means to him. It is "a lot of hard work where you do make good money sometimes, but you earn it." According to Simon, it takes a certain breed to be a trucker. You have to be born into it, stick it out for at least five years, love driving and have a woman who understands you.

For Simon the real trucker is a Teamster, company driver and professional. He was proud that for the twenty-three years in which he has driven for different carriers, he has always been a member of the Teamster's Union. His goal now was to retain his job as a company driver with M Transport and retire proudly as a Teamster.

Real Truckers

As we drove through the greenery offered by the Cascade Range, it became obvious that Simon had some fundamental, unshakeable views about "real" truckers. They are professionals who are hired as company drivers, get along with the company and their fellow workers, carry no animosity, resist taking drugs and they "keep their mouths shut and do what they're told without any hate or discontent." According to Simon, unprofessional drivers have "negative attitudes about their companies and their jobs," "take drugs," "always party at truck stops," "are always late with the loads" for which they "tell the dispatcher some phony excuse . . . like the truck broke down." Simon's view was that professional truckers are company drivers while unprofessional truckers represent owner operators.

By definition owner operators own and drive their tractors and perhaps their trailers, while company drivers operate company vehicles. Owner operators maintain themselves as businesses or single person proprietors, contracted or leased to haul freight. Company drivers are employees, working for specified remuneration and benefits. Owner operators usually lease themselves to carriers, working through the carriers' networks. Company drivers haul for one company. Furthermore, owner operators maintain their own vehicles, are usually not members of a union, are responsible for loading and unloading their freight, and they have, theoretically, the freedom to choose their own loads. Company drivers as a rule engage in little maintenance work, are generally Teamsters, get reimbursed for loading and unloading and they haul freight assigned, usually around a ten hour mandated time period.

In the public's eye, the image of trucker is usually synonymous with the image of owner operator. Crowe and Kinsey (1989; pg. 25) described it beautifully:

> Picture this – the last American cowboy, a rebel barreling down the highway in a rig either overloaded with chrome or so beat-up looking that it seems a miracle that it runs. Picture this latter-day Billy the Kid breaking all known speed laws, blaring Waylon and Willie from the truck's tape deck, screaming to his buddies on the C.B. radio all day long. Picture "Smokey and the Bandit." Picture "B.J. and the Bear."

The author's description is not without credibility in the real world. Witness Simon's description:

> They're leasers. They're probably on drugs and drive for thirty hours . . . Company's not paying them much money so they drive old wrecks . . . then they get on the CB and let loose.

According to Simon, the trucking world is composed of the two distinct and separate groups. It is cut and dry with no overlap. This became more obvious as my trip with Simon proceeded.

Starting Out

The roots of older owner operators and company drivers are planted in similar soil. Many learned to drive on the farm or within the family context where father, uncle, and/or brother drove. Training was on the job. Today's younger owner operators, however, are more likely to have graduated from a driver training school, gained a little experience, taken out a large loan and bought their own trucks. According to Simon, owner operators do not have to pass company hiring tests or employment screening tests, as do company drivers! Their driver records are not reviewed every year because the company does not pay for their insurance or their traffic violations. Consequently, according to Simon, they are not as safety conscious and as trustworthy as are company drivers.[1]

Yet, most of the owner operators with whom I traveled once were employed as company drivers. They quit to follow a dream of independence, freedom and economic advantage. They mirrored McRae's (1989;30) description of the typical owner operator being an "older family oriented man who has been able to raise the money to make that substantial investment in his own truck."[2]

The strategy of starting out as a company driver, eventually buying the truck and leasing it back to the company is, in Simon's mind, a "bad move." He has seen many drivers, who he judged to be "good truckers," "having a tough time of it," eventually "quitting trucking and digging ditches." Witness two truckers whose accounts illustrate their fate:

1. I've been hauling for about 12 years now and I can tell you that I'm starting to get worn down. I can hardly keep up with my payments as it is, never mind going out and buying that new truck that I need badly. My old Kenworth can only take so much. I don't know. My wife is after me to get out and maybe she's right. I got lots of debts, headaches and aggravation and really nothing to show for it. Maybe it is time for me to get out.
2. It's a real struggle and I have the ulcers to prove it. My father is after me to go work with him on the farm and I may just do that. I thought I could make it as an o/o but I'm not having too much luck. I'm working my tail off but I don't seem to be getting anywhere. (Robertson, 1989; pg. W12)

Some of the battle-scarred owner operators hit the podium to warn new recruits about entering their precarious world. One owner operator's version is:

I would tell a young guy not even to think about becoming an owner operator – stay as a company driver or get yourself another job. (Robertson, 1989; pg. W2)

A discussion with members of the United States Truck Driving School Inc., in San Bernardino, California, illustrated that although the ideal-type owner operator is older, most young trainee graduates are destined for this life. Their dream is to share in the image and earn a good income.

Most often the dream, the ideal of young owner operators fizzles. Rather than being free, independent, and selective they must contract themselves to carrier companies or other fleets, abiding by its policies, dispatching, freight rates and wishes. The independence left is only one of the imagination, and it is usually not enough to sustain them over a long period of time.

The company driver to owner operator route is one which Simon does not intend to follow, and one for which he has little sympathy. He envisions it as a sell out, company drivers going over to the other side.

Loading and Unloading

Simon considered himself to be an old, weathered, pro driver who can drive twenty consecutive hours if he wants to. He seldom gets tired because his extensive driving experience has helped him get used to driving for long hours at a time. The one thing about trucking that does tire him is loading. As Simon indicates:

> What tires you out is hand stacking a load or unloading physically. You've gotta take the pallets off this trailer then go over there and load.

Often truckers have to drive ten hours followed by "another eight hours of physical work."

As a company driver, Simon can escape the tiresome toil if he wishes. He receives sixteen dollars per hour for loading and unloading. With the company allotting a maximum of three hours for unloading, he can earn forty-eight dollars for his endeavors, whether he physically loads, supervises others, or helps intermittently. The rate is constant.

Simon takes advantage of the benefit by hiring dock gypsies or lumpers for sixteen dollars an hour, or up to forty-eight dollars gross pay, to unload while he sleeps. For him the economic value of three hours' sleep is greater than the money allotted. By gaining three hours, he is able to start earlier and not lose time in the log book. As Simon outlined, "I'm making my money when the truck's moving. I'm not making any money if I tire myself out." When he is rested he "can do miles." If he is stacking cargo for three or four hours, he doesn't feel like driving for the rest of the morning.

Owner operators are usually responsible for unloading the freight. If they subcontract the job they lose about $50, but they gain sleep time. If they wish to get a solid sleep in a motel they lose another $25 or more for room rental. To avoid the expense, they rest in their sleepers which may not promote a deep sleep and which have no toilet or washing facilities for a driver to freshen up and feel good. Drivers may have to pay another $2.50 to $5.00 in tokens for a shower at a truck stop in addition to losing valuable driving time.

The discrepancy in loading pay and responsibility hits owner operators hard. If an owner operator is unable to hire help at the warehouse he has little choice but to unload the cargo himself with no remuneration. The following scenario typified by Dale in Chapter Four often unfolds. Early in the morning the driver hand stacks his load for three to four hours. Becoming worn down, he drives for about twelve to fifteen hours. He sleeps for the next six hours. Upon waking, he unloads for three hours, drives to his next pick up spot where he, again, physically loads his trailer for a return trip. Once loaded with six to eight hours of manual labor already spent unloading and loading, the owner operator drives for twelves hours. In a twenty-four hour stretch, the trucker may have received five to six hours sleep, ten hours driving if he is running legal, and eight hours of hard physical work.

Dispatchers offer little support for the plight of the owner operators. Their job is to get the goods to their destination for a profit. The dispatcher's work is accomplished when the bills are handed to the driver. Any interference in the process results in the dispatcher becoming aggravated. According to Simon, if, for example, an owner operator complained to a dispatcher about insufficient sleep resulting from loading and/or unloading goods, the dispatcher will likely become "mad," and tell the trucker, "you can sleep all day then, because the loads are all gone."

Throughout the discussion, Simon explicated that he was personally unsympathetic to the owner operator's plight. He believed that they are responsible for undercutting company driver contracts by agreeing to load and unload cargo without pay. They are creating a major problem for unionized company drivers. Simon further believed that owner operators are out to destroy company drivers.[3] For instance:

> Our union contract used to say that there had to be more company trucks than leasor's trucks. That's changed where you now have more lease trucks than company trucks per company.

Because owner operators are willing to work more for less pay, company lease divisions are taking advantage of them. They push the owner operators to the edge of fatigue in order to reap greater profits, expecting them to drive longer, farther and faster, and to load and unload goods without remuneration.

Cost of Driving

Simon earns forty-three cents a mile, while owner operators get paid forty-four cents. But, Simon clarified, out of the rate per mile, owner operators "have to pay for their trucks, fuel, license, insurance for their wives and kids, state special insurance and stuff like that." You drop "two hundred dollars right there." On the basis of his experiences, although owner operators gross from forty to forty-eight thousand dollars, at most they net $28,000.

Simon was generally correct in his assessment. Based on figures in Driver/Owner magazine (1989), the owner operator's truck eats up a significant portion of the overhead. For example, thirty percent of the overhead or income received beyond the drivers personal mileage charge is spent on fuel, nineteen percent goes to truck payments, fifteen percent is lost on truck depreciation, eight percent is apportioned for tire and wheel maintenance and another two percent goes to fuel tax. In addition, thirteen percent of the overhead goes to insurance, licenses, tolls and other paper costs.

The bottom line for Simon is that owner operators clear about half of the income they make. According to Simon, "we make good money, they don't." As a result, owner operators are more apt to go bankrupt.[4] To make his point Simon offered the following insight:

> To prove my point, this company might have 200 leasors. The longest will stay maybe two years or so . . . but they don't last long. They may last three months, six months. They go under. Maintenance eats them up, company's not paying money.

My response was that if his figures were reasonably accurate, why would companies continue to contract with owner operators? Wouldn't the cost of turnover eventually even out the increase in profit? Simon had a ready answer. "The companies don't care, they're not out anything. They haven't paid for anything." They just collect. Much like a revolving door, there are always new owner operators willing to give independent driving a try.[5]

While we were driving through the Trinity Mountains in bright sunshine, Simon momentarily switched topics to describe the spiritual history of the caves found in the nearby mountain sides. Once we passed the points of interest, Simon returned to the topic of why companies continue to contract owner operators despite the high turnover. A major reason is ease of exploitation. Lease divisions can take advantage of owner operators in such areas as truck maintenance or trailer rental. Depending on the company, owner operators may be mandated by contract or pushed by threats to repair their tractors in the company's shop. According to Simon, the "catch is that the owner operators pay a lot more than it costs company trucks to be repaired." Also, some owner operators are expected to lease company trailer units with logos at unusually high costs. When you add these factors with companies saving money on loading, insurance, mileage reimbursement, truck maintenance and, in some cases, bookkeeping and administration, the reason for companies using owner operators becomes evident.

Random Issues and Owner Operators

On the way to Red Bluff, the freeway became hazardous, full of potholes, cracked cement and shifting roadbed. The truck was jerking back and forth, forcing Simon to drive in the left-hand lane, which in California is illegal. Simon was taking a chance on receiving a ticket for thirty-two dollars. He believed that it was legitimate to drive in the passing lane because he was not blocking any traffic behind him. But, according to the driver, "you have to watch it when you come to the off ramps." The police tend to "hang out there and if they see you, you'll get nailed."

After a few minutes of discussion, Simon began to damn the California freeway system. Witness:

> Roads are falling apart so fast that I could say another two years and they're gonna have a lot of construction on it. When that happens, everything's gonna damn near come to a standstill on account of there'll be a line of traffic 200 miles back there because they got one lane for fixing these roads.

Because twenty hour driving will likely take thirty hours, and owner operators depend on speed and time to maximize their earnings, the poor roads will likely "eliminate a lot of owner operators because they got to make their payments." Simon did not discuss the frightening possibilities owner operators may face in sympathetic terms. Rather, he gave a shrug and asked the rhetorical question, "What can you do?"

A short while later Simon related the roadway to snow and ice conditions. Whenever he encounters snow packed roads in daylight he "chains up." For him there is no exception to the rule. At night, he will not drive in snow because he is likely to be tired and would find it difficult to see.

Simon indicated that a person would not have to look far to see truckers who refuse to follow his safety rule. As with other problems, the culprits are owner operators. In his own words, "They will park their truck at a truck stop about ten in the morning, too damn lazy to put their chains on." Simon then moved the accusation towards a conspiracy where the owner operators will "lie to their dispatchers," and say, "oh, I'm snowed in, I can't move." "Well," Simon continued, "he can move, he can work the same damn way I do."

Simon's habit of pointing his finger at owner operators continued throughout the trip. If a driver had a "bad day," is "kind of crabby" and "lets loose on the CB," he is likely to be an owner operator. If there is a dirty, poorly maintained truck in sight, the driver has to be an owner operator. Whenever Simon spoke of truck wrecks, the driver was always an owner operator. The "rotten eggs" who take drugs and visit commercial beavers are owner operators. The list, quite extensive, continues.

To help him stay clear of truck stops and possible relationships with owner operators, Simon brings his own food and microwaves it at the unloading sites. During the conversation Simon focused on his cooler, inviting me to have another drink. The temperature was hot and rising, encouraging me to accept a ginger ale, while Simon opened a can of cola. While sipping our cold drinks, Simon continued his owner operator bashing. He hates stopping at truck stops, because that's where the owner operators hang out, "drinking coffee for two hours," "gettin' on drugs" and "bitchin'" about companies and dispatchers. Just the thought of truck stop restaurants disgusted him. He preferred to be driving as a professional trucker, ten hours on the road minding his own business. He refuses to greet owner operators with a hand wave or talk with them over the CB. In fact, on several occasions Simon did not give the customary light flick to passing trucks that were obviously driven by owner operators.

Consistent with the stereotype of owner operators, Simon considered them to be hedonists without restraint, slicing through freeway traffic, breaking laws at will, crashing into innocent victims, taking drugs and falling asleep behind the wheel. Witness:

> Ninety percent of these wrecks you see out here you'll find is owner operators. They're probably on drugs or they drove 30 hours, went to sleep, they run off the road. If you take a company driver, they very seldom have a wreck because the company's got guidelines to go by. They got charts of their truck, to show how fast we should be going, and when we stop, how long we stop. We got to stop in about ten hours so we're not running off the road killing people plus we can't take drugs and stuff 'cause we take drug tests all the time.

The Other Side of Red Bluff

Past Corning, on the way to Dunnigan, California, Simon began to present some consistent vignettes of his personality and his relationship with other drivers. When Simon believes he is right, he is right. He will go to any length to prove it.

His first rule is, obey the speed limit. He sticks to the company standard of fifty-eight mph, which I observed to be consistent. According to Simon, "One time a cop gave me a ticket and said I was going sixty-eight mph. No way." Simon took the tape inside his tachograph to court to prove his innocence. He won the case.

On another occasion, Simon stood toe to toe with a California trooper who wanted to ticket him for driving in the left-hand lane. The trucker asked the policeman to prove that a law exists which states that an eighteen wheeler cannot drive in the passing lane. The officer was unable to present the facts, instead giving Simon a ticket for a broken tail light. Although Simon was given a traffic violation, he translated the affair as a victory.

Simon has lately become suspicious of the California Highway Patrol. He is convinced that the police are picking on M Transport and on him personally. For example, a few weeks ago Simon was accused of moving his fifth wheel while traveling down the road. According to Simon, the feat is impossible. He took pictures and again went to court to "beat the rap." Several days later the same officer again stopped Simon for a fifth-wheel violation. As before, Simon was going to take a picture, but, according to him, "the cop said no, no, and gave me a ticket for unlawful order anyways."

Simon has, as of this trip, reported fifteen drunk drivers to the police over the CB. They were all "nailed." He not only reports car drivers but also fingers truckers. If he witnesses a drunk trucker, or one driving erratically, he will call the police, regardless of whether the driver works for his company. For Simon, if the trucker is unsafe you get him. Simon is "always on the lookout."

Not surprisingly Simon does not consider himself to be popular with his company colleagues. As he interprets it, the major reason for his unpopularity is that:

> I will run hard. They don't run hard and they drink a lot of coffee, go two hours and stop again. Here I am up here three, four hours before they are and they get mad at me.

Simon gets accused of being a company man, a guy "who'll do anything for the boss." Simon's response was:

> Christ, a lot of guys don't like me for that, but, the company likes it because, but I'm not out here to suck ass or brown nose, or whatever. I'm out here to make a living.

I think it is appropriate to include a footnote at this point in the text. Danny and B.J., two truckers, each with whom I rode after this segment of the trip, knew Simon. Independently they referred to him as "deep throat," "company rat," and "suck hole," who would squeal on anybody to get better loads, routes or equipment. To them, Simon was not a colleague, a man to be trusted. Their independent assessments, both drivers believed, are shared by other M Company drivers.

We approached Dunnigan around six p.m. The hamlet consisted of a hotel, restaurant and three houses. Simon drove me directly to the hotel. Throughout the trip he left the impression that he was an upright man, a real trucker fighting the ills not only of owner operators but also of non-union truckers and non-professionals. He chastised all drivers who did not meet his expectations, yet he always assumed that he could and did meet his own high expectations, making him an exemplar trucker.

Simon never had a reportable accident. This claim, I later found out while driving with Danny and B.J., can be disputed. According to Danny, a year ago he saw Simon's truck in the ditch. To avoid an accident report Simon called a tow truck to pull him out. He then drove to a body shop to straighten out minor bends. To keep his record clean he paid for the entire service "out of his own pocket." Simon stated that he would not break traffic laws. He spoke highly of company management. He described himself as a safe driver, always checking his mirrors. He would never tailgate. He was a company man who abided by laws and regulations whether they were good or not. Simon did not grant these qualities of a model driver to owner operators.

Notes to Chapter Five

1. As a group, owner operators experience greater exposure because they tend to drive greater distances more often. A survey of 1,416 truck and bus drivers located in East, West, Mid West and South regions, by Sanders (1977) illustrated that:

   > For truck drivers, those driving as owner – operators averaged more miles (mean = 362.9) than those driving exempt (mean = 348.9), certificated (mean = 343.5) or private (mean = 301.1). (1977; pg. 42)

2. There is surprisingly little accurate information about the differences between owner operators and company drivers? But a few points can be retrieved. When Wyckoff (1979) engaged a survey of American truck drivers, he learned that there are more young drivers under the age of 35 who are owner operators than company drivers. This is realized because (1) the increasing number of new owner operators being young and (2) the greater percentage of truck drivers being owner operators.

   In 1989 things have changed. In a personal interview with Edward Shea, editor for a major owner operator magazine, I discovered that two large surveys in 1977 and again in 1987 were done on owner operators. Several relevant findings were gleaned.

   In 1977 the owner operator's median age was 35 years. A driver's median truck driving experience was ten years of which three years were experienced as owner operator. In 1987, the owner operator's median age jumped to 43.5 years, of which a median of 16.5 years were spent in truck driving and 9.5 years were experienced as owner operators. It appears from these numbers that the trend is for owner operators to be older, wiser and more experienced. Or, the data could be interpreted as representing a closing field, one which young newcomers are not so ready to enter, or if they do, they are quick to leave.

In Canada, a recent study by Transport Canada was based on 1,509 drivers interviewed in four western provinces, Ontario, Quebec and New Brunswick:

> Drivers who owned the tractor they were driving tended to drive greater distances per year and had driven more hours in the past week. More owner – operators exceeded the federally prescribed hours of service than did employee operators. (Transport Canada 1987; pg. 2)

The fact that owner operators reported a mean of 58.5 hours of service for the past week as opposed to 53.9 hours for company drivers makes the finding statistically significant (at $p < .0001$).

3. It does not appear that based on freight hauling statistics owner operators are increasing their share of the trucking business. The **Commercial Carrier Journal** each year reports the top 100 carriers in the United States. Yellow, Roadway and Consolidated Freightways hold about 25 percent of the total Less Than Truck Load (LTL) market. Desmond (1988) found that a year later these three companies combined increased their total LTL tonnage by 38 percent. If UPS is added on large percentage of freight hauling is realized. In the 1989 report Desmond (pg. 77) projected:

> And, as has been the case since CCJ started providing data on the Top 100 in 1969, four less-than-truckload carriers have dominated the for-hire industry, based on revenues. As reflected in the chart, Yellow Freight system, United Parcel Service (UPS), Consolidated Freightways and Roadway Express continue to gradually increase their share of the nation's freight, to the point that they may soon control one-half of the traffic handled by the Top 100 fleets.

Yet, despite the large percentage of volume delivery undertaken by these companies in 1986, only 12,867 owner operators were recorded as being affiliated with these companies (Glines, 1987). The number shrunk to 11,877 in 1988, all of whom were contracted to Consolidated Freightways.

The downward trend for owner operators is closely monitored by many transportation analysts, as Brown and Sons of Baltimore. Researchers for this firm project that LTL carriers with nationwide distribution systems will attain an ever increasing share of the market and more shippers interested in reliable, cheaper country-wide haulers will hire LTL carriers.

The lease operators appear to maintain a solid footing in the trucking business. Proof is found in the *BCTA News and Views* (September 21, 1989; 2) where a study by the National Accounting and Finance Council of the American Trucking Association stated:

> Use of independent contractors has remained relatively stable over the past few years despite continuing speculation regarding their demise. Of 514

respondents to the survey conducted last year, 76.7% said they were using single or fleet contractors in 1987 and 99.5% of those companies said they would continue to use independents in the future. In previous surveys, respondents using independents were 78.7%, 1986; 82%, 1985; and 79%, in 1984. The study also indicates that smaller fleets rely on independent contractors rather than employ drivers to maintain and expand their businesses. Almost 35% of the companies using independents own one to nine power units and over ¾ own less than 50 power units. Though the data suggests a trend to smaller company-owned fleets, researchers said the numbers do reflect increased participation in the study by moving and storage companies and some specialized operations such as courier services.

Large furniture moving companies such as North American, United, Atlas, or Allied Van Lines, Mayflower Transit, and Bekins fall within the top 30 gross revenue freight companies in the United States. These companies, and others like them, operate entirely on owner operators. They have gained an increased presence in the freight hauling business because of transportation deregulation. On the basis of national policy American moving and storage companies are now able to haul any freight. They are no longer restricted to furniture.

Also predominant in trucking are mid-size geographically bound carriers whose fleets consist primarily of company drivers, but who also have lease divisions for which owner operators haul. For these companies the "us" (company drivers) and "them" (owner operators) paradigm becomes immediately relevant. The perceived or perhaps real threat that the lease division will eventually account for the company's entire trucking fleet is a possibility or maybe even a probability.

4. Corsi and Martin (1983) studied the turnover rate of owner operators between 1978 and 1979. Approximately five hundred owner operators responded to questionnaires in 1978 and again in 1979. They discovered that of the permanent lease operators (all those with a lease arrangement to a company for at least thirty days) 20 percent were no longer under any permanent lease, 8 percent were under permanent lease to a different carrier. Seventy-two percent were still under permanent lease to the same carrier.

In comparison, the stayer rate is similar to the average stayer rate between 1977 and 1978 according to estimates by the U.S. Department of Labour, Bureau of Statistics. The average stayer rate for "all industries combined" is 72 percent, for "construction" it is 62 percent and for all "transportation services" it is 70 percent. According to Corsi and Martin (1983), although direct comparison with the Bureau of Labor figures is "somewhat hampered by different definitions of the stayer rate," the owner operator stayer rates are not out of line with other industries.

5. Based on an explanatory model developed by Corsi and Martin (1983), the significant independent variable for explaining owner operator is

net income. The second most significant independent variable is the number of years that the owner operator has been in trucking. The third significant independent variable falls into the capital investment category. According to Corsi and Martin, it demonstrates a linkage between greater capital investment (represented by the number of tractors owned) and stability.

References

British Columbia Trucking Association. 1989. "U.S. Fleets Still Rely On Independents." **News and Views**, September 21, No. 339, pp. 1-2.

Corsi, M.T. and Martin, J. 1983. "An Explanatory Model for Turnover Among Owner Operators." Journal of Business Logistics, 3(2).

Crowe, J., and Kinsey, B. 1987. "Independents Shedding Cowboy Boots For Wing-Tip Shoes." **Transport Topics**, July 10, pg. 30.

Desmond, P. 1988. "The Top 100: Big Boys Crying Dereg Blues . . . All The Way To The Bank." **Commercial Carrier Journal**, July.

——— 1989. "Bigger, Better, But No Boomer." **Commercial Carrier Journal**, July.

Driver Owner (Editor). 1987. "A Standard Rate: Will It Fly?" **Driver Owner**, December

Glines, C. 1987. "In Search of Profits." **Commercial Carrier Journal**, July.

McRae, D. 1989. "There's Room At The Top for Committed Owner-Operators." **Transport Topics**. July 10, pg. 25.

Oregon Public Utility Commission. 1986. **Truck Driver Profiles In Traffic Offense Conviction Rates**. Salem, OR.

Robertson, Rob. 1989. "Making It At Mercury." **Independent Trucker**, June.

Robertson, R. 1989. "Keeping the Faith." **Independent Trucker**. September, pp. W12-W15.

Sanders, Mark. 1977. **A Nationwide Survey of Truck and Bus Drivers**. Washington, DC: U.S. Department of Transportation.

Transport Canada. 1987. **Driving Behaviour And Characteristics of Heavy Duty Truck Operators In Canada**. Ottawa, ON: Road Safety Directorate.

Wyckoff, D. Daryl. 1979. **Truck Drivers In America**. Lexington, MA: Lexington Books.

6

DISPATCHERS AND BENNIES

During his call to the Portland dispatcher, Danny was told to pick me up at the Dunnigan motel and provide me with a ride to Los Angeles. He was slightly suspicious when he arrived, asking about my intent and agenda. After I eased his mind about anonymity and confidentiality he helped me load my baggage into the bunk. We were off.

Danny drove for the same company that employed Simon. Inside the company truck things were amiss. The tachograph was out of service. The windshield had several major cracks. The passenger seat was broken. But, most importantly, the speedometer had been inoperative for two months, making it nearly impossible for Danny to judge precisely how fast he was traveling. So he improvised, approximating his speed according to the reading on the tachometer.

I learned that Danny made no effort to have the equipment repaired, and obviously the company did not engage in regular vehicle maintenance. According to Danny, the mechanical failures enhanced his freedom. Because the tachograph and speedometer were out of commission, the company lost its capabilities to monitor his driving. So he consistently downplays the vehicle failures with the maintenance crew, hoping to delay repair for as long as possible.

The day was hot, a scorcher. Blue clear sky and white sun. In the distance the air moved in waves. Sand, some fruit groves, more sand! And just beyond the horizon stood sand hills, looking occasionally like fading, distant adolescent mountains.

Danny was transporting three giant rolls of newsprint, which for the trucker was a routine load that demanded little more than standard conduct and few expectations. He knew of his destination and approximate arrival time. He drove confidently, loosely gesturing with his hands while he was talking.

Danny informed me that his tenure with M Transport is approaching two years. He has reached the point where he wishes to quit. He "gets no respect." He is expected to jump at the "whim" and "fancy" of the company "big shots" without them considering his feelings. At the age of twenty-five, Danny believed he has a long future ahead of him in trucking. So what would he like to do? "Drive for my uncle," he answered.

During our discussion, Danny told me that his uncle owned a few trucks which he leased to a large carrier. If all goes well, Danny expected to be driving for his uncle in a few months. He has not told company officials of his intentions to date. For Danny, the drama is in the impact of "quitting on the spot" not a long negotiated process of resigning.

The California portion of Interstate Five was still in terrible condition. Danny labelled this stretch of freeway "hell on truckers." The roadway is constructed of cement, not pavement. Between measured sections of concrete roadway are expansion joints. After years of neglect and a dramatic rise in the number of commercial vehicles, the California road has really deteriorated. Potholes and cracked concrete have not been repaired for a long time. So we hit potholes, ruts, and worn out joints every five seconds. Each time, we shook and rocked. The fact that Danny's truck was a cabover made the ride especially wearing. According to Danny:

> It's like the driver sits over the front wheel. Everything the tire feels, the driver feels. And then you get a load, heavy load you know, front loaded and you shake like, ah, on a roller coaster. It's wild.

As I stated in Chapter Five, a California law stipulates that tractor trailer units must stay in the right-hand lane. As a result, the heavy vehicle congestion in this lane is increasing its wear and tear, immediately evident and physically dramatic. There are potholes that, according to Danny, you could "lose a rig in." Although Danny obviously exaggerated, there was a kernel of truth. There were times Danny hit some potholes or deep ruts where, "things were flying off the dash over my (Danny's) head." Unlike Simon, who occasionally switched to the left-hand lane, Danny stayed on the right side, putting up with the bumps and shakes.

In the distance, to the east, a mass of moving figures came into view. It was the stockyards. About two miles before our approach Danny warned me of the impending stink, particularly if the wind came from the east. Although we closed all the cab windows, still the awful smell crept into the cab. Danny was right. It was putrid. It resembled the stench we experienced about 30 miles up the road at the Mobil Gas Station and truck stop.

As lunch time was approaching, Danny decided to stop here for a bite to eat. We entered the gas bay so that Danny could scrape the bugs off the windows. Once the chore was completed we parked the rig in the truck stop parking lot where Danny asked me if I could smell the stench that was "like that shit back on the road." Rather than the stockyard stink it was, according to Danny, "trucker smell."

The heat was stifling, surpassing the hundred degree Fahrenheit mark. The pavement was hot, the sun relentless and the stench awesome, forcing me to cover my nose. Danny explained why the nauseating smell:

See the truckers here. They sleep here, then open the door and piss out in the morning. Sometimes they shit too, y'know, but not that often. Lots of them are pigs.

Apparently the truck stop attendants seldom hose the parking lot. So during a heat wave like the one we were experiencing on this trip, the urine stench was overwhelming, all pervasive. Although Danny wanted to "puke," he found a lighter side of the issue, "what the hell, truckers gotta piss too ya know."

Once we set foot inside the restaurant, the air conditioning saved us. The offensive nasal attack was left outside. We sat down and ordered. Danny had a hamburger and french fries while I ordered from the salad bar.

Danny on Dispatchers

During the meal Danny took the opportunity to share his feeling about dispatchers. He disliked them immensely. He hated the way they generally "control" and "exploit" drivers, and how they mistreated him personally.

According to Danny, the dispatcher at M Transport believes that a driver must obey all commands. On numerous occasions Danny is ordered to take "hot loads" against his will. He is told to take freight that must reach its destination in the shortest possible time. To illustrate the meaning, Danny told me that three months ago he was told to take a hot load from Portland to Denver in only twenty-four hours. To prove his worth to the dispatcher Danny undertook the challenge and completed the task on time. He "busted his ass," struggling against the odds of law enforcement, accidents, and fatigue.

Instead of acclaim, Danny received a warning letter from the company safety supervisor who, upon review of the record, assessed that Danny's average speed was excessive. The dispatcher saw no reason to support Danny because he had achieved his goal of getting a load to its destination quickly.

Danny's practice of consenting to the dispatcher's demands, and fulfilling all of his expectations regardless of legality, has, according to Danny, led to the dispatcher becoming increasingly overbearing. Succumbing to M Transport dispatchers has cost him six warning letters for speeding from the safety supervisor, a seven-day company suspension, and two speeding citations from the police. For Danny, being a good employee was dangerous – "a waste of time." He realized that the odds were aginast him. Eventually the police will catch him cheating on his log books, a probability Danny wants to avoid.

In Danny's view, some dispatchers are prepared to be coercive to achieve their goals. Whenever they request a trucker to haul goods under severe time restrictions and distance specifications, the driver has the "official right" to refuse. But reality is not that simple. Truckers are fully aware that if they decline a request, they "will be punished." The disciplinary tactic used by the dispatcher is often embedded within a cover story. For example, a trucker who refuses to break a law or regulation upon a dispatcher's request may find that, although promised, there is no load available the next time the trucker calls. Consequently, the driver may "find himself in Oakland on a layover with little chance to leave until Tuesday." Downtime is costly to the operator.

Changing trip allocations for a driver is another popular form of punishment. A trucker who declines a dispatcher's requests receives the official line that because he arrived a little late, another driver was assigned his expected load. The victimized trucker is given a different trip, one which is less financially lucrative.

A simple right such as taking time off can create a tense reaction from a dispatcher. According to Danny, to discourage him from taking a day off, the dispatcher first says "Okay, take it off. But could you first clean your truck." When Danny returns to work a day later the dispatcher reassigns him to a piece of "filthy junk." During our discussion, Danny showed his anger over the dispatcher's actions. He pounded on his steering wheel, "Shit, they think they're God." I lightened the tenor of the conversation by telling Danny about a dispatcher joke told to me by Vic, the driver described in Chapters Two and Three:

> What's the difference between a dead dispatcher on the road and a dead dog? The skid marks in front of the dog. What's the difference between a dispatcher and a six month old baby? The baby quits crying after six months.

Danny laughed, nodding his approval of the jokes' content.

I continued to tell Danny that Vic's dispatcher forces compliance by sending him on an add-on trip to Nanaimo, a small city located on the tip of Vancouver Island, British Columbia. After a sixteen hour drive from the United States to Vancouver, Canada, the trucker is commanded to continue the journey to Nanaimo, a trip that takes a full day but includes only about twenty miles (thirty-six kilometers) actual driving distance. The reason for Vic's punishment was that he was overly tired to take a trip. The manager of Z Company came into play telling Vic, "You're going to pay for it." Vic soon discovered the meaning of those words. For five consecutive weeks Vic was dispatched to Nanaimo where most of the time is spent on a ferry. If we multiply the mileage by forty-six cents, the driver's earnings for an eight hour day is about $7.20. Small wonder the dispatcher is considered to be powerful by truckers.

Officially, the Federal Highways Administration (FHWA) has a process that allows truckers to grieve company officials who expect truckers to blatantly violate regulations or force them to operate beyond their physical limits. The FHWA does not want to see truckers, especially owner operators, be victims to the not-so-subtle message that if they refuse to take a load another driver will, because customers are valued and loads have to be hauled.[1]

Danny was aware of his right to complain. But pursuit of legal or administrative avenues is like turning your back on trucking. To "rat" is beyond anything Danny would consider, never mind a process in which he would participate.

Enter Drugs

We were hauling through the Kettleman Hills about sixty miles (106 kilometers) from Buttonwillow, when we passed Kettleman City, an eyeblink off the side of the freeway. Danny became more open, freely discussing his personal life as a trucker.

The young driver does not like alcohol. Whenever he drinks "a few beers" he gets a "pounding headache" and feels nauseous the next day. He proudly proclaimed his achievement of not touching "any booze" for three months. Cigarettes, are a different matter. Danny smokes about two packs a day. It's the boredom, he analyzed. "You're bored, you fidget, then you smoke."

But Danny does take illicit drugs. Trucking circumstances and lack of company policies make it easy for him to pop pills. According to Danny, M Transport has no policy or voluntary program for urinalysis. He proposed that any implementation of a drug detection program would be disadvantageous for the company. First, M Transport has a high driver turnover. Danny exposes:

> They lose most drivers before three months. Seven out of ten. I'm only two years here and already I am a senior driver.

In Danny's mind, to engage in a urinalysis test is expensive, about fifty dollars per driver per detection. When seven out of ten drivers tested quit within three months, the cost effectiveness ratio for urinalysis becomes problematic. A check with the company's management generally supported Danny's premise that over half of its drivers quit after a half a year.

The second reason for not having a drug detection program is contractual. That is, the Teamster – M Transport contract has no clause about drivers taking urinalysis tests. Danny believed that in the case of M Transport the Teamster representative plays along with the wishes of the company. For, according to Danny, "You only see him when contracts are negotiated or elections, union elections are on. He's never around any other time."

Finally, Danny believed that M Transport has no policy on urinalysis because of a secret deal with the United States Department of Transport. Every two years drivers are expected to undergo a thorough physical examination, which according to Danny entails urinalysis. But, in Danny's view, M Transport has an arrangement with the Department of Transport (DOT) to "hold back on pee tests." For proof, Danny cited his observation that not one driver at M Transport, regardless of tenure, had ever taken a urinalysis during a DOT physical examination.

Danny's awareness is generally correct but lacking in specifics. Further investigation showed that there was no sweetheart arrangement between the company and the Department of Transport restricting urinalysis during federally regulated physical examinations. The Department of Transport does not have a mandate requiring urine tests during medical examinations. If urinalysis is undertaken it is on the basis of driver volunteers or company policies, not federal regulations.

According to Danny, the fact that many drivers like him do drugs should come as no surprise to management. Last year Danny earned thirty-four thousand dollars (net). From this sum Danny developed a single logic. To earn such money requires driving long miles for many hours, which is impossible to do without taking drugs. "Anybody would know that." Yet no company official has ever sincerely questioned Danny about drugs. Although "all the dispatchers know," Danny believed that they cleared their conscience by superficially asking, "Do you do drugs?" Obviously the truckers says no. At this point the interview is completed.

Danny Takes Pink Hearts And . . .

When the need arises Danny pops two "Pink Hearts" – a heavy caffeine pill that "may have some speed in it." Danny smiled as he pulled out a small bag from his jean jacket lying on his sleeper. I counted twenty-five little tablets.

For a powerful kick, Danny swallows "Cross Tops," small white pills with little crosses. For a shot that will "get him home" he ingests "Black Beauties" because they "put a bounce" in his step.

When Danny first pops pink hearts, "nothing much happens." However, a short time later his "hair tingles" and his "head stretches like an elastic." The pills inspire him to urinate. When he does, most often at the side of the road, his heart begins to "pound and pump overtime" forcing Danny to stay wide awake. He "sees and hears" everything. This rush allows him to drive those extra hours demanded by the company.

Up to now, Danny had not been "busted" for drugs. To escape first round detection Danny wears shades. He knows that some of the California highway patrol are trained to detect early drug use.[2]

They look for eye movements, pupil dilation, alertness and conversation style. If they ask a question and it takes a trucker exaggerated time to answer, it tips off the drug recognition experts as to probable drug use. Whether sunglasses help deter drug recognition is doubtful, if a police officer is committed to investigate a driver for drug use.

Although cocaine is a popular road drug, Danny has never tried it. Neither does he smoke grass, although he once teamed up with a driver who "had 40 joints," toking-up on the entire trip. Danny felt at risk. Still he would not consider reporting his co-driver because, as before, his first loyalty is to the trucker, not to the authorities. He hates truckers like Simon in Chapter Five, who snitch to the company brass. According to Danny, M Transport has several older drivers like Simon who receive little perks like driving a newly purchased vehicle, or receiving a quality haul for "squealing" or "ratting" on other drivers.

Danny prefers to purchase his drugs in his home town in Oregon, where his supplier is cheaper and safer than road sellers. For example, Danny can buy pink hearts near the Mexican border at the price of twenty dollars for twenty-five pills, without knowing the quality of the drug. This equates to eighty cents a pill. In Oregon, Danny can buy the same drug at five for a dollar, or twenty cents a pill, knowing that it is "good stuff," or the "real thing."

Confidence in the quality of a drug is essential for a user. Because the seller knows Danny personally, service is direct, and guesswork about the strength of the drug is reduced. The pills bought near the Mexican border were defined by Danny as "real shit."

The drug trade is active. Danny believed that at least seventy percent of truckers use or have used drugs on the job. "You can buy 'em anywhere," he told me. But "you'd be damn stupid to do it."

As I discussed in Chapter Three, drugs can be easily bought over the CB. However, more importantly, according to Danny, truck stops are a key piece of the drug puzzle. Here prostitutes may come up to the truckers' sleepers and invite themselves for sexual services and/or drug sales. Although Danny has bought several favors from a few commercial beavers, he never purchased drugs from them. Danny knew the police may be running an undercover operation or a sting.

On the West Coast there are several truck stops that stand out for easy access to contraband. One of these is located in the Los Angeles – San Bernardino area, where truckers can buy anything they want – speed, crystal methadone, coke, black beauties. And cheap sex! Obviously, according to

Danny, if the truckers know the reputation of the truck stop, the police would also know. In fact, truckers and some police officers throughout southwestern United States know of the particular truck stop in question. Danny considers the truckers that hang out there as "rubbies" and "lazies." For Danny it is best to play it safe – to stay away from possible violence and police action.

Danny recognized the risk or the threat of undercover operations at truck stops. He, therefore, keeps his distance from certain ones and he refuses to buy drugs from strange persons. He buys at home believing in the advertising motto, "Don't leave home without it."

Enter The Dispatcher

Outside the heat was explosive. It was early afternoon, just past two thirty. We stopped at a roadside park for a pop and so that Danny could telephone his Los Angeles dispatcher. He wanted to project his approximate time of arrival and request further information about his backhaul.

As we pulled into the parking lot Danny spoke to me about his upcoming weekend. At minimum he will have a one night stay in Los Angeles. Whether the downtime stretches to two nights and whether he would be returning fully loaded or driving a deadhead were questions still left unanswered. But, for tonight at least, he wanted a motel, shower, good food and a few beers in a relaxing bar. But what he desired and what he expected are two different issues! Danny knew the company would not grant him the motel. With little cash in his possession, the trucker was left with little choice but to sleep in his truck parked in the loading yard in one hundred degree Fahrenheit weather, with no toilets or washing facilities.

Danny walked over to the curbside telephones, leaving me sitting by the truck, sipping a pop. Five minutes later he returned slapping his little note book against his hips. He was told that he may have another run. Instead of unloading in Norwalk, Danny would likely exchange trailers with a driver from Los Angeles. The rendevous point would be La Sacla. "What about your driving hours?" I asked. "What about them. Dispatcher knows. She don't give a shit," he answered.

Danny jumped into the truck angry. He updated his log book, the first time since he left at six thirty in the morning. He had two official hours of driving time left. He informed the dispatcher about his remaining driving time, but she paid little attention. With the trip to Oakland added to his present drive, Danny will accumulate more than sixteen hours of consecutive driving time.

But all may be wasted anger. The key word in Danny's telephone exchange with the dispatcher was "maybe." There was still a chance that the extra run would not happen. The dispatcher advised Danny to telephone her from the next truck stop. After that call, the decision was "yes," Danny must take a load of chemicals from Los Angeles to Oakland. He was ordered to exchange trailers in La Scala with a driver named B.J. According to Danny, he was to arrive in Oakland by four a.m. Saturday. The trailer would be unloaded; Danny would stay over Sunday and return with a load Monday.

The dispatcher had formulated the following strategy. Danny was to travel to Oakland late at night, a time when the weigh scales near Oakland are usually closed. This ploy would reduce Danny's chances of being caught by the police. Furthermore, by forcing Danny to wait until Monday for the return trip, the dispatcher encouraged Danny to graduate the ten hour shifts over three days. This is consistent with the strategy of faking the log outlined by Agar (1986), where the driver lets the log stay a few days behind to fill in or even things out.

The changed plans angered Danny. He was aware of the dispatcher's strategy and motives. He was again expected to break laws. He felt for his pocket in the blue jean jacket, pulled out the "pink ladies" and told me defeatedly that to stay awake he would have to "pop a couple." Ninety minutes from Los Angeles and Danny was yawning, noticeably.

Danny argued that if he declined this trip the dispatcher would "slap a one day suspension" on him. Worse yet, if he decided to report the incident to the authorities, he would be fired.[3] Although he kept talking about becoming more assertive with dispatchers, when a situation arose Danny was unable to defend his rights with candor and confidence. Instead Danny compromised, then stewed. The more furious he became, the faster he drove. The truck began to shake. Danny felt victimized. He has been "keeping his (my) mouth shut, running illegal all the time and this is the thanks he (I) get(s)."

Twenty minutes later we turned off Interstate Five heading towards La Scala for a rendezvous with B.J. They were friends. Behind a Mexican food restaurant, on a gravel truck lot, Danny and B.J. exchanged trailers. Danny was still steaming about the dispatcher demands, whereupon B.J. took Danny to the side of the truck and recommended that he calm down. After all, to be a trucker means to meet the needs of the dispatcher.

While exchanging views with Danny it became evident that he was naive about the dispatchers' politics, role definitions and perspectives on trucking. I followed up on my suspicions to interview ten dispatchers, whose descriptions are found in the Notes[4]. Also included in the Notes is an account on the empirical findings of truckers and drug use.[5]

Conclusion

While I was writing this report in my office, Danny was probably living trucking as he best knew how – driving a rig, listening to loud country and western music, smoking cigarettes and popping bennies. Regardless of the stigma, trucker drug taking is more of a response to road problems than it is a lifestyle enhancer.

The economic pressures, dispatcher authorities, and boredom-enhancing working conditions are three major reasons why truckers risk taking drugs. How unsafe are drugs – naturally very unsafe. How do we know? Laboratory equipment mainly! So we need more exposure data before we can answer with any **definite confidence**, use of drugs is more risky than non-use.

Notes on Chapter Six

1. Federal Highway Administration regulations provide a mechanism for filing a written complaint and having an investigation started.

   All FHWA Regional Offices (Albany, NY; Baltimore, MD; Atlanta, GA; Homewood, IL; Fort Worth, TX; Kansas City, MO; Lakewood, CO; San Francisco, CA; and Portland, OR) will accept written complaints requesting investigations when a driver believes that a motor carrier has violated Agency regulations. Each complaint must contain: (1) the name and address of the party filing it, although complaints MAY be filed anonymously; (2) the name and address of the motor carrier against whom the complaint is directed; (3) the specific regulations that are being violated (for example, the 10-hour rules, or the 15-hour rules); (4) the reasons why the party believes that a notice of investigation should be issued; and most importantly, (5) specific examples of the violations – when they occurred, who was involved, how widespread the problem is, etc. The more accurate and detailed the complaint letter, the better the chances that the allegations will be thoroughly and promptly investigated. Although anonymous complaints are given the same attention as signed complaints, an anonymous complaining party obviously will not be privy to the Agency's findings. FHWA regulations specifically state that a motor carrier cannot punish, harass, or fire a driver because a complaint has been filed against it. (Land Line, 1989, pg. 14)

2. In California, the Los Angeles Police Department has implemented a drug recognition program that involves training officers to detect on site patterns of behavioral and psychological symptoms associated with major drug categories (Compton, 1986). The city courts accept the expertise and court testimony of officers certified through the police department program, otherwise known as Drug Recognition Experts (DREs).

In 1986 the National Highway Transportation Safety Administration evaluated the program. Twenty-five experts processed 201 drug-taking suspects. The process, or drug recognition procedures consisted of the following steps:

A. Interview

The DRE would conduct a brief interview with the suspect concerning the suspect's medical and drug use history, recent eating, sleep and alcohol/drug use. During this interrogation the officer would evaluate the suspect's alertness and responsiveness, speech characteristics, mood, attitude, cooperativeness, etc.

B. Psychological Symptoms

This includes measuring pulse rate (three times during the examination), blood pressure, oral temperature, pupil size, pupillary reaction to light and dark, nystagmus (horizontal and vertical), smoothness of visual pursuit, perspiration, condition of the tongue, and salivation. The officers also examined the suspects closely for skin signs of substance abuse (e.g., needle marks, skin rashes, perforation of the nasal septum).

C. Behavioral Tests

These tests were designed to assess psychomotor performance, the ability to follow and remember instructions, and divided attention. The tests used were:

1. Rhomberg balance test: a modified attention test in which the suspect is instructed to stand with his feet together, arms at his side and eyes closed for 30 seconds. The officer observes the amount of sway, loss of balance, and suspect's perception of elapsed time.

2. One-leg-stand: The suspect is instructed to stand on one foot, lift the other foot six inches off the ground and to hold that position while counting out loud to 30; this is repeated for the other foot. Loss of balance is observed.

3. Finger-to-nose: The suspect stands erect with the feet together, eyes closed and arms to the side. Alternating with his right and left hands, the suspect is directed to touch the tip of his nose with the tip of his extended index finger. The location of the touches, balance, and ability to follow simple instructions are recorded.

4. Walk-and-Turn: The suspect is told to stand heel-to-toe on a line, hands at sides, while the officer gives instructions on how he is to walk the line. He is told to take nine steps down the line, told exactly how to turn, take nine steps back, counting the steps out loud. His ability to maintain his balance and to divide his attention are noted. (Compton, 1986; pp. 5-6)

The officers' accuracy at discrimination was uncanny. For example, Compton (1986) established that the DREs were totally correct in their judgment on 49 percent of the suspects, and partially correct, where at least one drug was identified, on 38 percent of the participants. They identified one or more drugs correctly in 87 percent of the suspects. From another perspective, they erred only 13 percent of the time (Compton, 1986).

3. In the trucking magazine **Land Line** (1989, pg. 14), is a statement of truckers' rights when they are told by dispatchers to drive illegally:

> Should you find yourself in a situation like this, there is a way to air your grievances. Federal Highway Administration regulations provide a mechanism for filing a written complaint and having an investigation started.
>
> All FHWA Regional Offices (Albany, NY; Baltimore, MD; Atlanta, GA; Homewood, Il; Fort Worth, TX; Kansas City, MO; Lakewood, CO; San Francisco, CA; and Portland, OR) will accept written complaints requesting investigations when a driver believes that a motor carrier has violated Agency regulations. Each complaint must contain: (1) the name and address of the party filing it, although complaints MAY be filed anonymously; (2) the name and address of the motor carrier against whom the complaint is directed; (3) the specific regulations that are being violated (for example, the 10-hour rules, or the 15-hour rules); (4) the reasons why the party believes that a notice of investigation should be issued; and most importantly, (5) specific examples of the violations – when they occurred, who was involved, how widespread the problem is, etc. The more accurate and detailed the complaint letter, the better the chances that the allegations will be thoroughly and promptly investigated. Although anonymous complaints are given the same attention as signed complaints, an anonymous complaining party obviously will not be privy to the Agency's findings. FHWA regulations specifically state that a motor carrier cannot punish, harass, or fire a driver because a complaint has been filed against it. (Land Line, 1989, pg. 14)

4. Dispatcher Interviews, on the definition of roles, making of a dispatcher and safety.

Out of the ten interviews, the following four verbatim answers to the question, "How would you describe your job?" represent the feel expressed by all of the dispatchers:

Dispatcher 1:   I am responsible for dispatching the trucks across Canada, looking for their loads, matching their loads to the type of equipment, servicing the customer basically. He wants a truck and you tell him what kind you have. You match the equipment you have in the different areas, B-train, regular, or van, or step deck or hopper bottom.

Dispatcher 2:   Okay, basically I think dispatcher is kind of a misnomer. I do dispatching, I do many other things as well. I look after the drivers' instructions and I look after the origin of service. I make sure the maintenance is all done. I am actually what you would call one step above a straight dispatcher. I have a dispatcher that works for me. I do whatever needs to be done in the daytime,

Dispatcher 3:

Dispatcher 4:

as far as dispatching goes, and then he takes over in the evening. I set it up roughly for him and then he does the fine tuning of it in the evening. I'm more a driver supervisor than a dispatcher. Scheduling mostly. You're planning ahead. You have got 25 trucks going into the California area on a Monday morning and you have 25 loads coming back, now all you have to do is lay out your game plan for Monday morning. You do this on Friday to allocate the proper truck to the proper load in the closest area that he is. The less miles we have to run the better. Depending on the size of the trailer, some loads require bigger trailers than others.

I'm like an Operations Manager, it is just a matter of getting the trucks where they are supposed to be at the right time.

To become a dispatcher the candidate usually has extensive truck driving experience. This gives the dispatcher-to-be first hand knowledge of the day-to-day reality of truckers and it helps future dispatchers gain respect and allegiance from truckers. The following account displays the dispatching apprenticeship model:

The ideal way is to have a fellow who has been a driver, because he kind of understands a little more really, you know, some of the problems that we have got out there. A fellow can phone up and say "Hey, this is happening . . ." I'm not sure what it could be. Once you have been a driver it gives you kind of a better idea of what is going on out there. A fellow that hasn't been a driver would turn round and be in a bad position when this happened, because they really don't have any idea at all, so whenever possible we try to get a fellow who has been a driver.

Cognitive resources for the job are a good memory, quick thinking, a knowledge of time, speed and distance, an appreciation of driver capability, a calm attitude and the skill to make quick decisions. As a city dispatcher for a freight company said:

Oh, yeah. There are days where you might have had a tough night the night before and you come in and are not really looking forward to facing 400 or 500 calls a day. But you get used to it. About all I can say is it really isn't as bad. If you sat in here Friday afternoon totally blind to what was going on you said you were amazed at what takes place, but it isn't if you have two or three people in here that have done it before and know what is going on. It sounds more confusing than it really is. There is more repetition, knowing who is calling, where they are, what they are doing, and it is just basic planning. If you plan it right things should go okay. There are days where, you know we are only human, under that kind of pressure 10 hours a day, there are things you forget. Little simple things, you forgot to write something down or you messed up on a trailer number but as far as serious stuff happening, not really.

For dispatchers, expedient hauling expected by a client shipper is their premise of operation. Cargo must be hauled in the shortest period of time yet travel a maximum distance. This premise invokes a mistrust amongst the police. Officers consider dispatchers to be at the root of poor trucking safety. Witness Phil, a sergeant for the Arizona Highway Patrol:

> Dispatchers are co-conspirators over hours. A guy calls in, he's in say Albuquerque, and he left Louisiana 12 hours before. No way can he make the trip from New Orleans to Albuquerque in 12 hours legally. The dispatcher says, "Well, I need you in Phoenix and I'm looking for an 8:00 o'clock drop." Well the guy's already driven 12 to 18 hours straight, hasn't had any sleep, lie on your log book, do whatever you do but get that load there. And dispatchers know where these guys (drivers) are. They can figure out if this guy is over hours or not. When we do our audits, we check to see that the dispatchers keep track of where these guys are. They are the key player in the whole thing.
>
> We can go after them criminally in this state. You get a driver with a gross falsification of his log book, and he says, "Well, the company knows I'm doing this." We go in and talk to the company and say, "Does he call in daily to the dispatcher and report his location?" And, "Yes, he does." And when they call in they log it, they know the times and places of the drivers.

A company dispatcher reasoned the relationship between safety and dispatching:

> Safety is not our problem, that's the driver's responsibility. If his truck isn't up to standard, then he shouldn't take the load. Safety is not the dispatcher's problem, that's the driver's. The dispatchers outlook on life is to move that freight, to get that truck out of the yard . . .

Some dispatchers agreed that there is an incongruence between safety and dispatching. They argued that their companies have safety supervisors, accident review boards and maintenance departments whose job it is to assure and maintain safety. Drivers have the responsibility to assure that loads are properly distributed and tied down, and to look after themselves according to roadworthiness.

When questioned further, dispatchers conceded that safety is a factor in their work. "They won't push a guy" beyond his limit. They "don't condone alcohol or drugs." They don't "support running two log books." They don't "like drivers not sleeping." They "don't ask a driver to take out a truck that isn't safe." But in a crunch the above principles are negotiated:

> We have to comply with the log book in the U.S. They are only allowed so much time. I'm not saying we don't cheat. Everybody cheats. I'll be damned if I was a driver if I got to the border on my way home and I had already had my 80 hours in for another hour. I'm not going to stop 30 miles from home and wait eight hours.

The negotiated element of safety reflects the entire foundation of dispatching. Dispatchers, like foremen at a manufacturing plant, come through the ranks, only to be perceived by truckers as sitting on the "other side of the fence." They are part of management, yet feel a friendship for drivers, most likely members of the Teamsters union, or owner operators. The dispatchers are a denizen of two worlds. They may join drivers in company "baseball games," but when it matters, they side with management.

Dispatchers make decisions that are preferable for business and profit. They expedite loads for survival. Top priority is given to the shippers or clients. A delay in minor truck repairs or general maintenance duties may happen if a shipper wants to secure a shipping contract. With the costs of truck operations increasing, available loads decreasing due to greater competition, and company profit margins becoming thinner, some maintenance work may suffer and some driver difficulties or legal rights be dismissed by the dispatchers.

On record dispatchers do not negotiate safety pertaining to truckers' use of drugs and alcohol. They quote company policies as proof of their determination to rid the use of illicit substances and liquor. Yet dispatchers generalize that anywhere from 50 to 97 percent of the drivers take drugs.

5. There is a shortage of rigorous empirical investigation on truckers and drug use. This was brought to the forefront at a November 14, 1989, National Trucking Industrial Relations Association conference by Mr. Michael Trentacoste, director of Motor Carrier Standards for the American Federal Highway Administration.

The Insurance Institute of Highway Safety undertook a 1986 study to establish the extent to which truck drivers operate their rigs under the influence of such drugs as alcohol, marijuana or cocaine and to establish if stimulants such as amphetamines or "look alikes" are used by truckers who drive for excessive hours (Lund et al., 1987).

Lund et al. collected a sample of 317 tractor-trailer truck drivers who stopped at the Brownsville, Tennessee, weigh scales during the week of December 15, 1986. Urine tests, blood tests and questionnaire items on general health status of truck drivers and views on drugs were undertaken on drivers who volunteered after undergoing Tennessee Public Service Commission log book checks. Each participating driver received $30. Co-drivers, women drivers, tandem or "double bottom" rig drivers and single unit operators were excluded from the study. In short, the researchers provided the following findings:

> Altogether, 29 percent of the drivers had evidence of alcohol, marijuana, cocaine, and/or prescription or nonprescription stimulants in either blood or urine; nonprescription stimulants, such as phenylpropanolamine were found in 12 percent; prescription stimulants such as amphetamine were found in five percent; cocaine metabolites were found in two percent; and alcohol was found in less than one percent. (Lund et al., 1987, Abstract)

Several questions on study methodology came to mind. Researchers stopped trucks westbound on Interstate 40, near Brownsville, Tennessee. The CB is a focal communication device amongst drivers. They communicate visible police action, roadside checks, unusual circumstances, road closures, and dangerous road sections. It is likely that truckers who observed the research activities would communicate the news to other truckers regardless of voluntarism or a $30 profit. The presence of the police, DOT officials and researchers checking for drugs plus the truckers' natural suspicion of bureaucracy and authority is worth a warning.

If the above holds true, westbound truckers, having been warned could have swung off Interstate 40, down Highway 70 to Highway 79, back to Interstate 40 at Stanton or Braden. Because there were no other testing risks, any escape route from Memphis to Nashville would prove productive for truckers.

A second concern is the size of the sample. As of 1986, there were 1,833,000 truck drivers in the United States (U.S. Department of Commerce, 1987). A sample of 317 drivers who went through despite probable warnings of other truckers is limited.

Getson (1987; pg. 4), critiqued the sampling process:

> Based on the supplied ATA figure of approximately 1.8M total truckers, a true random sample of approximately 322 drivers would have been sufficient to conclude with 95% confidence, that the actual population rate was within 5 percentage points of the drug incidence rate observed in the study. This would only be true if the sample had been a representative random one, which it was not . . . the limitations of the study are serious, and particularly jeopardize generalizability. They include: exclusion of female drivers, nonstandardized period of day for sampling (i.e. overrepresentation of 6pm – 6am), nonconsecutive truck selection (i.e. certain trucks were excluded based on size, and type, while other 'appropriate' trucks were missed if inspectors were busy with violators at the time they entered the facility), allowance of inclusion of drivers not really operating a "truck" at the time (i.e. tractor-only), lack of stratification or control for other potentially confounding variables, such as geographic area, time of day, time of year as related to weather, time of year as related to increased upper respiratory problems and OTC drug use, prevalence of truck type on this specific roadway, increase in holiday period business and related enhanced requirements for schedule adherence by drivers, changes in usual routes to either include/exclude passing through Brownsville, Tn.

Summarizing the entire report Getson (1987; pg. 7) wrote:

> In summary, the IIHS conducted an extremely thorough drug incidence study, the results of which have flawed interpretation. Most grievous fault derives from the sampling plan employed and the resulting lack of randomization among the drivers who were enrolled. Exclusions and lack of stratification

or control for confounding variables are also strong negative issues. The reported incidence of 30% was incorrect, with the correct comprehensive percentage being 20%, although only about a third of these drivers (6-7%) used an identified illegal substance frequently or recently, or were involved with the use of an Rx drug associated with abuse. There is nothing to indicate that this smaller percentage (6-7%) is different from that which could be established for use of these same substances in the population of all drivers of all types of vehicles using our nation's major highways.

Some general driver performance and drug use studies are worth reporting. In June 1980 Warren et al. reported on a study entitled "Characteristics of Fatally Injured Drivers Testing Positive for Drugs Other Than Alcohol."

With a sample of 401 Ontario victim drivers, all of whom were 14 years or older and proclaimed dead on arrival at hospital or shortly thereafter, Warren and colleagues proceeded to take blood and urine samples. In short, the findings were:

> Alcohol was detected in 57 percent of the fatally injured drivers; other drugs were detected in 26 percent of the victims. In 43 percent of the cases, alcohol was present, but no other drugs were detected; in 14 percent alcohol was present in combination with other drugs, and in 12 percent drugs were detected, but no alcohol was present. In only 31 percent of the victims were neither alcohol nor other drugs detected. (Warren et al., 1980; pg. 3)

Terhune and Fell (1982) used a similar methodology for American drivers. The results of testing 497 drivers injured in a motor vehicle accident and treated in a hospital were:

> The results showed that fully 38 percent of the drivers had alcohol or some other drug in their systems; alcohol was found in 25 percent, tetrahydrocannabinol in 9.5 percent and tranquilizers in 7.5 percent. Ten percent of the drivers had ingested two or more drugs. It was found that legally intoxicated drivers (BAC $\geq$ .10 percent) had the highest culpability rate (74 percent) followed by drivers with lower alcohol levels (54 percent) and with THC (53 percent). The drug-free drivers in contrast had a culpability rate of 34 percent while the drivers with tranquilizers were judged culpable in 22 percent of their accidents. (1982; pg. 13)

Owens, McBay and Cook (1983) and Mason and McBay (1984) analyzed 600 fatally injured drivers killed in single vehicle crashes in North Carolina during the period of 1978 to 1981. Collisions or second party involved accidents were excluded for easier determination of accident fault.

About 14 percent of the drivers used the specific drugs of interest for the study (alcohol, marijuana, barbiturates, cocaine, opiates, phencyclidine, amphetamines and methaqualone). Ninety-seven percent of drivers who had used drugs also consumed alcohol.

The use of multiple drugs is more common than ingestation of one drug type. Joscelyn and Donelson (1980) analyzed 440 auto accident victims aged 15 to 34. They discovered that the use of multiple drugs was common with 43 percent of the drivers. Alcohol alone, or in common with drugs, was present in 70 percent of the drivers. Fifty-one percent of the drivers were reported to have used drugs other than alcohol.

A question raised is why, contrary to other drug analysis studies, Joscelyn and Donelson found such high use as, for example, 37 percent cannabinoids (constituents of marijuana). Compton and Anderson (1985) helped us with the answer:

> The fairly high incidence of marijuana, 37 percent of the drivers, should be interpreted cautiously as it includes drivers in whom only very small quantities of THC were found. At least 40 percent of these drivers would have been treated as false positives and would not have been counted by other authors, based on the THC levels detected (i.e., concentrations of less than 1 mg/ml in hemolyzed blood). (1985; pg. 6)

The frequency with which motorists combine drugs with alcohol makes it almost impossible to determine if an isolated drug increases accident risk. Also, to date few of the studies have collected exposure data from non accident involved drivers to help establish the extent to which drugs other than alcohol are safety problems for drivers. One exception was Honkanen et al. (1980) who attempted to compare drug use rates between injured and control drivers. The researchers concluded that almost twice as many injured drivers than control drivers had used drugs. They inferred that the use of drugs could have increased the risk of being involved in an accident.

Unfortunately Honkanen et al. (1980) failed to analyze the combined effects of alcohol and drugs that may have contributed to increased accident risk. Also, the researchers failed to screen for a number of relevant, often used, potentially hazardous drugs as marijuana and cocaine.

Some laboratory experiments should be presented. Moskowitz, Shauma and Ziedman (1981), Attwood and Williams (1980) and Shauma (1975), among others, concentrated on marijuana and driving tasks. All three experiments showed some drug-induced impairment of driving tasks such as visual search task, compensatory tracking task, critical tracking task and lateral control ability. The experiments established that the duration of the behavioral effects of marijuana extends beyond the psychological effects as evidenced by cardiac rates.

Controlled driving studies (discussed in Shinar 1978) have revealed that marijuana smoking can result in missing traffic control signals, forgetting the experimenters' directional instructions during the study, less awareness of parked vehicles and pedestrians, passing other vehicles with insufficient caution and slower responses to green traffic signals. However, as in the case of alcohol, heavy marijuana smokers are better able to compensate for behavioral deficits associated with consumption of a particular amount of marijuana than are moderate smokers. Shinar suggests that the mixed statistical results regarding marijuana use and traffic accidents may be due to other sociodemographic factors associated with marijuana smoking. The effects of mixing marijuana with other substances, such as alcohol, are quite common and are worthy of further study (e.g., Sutton, 1983) in spite of the large individual differences found in research on the effects of marijuana alone.

Similar studies on other drugs have been carried out in laboratories. Few involved truck drivers. However, the extent to which laboratory study results can be used to generalize a roadway problem is outlined in Compton and Anderson (1985):

> There have been a number of laboratory studies that have shown that performance on tasks that utilize driving related skills (e.g., divided attention, tracking) is impaired by some of these drugs. Given these results, it might be argued that there is a drug related highway safety problem and that the laboratory data could be used to specify its nature and magnitude. Unfortunately, this is not possible for the following reasons:
>
> - For a given driving related task, large differences in the degree of performance decrement are often exhibited between subjects consuming the same drug (and dosage level). Also, the average degree of drug related performance impairment may differ substantially between tasks.
> - Perhaps even more important is the fact that there is no agreement as to which of the many driving-related tasks used in the laboratory contain the **critical** combination of skills necessary to the safe operation of an automobile. Even if this ideal set of performance tasks could be developed, the **exact degree** of performance impairment that would be required to increase accident risk would be very difficult to determine. Also, the fact that a specific performance impairment results under the artificial and nonlife threatening situations necessary in the laboratory, does not mean that this same performance impairment will be evident in the real world. It may be increased or reduced depending on the driver's physical and mental reactions to the specific traffic situations being experienced.
> - Finally, laboratory performance data do not provide any indication how frequently drivers in the real world are consuming drugs that increase accident risk. If a drug has the potential for producing severe impairment of the driving task, but the driving public is not consuming drugs prior to driving, it can be concluded that there is no highway safety problem associated with that particular drug at the present time. (1985; pp. 1-2)

More study is required for all drivers, but especially so for truckers and drugs. Field research should focus on (1) the truck drivers frequency of occurrence in accidents, (2) the extent to which they contribute to the accidents, (3) the frequency of use on the roadway, and (4) reasons for usage.

Recently a major study on truckers and drug use was undertaken in British Columbia, where the provincial trucking association wanted a conservative estimate on drug use amongst tuckers in British Columbia. Quantity of use was not a question.

To accomplish the objective, personal interviews were conducted with a sample of 1,000 truck drivers, randomly selected from all trucks crossing the weigh scales in six different parts of the province of British Columbia. Also, urine samples were collected from another 500 truck drivers. The specimens were subjected to laboratory analysis.

The sample frame was based on truck drivers stopping at weigh scales in the province of British Columbia. The locations of the weigh scales' samples were as follows:

Nordel	–	at South end of Alex Fraser Bridge, Annacis Island
Haig	–	3 km North of Hope on Highway 7
Kamloops	–	(eastbound) – 10 km West of Kamloops on Highway 1
Parksville	–	5 km South of Parksville, Highway 19, Vancouver Island
Port Mann	–	(westbound) – 3 km East of the bridge on Highway 1, Surrey
Pouce Coupe	–	18 km Southeast of Dawson Creek on Highway 2.

When the interviewer was ready to begin an interview, the Inspector operating the weigh scale stopped the next truck arriving at the scale. (Drivers being cited for violations were excluded.) When the truck parked, the interviewer approached the driver and asked for cooperation. In a motor home parked on-site, the interviewer read the instructions and questions from the questionnaire, while the driver marked his/her answers on a preprinted answer sheet. At the conclusion of the interview, the driver sealed the answer sheet in an envelope and placed it at random in a bin of previously-completed answer sheets.

Every third driver was asked to provide a urine sample, following much the same procedure and being promised anonymity. Each driver who completed an interview or provided a urine sample was paid $25 in cash. The interviews were conducted, and the urine samples collected, during the period of April 4 – May 4, 1989. In all, 1006 interviews were completed, and 500 urine samples were collected.

It was learned that among the drivers interviewed 7.6 percent admitted to occasional or frequent use of marijuana. The urine samples of another group of truckers showed the 5.2 percent had used marijuana within the past 30 days or so.

In two percent of the urine samples codeine was detected. In the interviews ten percent of the truckers answered that they take codeine by prescriptions while another ten percent take it without prescriptions. A further analysis showed that the groups who reported using codeine regularly or occasionally with a doctor's prescription, and without one, are overlapping groups; with 6.3 percent of the drivers reporting usage under both conditions. Although certainly a potential problem, codeine has a rather ambiguous status as a restricted drug given that it is readily available and not illegal. Therefore, secondary analysis was done which omitted codeine use. The breakdown of this variable showed that of the truckers interviewed, 9.5 percent reported the use of one **or more** of the following illegal drugs: marijuana, cocaine, amphetamines, barbiturates, and opiates.

As with the Lund et al. study, for the Insurance Institute for Highway Safety, this research also had a few problematic edges to it. First, weigh scales do not cater to random truckers. As mentioned before, warning amongst truckers via the CB is real. Second, voluntary participation in urinalysis leaves a conceptual gap for generalization of the findings. Finally, no comparison group data were retrieved with which to measure truck driver involvement in drugs.

References

Agar, M.H. 1986 **Independents Declared**. Washington, D.C.: Smithsonian Institute Press.

Attwood, D.A., and Williams, R.D. 1981. "Cannabis, Alcohol and Driving: Effects on Selected Closed-Course Tasks." 180. In AAAM (ed.) Proceedings of 24th Conference of the American Association of Automotive Medicine. Morton Grove, IL: AAAM, pp. 938-953.

Campbell, B.; Goodell, R.; and Linifield, J. 1989. **A Survey of Truck Drivers in British Columbia**. Report submitted to British Columbia Trucking Association, July 10.

Compton, Richard. 1986. Field Evaluation of the Los Angeles Police Department Drug Detection Procedure. NHTSA Technical Report No. HS 807-012. Washington, DC.

Compton, Richard, and Anderson, Theodore. 1985. The Incidence of Driving Under the Influence of Drugs 1985: An Update of the State of Knowledge. NHTSA Staff Technical Report, Washington, DC.

Desmond, P. 1989. "1988: Bigger, Better But No Boomer." **Commercial Carrier Journal**, July, pp. 70-84.

Editor, **Land Line**, 1989. "Problems with Hours of Service Violations." April, pg. 14.

Editorial "Federal Drug Testing Rules Are Scrutinized." 1989. **Transport Topics**. No. 2787. January 2, p. 18.

Getson, P. 1987. "A Critical Review of: 'Drug Use by Tractor-Trailer Drivers'. " A report submitted to the IIHS, June.

Honkanen, R.; Ertama, L.; Kinnoila, M.; Alah, M.; Lukkari, I.; Karlsson, M.; Kiviluto, O.; and Puro, M. 1980. "Role of drugs in traffic accidents." **British Medical Journal**, Vol. 281, pp. 1309-1312.

Joscelyn, K.B., and Donelson, A.C. 1980. **Drugs Research Methodology. Vol. II. The Identification of Drugs of Interest in Highway Safety.** National Highway Traffic Safety Administration, Report No. DOT HS-805-299, U.S. Department of Transportation, Washington, DC.

Lund, Adrian; Preusser, David; Blomberg, Richard; and Williams, Allan. 1987. "Drug Use by Tractor-Trailer Drivers." **Journal of Forensic Sciences,** September.

Mason, A.P., and McBay, A.J. 1984. "Ethanol, Marijuana, and Other Drug use in 600 Drivers Killed in Single-Vehicle Crashes in North Carolina, 1978-1981." **Journal of Forensic Sciences,** Vol. 29, No. 4, October, pp. 987-1026.

Moskowitz, H.; Sharma, S.; and Ziedman K. 1981. "Duration of Skills Performance Impairment." In AAAM (ed.) Proceedings of 25th Conference of the American Association of Automotive Medicine. Morton Grove, IL: AAAM, pp. 87-103.

Owens, S.M.; McBay, A.J.; and Cook, C.E. 1983. "The Use of Marijuana, Ethanol, and Other Drugs Among Drivers Killed in Single-Vehicle Crashes." **Journal of Forensic Sciences,** Vol. 28, No. 2, April, pp. 372-379.

Pollock, James. 1989. "How Are You Coping With The Stress of Trucking." **Independent Trucker,** April, pp. 14-15.

Sharma, Satanad. 1975. "Marihuana Effects on a Critical Tracking Task." In AAAM (ed.), **Proceedings of Nineteenth Conference of the American Association for Automotive Medicine.** Lake Bluff, IL: AAAM, pp. 285-291.

Sharma, S.; and Moskowitz, H. 1973. "Marihuana Dose Study of Vigilance Performance." Proceedings of 81st Annual Convention, APA, pp. 1031-1032.

Shinar, D. 1978. **Psychology on the Road.** New York: John Wiley and Sons.

Sutton, L.R. 1983. "The Effects of Alcohol, Marihuana and Their Combination on Driving Ability." **Journal of Studies on Alcohol,** Vol. 44(3), pp. 438-445.

Terhune, Kenneth, and Fell, James. 1982. "The Role of Alcohol, Marijuana And Other Drugs In The Accidents of Injured Drivers." NHTSA Technical Report No. HS 806-181, Washington, DC.

U.S. Department of Commerce. 1987. **Statistical Abstracts of the United States.** Washington, DC: U.S. Government Printing Office.

Warren, R.; Simpson, H.; Hilche, J.; Cimbura, G.; Lucas, D.; and Bennett, R. 1988. "Characteristics of Fatally Injured Drivers Testing Positive For Drugs Other Than Alcohol." Presented at 8th International Conference On Alcohol, Drugs and Traffic Safety, Stockholm, Sweden, June.

7

THREE BEERS FOR THE ROAD

La Scala was a Mexican-like border town which resembled an oasis for drivers. Trucks were parked everywhere, along the side of every street, in the back alleys and in every parking lot available. Danny inched his way down the street through the maze of trucks and turned into a gravel lane that ended in a hidden parking lot behind a small rundown Mexican cafe. BJ was already waiting for him.

For a brief period of time I became an outsider, a non-entity as Danny met his old compatriot. I stood aside as the two drivers unhooked the trailers in the lane part of the parking lot bounded by two buildings, packed with trucks. It took several tries before they could maneuver their tractors to hitch up the trailers.

Changing trailers with Danny under a blistering sun magnified BJ's thirst and hunger. He craved a cold drink and some good food. While Danny telephoned Oakland about his anticipated time of arrival, BJ and I walked over to the coffee shop and corralled the first table that became available.

BJ was a fifty-five year old company driver eagerly awaiting early retirement. Similar to other drivers I met in his age bracket, a central and indispensable part of BJ's work-related thinking was retirement. In short, he was filling in time with a company for the retirement benefits offered by the union and company. He had few expectations of trucking left. According to BJ he's "seen it all." The thing now was to save and plan for the future.

I ordered a coke. BJ called for a "nice cold beer" then scanned the menu and ordered a hamburger steak with fries. As the waitress arrived with our drinks, Danny returned for a quick visit with BJ before heading north. During his short visit BJ offered Danny comfort and solace. He acknowledged Danny's complaints about company policies, soothed his outrage over the dispatcher and sympathized over the probability that Danny will end up with a deadhead run. After calmly listening to Danny's grumblings and outpourings for five minutes, BJ changed his tone. He became more authoritarian or parental, telling Danny not to do anything stupid like "quit his job." BJ advised Danny that he must recognize that his role is a hired hand paid to haul freight.

BJ's attitude

Once Danny calmed down and reluctantly accepted his fate, BJ changed the tenor and topic of conversation. He eyed me suspiciously, asking me who I "really" was and why I wanted a ride with him. He believed that I had a cover story that needed to be cracked. Was my real agenda to "snoop for the company?" I spent several minutes assuring him of my intent and credentials.

BJ let it be known that he does not like giving people rides. Five years ago, "a long haired bum" approached him at a truck stop and asked him for a ride. BJ paid dearly for the favor, having his wallet stolen out of his jacket. As a result, he sticks to his rule, "No pickup rides."

At this time Danny jumped into the conversation and told BJ that I had clearance from the company president to ride with any trucker I desired. Because the Los Angeles dispatcher forgot to tell BJ about me, he was still suspicious. After a little more convincing, BJ felt more comfortable and agreed to me being his passenger. It was not the official line that convinced him, rather it was Danny's judgement that I was a "legit guy." As a truck friend, BJ trusted Danny before he trusted anyone else. Witness:

> If Danny says you're ok, it's ok by me. A guy's gotta be careful around truck stops . . . It's a place where bums come and want rides. When you give 'em one the next thing you know is they're hitting you up for money or a ride to a special place.

Ten minutes later Danny excused himself from the table to proceed with his trip. He gave BJ and I hearty handshakes as he left the stuffy, overcrowded, sweaty American-Mexican cafe. "He's a good boy, a little young and green around the ears. He's still got a lot to learn," BJ told me after Danny's departure.

The Second and Third Beer

As Danny left, the waitress re-appeared and brought BJ a second beer. BJ attacked the cold bottle, chugging half of it in a single swig. The experience of a working man quenching a heavy thirst did not promote negative images, but for a driver it left an opening for questions. I asked about BJ's views on drinking beer on the job. BJ answered, "Yeah sure, no problem. I'll just have one more." The trucker justified his actions on the grounds of hard work. It was four p.m. and he already "single stacked a load of apples, unloaded them and loaded other cargo." According to BJ, he was absolutely "wiped," as he cleared the sweat off his brow.

For his Los Angeles to La Scala run BJ was paid by the hour, not by the mile. It is company policy that any freight hauled under a hundred and twenty mile radius went by the hour. This afforded BJ time to relax and have a few beers without loss of pay. In our discussion I noted BJ's attempts at normalizing his drinking. His rule of thumb was that "he doesn't drink on the job." But, if the weather is humid, ranging from ninety to a hundred degrees Fahrenheit and he is required to do physical labor, the rule is negotiated or neutralized. The "real" issue becomes how many beers BJ drinks, not whether he drinks. Three bottles is his self-imposed limit because according to BJ it is a safe amount, just enough to "replace water lost through sweat."

With three beers BJ is most likely in compliance with the law, and in harmony with his competencies as a trucker.[1] He expressed trenchantly that he had the special abilities needed as a trucker and the life long driver experiences to arrive safely in LA. Combined, the two factors became the great compensator, controlling for any difficulties that may arise on the road. In a period of half an hour, BJ finished three bottles of beer with his meal. He was "raring to go" and hit Los Angeles at a reasonable hour.

BJ's views on driving, drinking three beers and safety may be applicable at a common sense level, but they are not fully supported in the research literature. Although he could probably drive legally in California, falling below the .1 BAC level, his reaction time and physical coordination are impacted. Rather than provide the evidence here I included significant counter arguments and research findings in the "Notes to Chapter Seven" section.[2]

According to BJ, M Company has no disciplinary code that pertains to consumption of liquor. If a driver receives a drinking driving charge he will be suspended. But for a driver who has a few drinks without breaking the law, M Transport has no policy. This places a lot of de facto power into the driver's hands. He sets the standards for drinking and driving according to his view of the law and manifest danger.

Relevant Issues for BJ

As we trucked down Interstate Five, several things pertaining to trucker communication came to my attention. BJ did not have a CB. Like Vic, the slander and foul language on the air encouraged him to remove the radio from the cab. Also, BJ seldom waved to other truckers whenever they passed him. Because of what truckers have become, BJ feels little allegiance to them. For him the old "knight" of the road is replaced by the greedy, vulgar individualist who cannot be trusted. According to BJ, lack of collegiality amongst truckers is the new reality for which he blamed the CB. More than any other innovation the CB reduced the need and enjoyment truckers had sharing each other's company, or as BJ said, "The personal touch is gone."

When I asked BJ to expand on his thoughts on trucker changes, he explained that the worsening situation was not isolated in trucking, rather it typified social change in society. BJ provided a parallel example in agriculture. Because of progress farmers have become fully mechanized and self sufficient resulting in a lack of sharing and helping others. So it is with truckers:

> If you're broken down on the side of the road and need help . . . there used to be a time when everyone would stop to help. Any trucker that came and saw would lend a hand. Today no one does.

The emphasis on competition and economic survival appeared to have sapped the moral energy that once sparked truckers. Collegiality has largely been replaced by anonymity and self-interest.

We neared Valencia, just before the Highway 210 turnoff. BJ was traveling steadily at sixty mph. I watched carefully, but could not detect any obvious detriment in his driving co-ordination, vigilance or alertness. We both sweated profusely because the truck's air conditioning system was broken and the air outside was hot and sticky. As we were discussing the effect of muggy weather on a driver without air conditioning BJ, without warning, became excited and gave a couple of full blasts on the airhorn. "What's up?" I asked. "Did you see that short skirt on that one, that blonde passing us in the small Honda," he asked excitedly. To my dismay I was unable to see from the passenger side. BJ helped me by describing, "what a set of legs."

Although BJ was married for the second time, he felt it was still "all right to look." But he has a rule, "don't touch." His family consists of three teenage sons ranging from thirteen to seventeen years of age. He hopes that they do not become truckers like their "old man," and experience the money frustration. After twenty years of driving experience he is still struggling financially. The only strong point is that he still loves the thrill of freedom. As he said:

> Trucking is the remaining job where someone tells you what you have to do and you do it how and when you want. It's the last remaining freedom.

The sun was slowly setting in the west, providing us with much needed relief from the scorching heat. As we passed Saugus, BJ spoke about his experiences as an owner operator. Several years ago he owned four trucks and leased them all to one company. According to the trucker, he "did all right, making a few dollars." However, as the trucks needed more repairs, competition for loads increased and the price per mile lowered, BJ was forced to sell his vehicles. Today he is grateful for being a company employee. The owner operators, he believed, are "just hanging in there," forcing their wives to work to succeed. Despite the severe difficulties there is still, in BJ's frame of mind, a romantic or idealized side to lease operating. It represented the "guts" or "stuff" of owner operators:

> Lease driving gets into your blood like stock car racing or something like that. It's something you just have to do . . . If someone don't like it, or don't like how I do it, they can kiss my butt. That's how leasers think. I'm pretty independent, a bit like that.

BJ considered trucking to be a reflection of society. Problems in trucking mirror problems in society. For example, to blame the trucker for illegal acts like drug use is irrational. According to BJ, drugs are used by all groups in society, doctors, lawyers and people in many other jobs. "Why pick on the truckers?" he asked rhetorically. Why "get on the trucker's case?" According to this driver the drug problem with truckers is highly overrated.

BJ knew that Danny popped pills. In the mid-seventies, BJ was a "heavy drug user," most of the time popping "cross tops" which he used to get illegally at truck stop counters. They were like tokens given to the truckers "under the table" for having fuelled at a particular truck stop. Also, in those days dispatchers provided truckers free pills for "running on time or running early."

In the early 1980s BJ decided to quit drugs and cigarettes for health reasons. "Why kill yourself?" he asked. However, drinking beer was one essential habit he refused to break. Although BJ had not taken drugs for eight years, he still believed that truckers should not undergo urinalysis if the government authorities desire. "Not on your life," said BJ. He answered with a question, "Why should truckers undergo urinalysis when the CHIPs (California Highway Patrol) don't have to?" According to BJ, CHIP members fought the mandatory urinalysis policy and won. "They got away with it." To BJ it is a matter of constitutional rights. "If you have no constitutional rights, what've you got? Nothing, absolutely nothing. So why live in America?"

Near San Fernando BJ and I discussed the use and abuse of log books. Without apology BJ acknowledged that he has cheated on log entries and number of log books carried by a driver during his entire career. To his way of thinking, "every trucker cheats on his log book as everyone cheats on their taxes . . . What's the difference?"

Darkness was falling as we were in the midst of Los Angeles traffic. Near the Hollywood turnoff, in the middle of multiple lanes of traffic, BJ pointed to a beautiful looking Peterbilt semitrailer, calling its driver a "damn idiot!" The truck had just passed us returning into our lane. Ahead of the Peterbilt was a car full of senior citizens. The trucker tailgated them, his bumper nearly touching theirs at high speed. He then snapped over to the left lane, trailer whipping, cutting off a half ton truck in the process, passing the elderly people. There was no signal of intent, just rapid fire motion. BJ believed that there were about fifteen percent of such "bad eggs" in trucking, "lots of idiots on the road here." In fact, on my trip I saw this kind of driving more often in California than in any other state or province.

We arrived in Norwalk at seven thirty p.m. Traffic was heavy but BJ calmly steered the truck through the congestion and tight corners to his company's space rented from a large trucking yard in Norwalk. The compound looked depressing. In the shallow light provided by the single lamp located at the entrance, I could see acres and acres of land where a large number of trailers were arranged in formation. An old leaning outhouse was the only visible sign of anyone addressing a trucker's personal needs. Around the yard was a chain-link fence topped by barbed wire. The driving area was unpaved. A fine dust seeped through the pores of my skin collecting at the corners of my mouth. It forced me to lick my lips, then wipe them with my forearms. The dust crept inside my skin.

These surroundings were BJ's home away from home. He intended to sleep here overnight, leaving early next morning for Portland, Oregon. There was no running water and his truck lacked air conditioning to make his life a little more comfortable. It was destined to be another rough night for him, much like the previous two had been. His chance of getting a deep sleep was slim. Will it affect his driving the next day? "Na, not really. It's life on the road," he answered optimistically.

BJ unlatched the trailer and drove me to a Norwalk hotel. It was comfortable but noisy. I wished BJ well, thanked him for the ride, and prepared myself for the stay.

Notes to Chapter Seven

1. Flanagan (1983) studied drivers who consumed various amounts of liquor in a structured performance test on a planned course. He concluded that:

   > Many drivers are significantly impaired at blood alcohol levels well below the 80 mgms/100 ml limit (0.08) . . . The willingness to take risks . . . was . . . demonstrated by our drivers by their attempts to negotiate hazards when their angle of approach was clearly unsuitable.

   In a booklet entitled, "Smashed" (1987; pg. 19), Transport Canada officials analyzed the research and proposed the following BAC motivated driving changes:

Our ability to judge distances between stationary objects is reduced at BACs over 80 mg%. This ability can be impaired at BACs between 50 mg% and 80 mg%.

Once on the road, the ability to estimate distances between moving objects is also reduced. Some people are affected this way if their BAC is as low as 20 mg%. Virtually everyone's vision is affected at BACs of 100 mg%.

The ability to adjust to sudden darkness, called dark adaptation, is impaired at BACs of 80 mg% and higher. The greater the concentration of alcohol in blood, the longer the glare recovery time. This refers to the period during which a person is partially blinded when exposed briefly to bright lights and then to darkness. This happens each time the headlights of an oncoming vehicle pass you. (Transport Canada, 1987; pg. 19)

In Canada the legal BAC level is be .08. American states have different limits. Under Connecticut law a BAC between .07 and .1 constitutes an infraction (Jacobs, 1989). In Washington it is .08 and in Minnesota it is .05. Some states are moving toward zero tolerance. New York's Vehicle and Traffic Law, section 192[1] states:

"I charge you that a person's ability to operate a motor vehicle is impaired when he has voluntarily consumed alcohol to such an extent as to diminish or reduce his ability to operate the motor vehicle, even in the slightest degree. If the consumption of alcohol has any effect at all, even the slightest, upon the physical or mental ability of the defendant to operate the motor vehicle, this is sufficient to constitute driving while impaired" (Vehicle and Traffic Law, sec. 192[1]). (Jacobs, 1989; pg. 211)

Shinar (1978) associated driving with a blood alcohol concentration (BAC) of greater than .08. He concluded that there is a significantly increased probability of being involved in a traffic accident due to decreased visual, perceptual and judgment abilities. Higher BACs (greater than .1) are associated with: poor detection of roadway signs in night driving; misjudgment of speed and distance; driving through stop signs and red signal lights; narrowed effective field of vision ("tunnel vision"); decreased ability to allocate attention appropriately; decreased visual scanning; and motor inco-ordination. Such perceptual (e.g., Harris 1982) and performance (e.g., Ranny and Gawron, 1986) deficits combine to result in drastically degraded driving performance that commonly results in a single-car accident where the car leaves the road and strikes an obstacle, seriously injuring the driver (Johnston, 1982).

According to Shinar, there are individual differences in the degree of driving impairment associated with particular BACs. A heavy drinker suffers less driving impairment than a moderate drinker when both consume the same amount of alcohol per body weight.

As a rule, truckers do not use alcohol to enhance driving performance. It is more of a lifestyle drug, the aftereffects which creep into the driving world. It is not unusual, therefore, to find truck driving studies where alcohol is a questionable factor. The Transportation Research Board (1987; pg. 31) reported:

> The available information about commercial vehicle driver impairment by alcohol and the extent of alcohol involvement in truck crashes indicates that alcohol plays a much smaller role in truck crashes than would be expected on the basis of the estimates of alcohol involvement for all crashes presented in the preceding section. This lower percentage of alcohol-impaired driving for commercial vehicle drivers compared with passenger vehicle drivers is to be expected. Commercial vehicle drivers are at work and alcohol consumption in the work place is not generally accepted. The majority of passenger vehicle drivers are not at work; indeed, most are driving for recreational purposes.

It is premature to generalize that truck drivers engage in less drinking and driving than other drivers. The problem may lie in low police reporting of Blood Alcohol Concentration (BAC). Based on the Fatal Accident Reporting System (FARS) data, 1982-1985, BACs were reported for only 11.3 percent of crash surviving truck drivers of whom about 14 percent had some alcohol in their bloodstream (Transportation Research Board, 1987). Because in more than seventy-five percent of fatal truck crashes the victim was riding in the other vehicle, it is difficult to estimate the role of alcohol in fatal truck crashes.

Whereas truck driver alcohol use in fatal crashes is underreported, more emphasis has been given to surveys. Lund et al. (1987) engaged a urinalysis for drug use, one of which was alcohol. (See Note to Chapter Six.) The research team estimated that about one percent of the drivers had been drinking alcohol. But, because twelve percent of the drivers refused to give blood or urine samples, and an unknown number of drivers, through active CB communication, may have skirted the weigh scales where testing was being done, reliance on the percent estimate is questionable.

The 1989 weigh scale urinalysis study in British Columbia also reported in Chapter Six was not designed to highlight truck driver alcohol use through measurement of urine samples. It sought a conservative estimate of truck driver alcohol use based on self-reported data.

A fill-in questionnaire with fourteen questions pertaining to alcohol was presented to truckers. Of the 1,006 truckers that were surveyed, 78.5 percent answered that they had a drink two or more days previous to the survey. Averaged out over the last three months, 81.1 percent of the truckers stated that they use alcohol about once a week or less.

Responding to the question, "On a typical workday, how much do you drink before beginning work?," only 0.5 percent answered one or two drinks. Furthermore, 2.1 percent remarked that on a typical workday they have one or two drinks, typically during lunch or coffee breaks.

A question that produced answers with impact was, "In the past three months, how often have you driven your truck within two hours of drinking three or more drinks?" About four percent (3.9 percent) answered "occasionally" and 0.1 percent responded "regularly."

Each year British Columbia's Ministry of Solicitor General analyzes provincial traffic accident statistics. Recognizing that underreporting is a problem, still 3.5 percent of all truckers involved in 1987 heavy commercial vehicle accidents had alcohol involvement assigned as the major contributing factor in truck related crashes. In comparison, all accidents recorded in British Columbia included 9.2 percent alcohol involvement as the major contributing factor. The numbers reflect police completion of accident forms, and the probable underreporting of truck drivers. Based on a review of 32,000 hard copy accident reports in the United States, Boyer et al. (1985) established that only 0.6 percent listed alcohol as the prime cause.

More rigorous and comprehensive research on alcohol use in trucking is necessary before we can moralize on truckers' lifestyles. Truck driver data need to include information on employment settings and roles, social norms, accepted behavior, and legal sanctions. More data on the fundamental nature of alcohol effects on the nervous system as it relates to operating a truck is also required.

References

Boyar, U.W.; Couts, D.A.; Joshi, A.J.; and Klein, T.M. 1985. **Identification Of Preventable Commercial Accidents And Their Causes.** Submitted to Federal Highway Administration, under contract No. C-00034.

British Columbia Ministry of Attorney General. 1988. **1987 Traffic Accident Statistics.** Victoria, BC: Motor Vehicle Branch.

Campbell, B.; Goodell, R.; and Linifield, J. 1989. **A Survey Of Truck Drivers In British Columbia, Canada.** A report submitted to the British Columbia Trucking Association, Vancouver, BC, July 10.

Flanagan, N.G. 1983. "Effects of Low Doses of Alcohol on Driving Performance." **Medical Science Law,** 23, pp. 203-208.

Harris, D.H. 1982. "Visual Detection of Driving While Intoxicated." **Human Factors,** 22(6), pp. 725-732.

Jacobs, J.B. 1989. **Drunk Driving, An American Dilemma.** Chicago: University of Chicago Press.

Johnston, I.R. 1982. "The Role of Alcohol in Road Crashes." **Ergonomics,** 25(10).

Ranny, T.A., and Gawron, V.J. 1986. "The Effects of Pavement Edgelines on Performance in Driving Simulator under Sober and Alcohol-Dosed Conditions." **Human Factors,** 28(5), pp. 511-525.

Shinar, D. 1978. **Psychology on the Road.** New York: John Wiley and Sons.

Transport Canada. 1987. **Smashed.** Ottawa, ON: Road Safety and Regulation Directorate.

Transportation Research Board. 1987. **Zero Alcohol And Other Options Limits For Truck And Bus Drivers.** Washington, DC: National Research Council.
Wick, R.L. 1989. "Everything You Need To Know About Drinking Alcohol." **Transport Topics,** July 10, pp. 28-40.

8

HUSBAND AND WIFE TEAMS FOR LOVE AND SAFETY

On Monday, two a.m., I left my comfortable hotel in Long Beach for W Freightlines near East Los Angeles. My taxi driver was reluctant to drive here in the middle of the night. When I bribed him with cash, he took the extra money, feeling a little ambivalent about safety, the fare and the bribe. Our short journey to the marshaling yard was uneventful, for which the cab driver was thankful.

While I was waiting for Ted and Lisa, I sat around in the office, drank a cup of coffee and spoke to the dispatcher. He was "sold" on husband and wife teams. As he put it, "they're safer, faster, cheaper and they bitch less." Whenever a lucrative run becomes available, the dispatcher tries to assign it to a spouse team. On this night Ted and Lisa were scheduled for a trip to Jacksonville.

While Ted was preparing the paper work for the journey, I introduced myself to the couple. Ted was a little apprehensive about me becoming a passenger. He asked the dispatcher whether I received administrative clearance, if I passed company safety regulations and if I signed liability waiver forms. Fortunately, the company's senior management in Jacksonville made sure that my request to do some research with W company drivers was granted. Ted was satisfied with the news.

Once we were in the truck, Lisa jumped on the bunk, I sat in the passenger seat, and Ted drove. Since Lisa was not scheduled to drive until later in the afternoon she intended to sleep to Phoenix.

At four o'clock Monday morning, the traffic leaving the Los Angeles area was light, but steady. Few cars–mostly trucks! This is a common scene – truckers escaping Los Angeles at the crack of dawn trying to stay ahead of the traffic congestion.

The environmental and social impact of rush-hour traffic in the Los Angeles basin is the major reason underlying the Los Angeles municipal government's intent to regulate trucks more tightly. To reduce peak rush hour traffic, street congestion and air pollution, carriers must keep seventy percent of their heavy and medium-duty rigs off city streets from six to nine a.m. and four to seven p.m. (Ponzani, 1988).

Truckers are not happy with rush-hour traffic either. During the six to eight a.m. rush they can lose up to five hours' driving time. To miss the six a.m. traffic onslaught and to avoid the loss of valuable time, truckers leave extra early. It was for this reason that Ted and Lisa departed at four in the morning.

Once we neared San Bernardino, the two drivers and I discussed trucking. Ted has operated a truck for twenty-five years. As a team he and Lisa have been driving for five years, the last three of which were with the same company. Their home is in Florida, to which they return about once every three weeks. The rest of the time Ted and Lisa are on the road. The question that naturally arose was why Lisa entered trucking with her husband.

Ted told me that Lisa's decision was based on him. He didn't want to be driving long distance without his wife anymore. He wanted her to keep him company. Since she was a good driver, Ted believed she was also capable of handling a truck. He asked her to try it. Because Lisa was lonely at home, she consented. According to Ted, "the rest is history."

Dawn showed us the first signs of daylight while we were heading south towards the Arizona border. Lisa decided to sleep. She excused herself, zipped up the bunk and left Ted and I alone to speak.

Ted confirmed the point earlier made by the dispatcher; namely, that freight companies prefer spouse teams. However, such teams are difficult to find because married women are reluctant to become truckers. Whenever a company manages to contract one, the dispatchers and supervisors try not to hassle the team. As the W Freightlines dispatcher previously told me, "husband and wife teams are money in the bank, an investment you want to protect." Ted's views were further echoed by a Jerry and Cindy, a husband and wife team I met at the Portland truck stop. Jerry said:

We're a team, so we don't get the hassles because they know that we're going to get it there as quick as we can. If a solo driver takes the same run, there's no way that solo driver can get back from New York in three days.

The definition of driving that is used by husband and wife tends to be different from one used by other drivers. The spouses interpret trucking with reference to family matters typified in settling disagreements, negotiating marital roles such as doing the laundry, cooking or paying the bills and maintaining a love life on the road. The close proximity in a cab between husband and wife provided little difficulty for Ted or Lisa. Their roles as truckers were linked to their marital roles where the happiness of each spouse is an important goal. Rather than toiling for pay they share experiences for which they receive money.

According to Ted, driving with Lisa produces a contentment and an overall better attitude. When Ted drove alone he was like other solo truckers whose minds are preoccupied with thoughts about getting home. In Ted's words, "I'd push harder, . . . used to drive longer periods of time to get home." Now he drives easier, has better personal habits and enjoys trucking much more.

The morning was quickly heating up. We were in the desert cruising comfortably between fifty-five to sixty mph. Ted seemed very confident in his abilities as he calmly reasoned his views and beliefs. He was dressed in a pink California shirt, looking casual and neat. Lisa was dressed in a blouse and slacks, appearing well groomed. The inside of the truck was spotless. The manners displayed by Ted were polite. The total appearance of these two truckers was different from any others I had met.

Neither spouse took drugs or smoked. Their primary concern was for each other's welfare. Ted and Lisa's view on time was not to challenge it with maximum distance traveled, but to use it wisely for getting to their destination safely and contentedly. While on the road they follow a simple rule, "the person behind the wheel's the boss." According to Ted, this rule is important because:

> That's exactly the way it's been set up. It's got to be that way. If I'm sitting over there and something comes up, she don't have time to ask me how she should handle this or anything, you know.

As a pair of drivers, Ted and Lisa are "making a pretty good living." If one decided to quit "things would get tight." Their situation would be the same as other single drivers who experience increasing road expenses without a parallel rise in wages. For Ted, paying three to four dollars for a simple hamburger illustrates the point. Several years ago the same hamburger cost him a dollar.

Team driving entails an economic spirit not only for today but also for tomorrow. Partners are planning for life after retirement. They drive as a team to prepare for the major event by maximizing their earnings and savings. With children having left home, both spouses drive together to re-establish their relationship while making a living.

Ted and Lisa haul for W Freightlines, in part, because of its excellent pension plan. After having been a Teamster for eighteen years, Ted decided to quit the union and work for a non-union outfit. He was upset that the Teamster union short-changed him by six years of his retirement fund. Ted explained:

> I was a Teamster for . . . almost 18 years. I sent in for, to see how much time I had valid. They come back and tell me, well, you only got 12 years because this one person didn't pay a retirement fund on you and we can't find the records, right . . . So I lost six years of Teamster time right there. Well, they ain't kiddin'

nobody. The company that they're talking about that didn't pay it, went out of business. So somebody just took it off the records and put that money in their pocket.

Ted mistrusted the Teamsters because he believes that in the final event, they don't give a damn about him as a driver. The union representatives only look out for themselves, even if it means joining with a company against the driver.

Around seven, Lisa unzipped the bunk sat up and prepared to enter our conversation. She presented her point of view while Ted and I discussed the amount of driving Ted and she were prepared to do before retirement. "I think ten years will do me," Lisa said. Ted anticipates another fifteen years. But if the money is saved, he could easily be persuaded to retire when Lisa does.

The First Stop

"There's scales ahead. Banning has trucker scales," Ted remarked as we approached Banning, California. Ted geared down and braked so he could have his truck weighed and his papers reviewed. The state transportation authorities in California have a reputation of rigor and hard nosed enforcement, qualities not appreciated by many truckers, but well accepted by Ted. He appreciates the California agents pulling over truckers who have not obtained inspection stickers over the last three to six months to get the bad trucks off the road and to make the companies "toe the line." He reasoned that, "If the trucks have defects in them and the company ain't fixin' them, I gotta face that guy." Ted continued:

So I'd rather face somebody whose truck is in good shape brakewise, tirewise, steering mechanism. The whole thing is, I'd rather, I'd rather be, the guy coming at me, he's got good equipment, rather than junk, you know, not knowing when he's gonna blow a tire or whatever, uh, so I believe in inspections, I really do, I, I think it's a, there's no such thing as too much of it.

Ted supported rigorous equipment checks at weigh scales. He personalized possible ramifications if inspections were relaxed. According to Ted, if weigh scale attendants are slack, the next truck that hits him may have faulty equipment because weigh masters or the police "were not doing their jobs inspecting the big rigs."

Ted stopped the truck and handed the weigh master his documents. After a brief survey, the agent flashed the "Proceed" light on the outside instruction board. Ted explained that his company enjoyed a good safety image. Officers usually let him continue on his trips because "W" Company is recognized as being safe.

Six miles up the freeway we stopped at Cabazon, a small roadside cafe located in the desert. It had similarities to "Baghdad Cafe," the movie; an old log building in nowhere land surrounded by several smaller buildings. Ted wanted to stop here for breakfast. Lisa supported his plan. We were all hungry. While we were waiting to place our order in this rundown yet lively cafe, food became the focus for discussion. Up to this point in my voyage most truckers I met believed that nutrition was not synonymous with truck cafes. Fast, greasy foods are the mainstays of truck stop menus. It is not surprising, therefore, that truckers have a tendency to become fat. In the trucking world, the observation is a truism. In response to their poor physical fitness, truckers invariably mention diets or, more precisely, the lack of healthy foods at truck stops. They have a ponch because they sit all day in a bouncing truck, eating "garbage food." I pondered over the question, if truckers recognize that truck stop restaurants serve poor food, why do they not eat elsewhere? The answer is straightforward. Choosing an eating establishment is premised on truck parking facilities not quality of food.

Lisa openly stated that the food at truck stop restaurants, "is not good for you cause its all fried food. You can't get the truck into a normal restaurant. There's no parking for you." According to Lisa, unless a person is "naturally skinny," the majority of trucking people are overweight.

For Lisa, gaining weight has become a personal battle which began when she started driving with Ted. Her net weight gain over five years has been sixty pounds. Ted also conceded that he gained weight and now was overweight, but, unlike Lisa, he refused to quote numbers. His commonplace phrase was "Truckers are like that." It served as Ted's shorthand rationale to illustrate that operating a truck takes up so much time and energy, he can't be concerned about his physical fitness. Ted works "so much" that he does not "have as much time to work out a bit." Lisa piggybacked on Ted's fatalistic reasoning. She emphasized that truckers sit and drive, then go to bed with whatever they have eaten. They cannot stop the truck, step out and jog for an hour. The trucker's schedule is too tight to allow for exercising. If a trucker does walk a few miles, then, according to Lisa, he goes back to work sore.

It became evident that the demanding driving schedule leaves little time for physical fitness activities. Ted admitted that becoming "fat" is unhealthy, but he took a passive stance concerning his role in the problem. He blamed delivery schedules and restaurant menus. Lunch bags disinterested him because they were time-consuming, cumbersome and boring. Lisa took comfort in Ted's justifications, stressing that the stereotype of truckers as fat is not fully deserved. It is an individual thing.

Some truckers may run a couple of shifts before they eat. As a result they over eat. It usually catches up to them once they reach their thirties.

For Lisa, maintaining proper weight is a battle. On her last trip she stuck to salad bars. In the morning she ate oatmeal and in the evening she had salad. She feels that on this trip she can treat herself and "have something good." So the battle begins, trying to stay psyched for salad. As she said, "its hard to eat salads three hundred and sixty-five days a year, you get tired of salad."

The waitress' service temporarily halted our conversation. Ted and Lisa each received an order of bacon and eggs, toast, hash browns and coffee. I had the same minus the bacon. The food was greasy, which now was an expectation in all truck stop cafes I visited. As Ted and Lisa mentioned, it's a fact of trucking many "thousands, if not millions of drivers" have discovered over the years.

The common trucker assessment is that the quality of food in truck stop restaurants has worsened over the years. Diners no longer provide, as they did in the 1960s, a "home-cooked meal" at reasonable prices. Today their mainstays are fast fried foods, with occasional "boring" salad bars. The old folk wisdom passed on from traveler to traveler that a person should eat where truckers dine because the quality is excellent, the quantity of food is ample and the price is right, no longer prevails. Truckers eat where they do because they can conveniently park their trucks. Quality of food is more likely "to be bad than good," and prices are as high if not higher than in other eating establishments.

Unfortunately there are few research studies that examine the relationship between weight, diet, obesity and lack of exercise; and driver reaction time, coordination and alertness. Studies sometimes quoted on weight and activity are, for example, Tevlin (1980) and Laser (1984), where the samples are obese women, physical involvement and energy exertion. The extent to which findings can be translated to the trucker driving reality is limited.

To Phoenix

Once I paid the bill we were on our way. The weather became extremely hot and dry. I took a few snapshots of the truck and the countryside. In the distance I heard a trucker yell to Ted, "Hey who's your new driver, hasn't he seen a truck before?" Ted and Lisa smiled. To the truckers I was an anomaly, one that demanded commentary.

Ted was satisfied with the time we were making, willing to slow down so that I could survey the land more leisurely. Lisa returned to the sleeper to get more rest. A few minutes later Ted pointed to Palm Springs and joked that the best age for visiting this resort is seventy, as long as the seventy-year-olds fly to Palm Springs and not drive. Between the Orocopia Mountains to the south and the Colorado River to the north we headed towards Blythe, the last California city before the Arizona border. While we were discussing driver skills and close calls the two drivers experienced, Ted, unsolicited, praised Lisa's driving abilities.

According to Ted, the other night while they were approaching California a truck travelling in the opposite direction crossed the center divider and came directly towards her. He was asleep at the time. She kept her cool as the other trucker woke up in time. Another time they were driving down Highway 75 when, as Ted described, the wheel on a camper "came apart, axles and parts scattered all over the highway." Lisa "just drove through that junk like it was an obstacle course." Based on these observations Ted considered his wife to be a very skillful driver.

Unlike most male truckers I met, Ted appreciates "the woman" as a "capable driver." He believed that they had personal characteristics that make them superior drivers to men. According to Ted, calmness, common sense and awareness of personal limitations are factors female drivers possess. Lisa illustrates this daily. Strength was not a quality Ted believed was necessary to be a "professional trucker." He challenged one of trucking's basic premise. If physically weaker females can control an 80,000 pound rig, then the all-embracing, age-old belief that only man's strength and abilities are prerequisites for trucking loses its status. Ted has fully integrated the woman driver into what has been traditionally a man's world.

At this point I posed a vital question to Ted, "Are husband and wife teams safer than solo drivers?" With little hesitation, Ted answered, "Yes, there's no doubt about it." Police officers in Canada, Arizona and California agreed, that based on their experiences, spouse teams are safer than solo drivers. Law officers reasoned that women moderate male aggressive driving tendencies, they check men's possible adventures with drugs and prostitutes, they are better organized with paperwork, and they are more emphatic about driving clean tractors – inside and out. Furthermore, because the wives accompany male truckers, the latter are less likely to race home.

The view that women in trucks increased the potential for safety was extended to their involvement in truck inspections. Truckers like Dale and Phil complained loudly that female inspectors at weigh scales do not follow customary rules appreciated by men. They are too thorough, too picky, or as Phil said, "They don't know the rules or know how to follow the rules of the game." Both drivers agreed that they are less likely to grant concessions for certain mechanical faults, concessions likely to be offered by men who "really know trucks." No truck is faultless, so the rationalization goes. Where you start and stop finding fault depends on the extremeness of the problem, the financial capability of the truck owner and feelings shared between men in the same industry. According to Ted, women are more conservative on the side of safety and rule-breaking than are male inspectors. Women have a personal feel for hurt and danger. Ted described:

> You know, women read the paper about this trucker running over so-and-so, you know, killing these people in this car, you know, uh, that brings the woman about saying, 'Well', you know, 'This, I'm not going to let this guy loose if he's in potential, his truck is a potential killer', you know. Women are thorough lookers.

Through husband and wife teams, alternate views of professional drivers are slowly gaining an audience. The female is becoming recognized as professional on the basis of being competent, levelheaded and by retaining enough sense of femininity to make the husband "feel proud." Similarly, the male driver of a spouse team is aware of the woman's expectations. He becomes more professional, skillful and safe besides being clean, shaven and looking presentable. Combined, the two ideal-type definitions of professional driver would give "trucking a better and cleaner image," or according to Ted, the dignity of "all drivers rises."

We entered Arizona. I was in awe of the large cactus standing in front of the distant Eagle Tail Mountains. Our stop at the Arizona point of entry station produced no problems. However, just ahead I noticed a state trooper ticketing a half-ton-truck driver. Ted spotted the scene and smiled sarcastically. He had a story to tell, one that included economics and police violations.

Ted believed that the police have joined forces with the government and with insurance companies to conspire against truckers. His example concerns Texas. Ted received a ticket for speeding, a charge Ted denied he deserved. He thought that the police were ticketing truckers to help the state survive after the "oil business went to pieces." Ted described:

> I told that officer there, I said, 'You know, it wouldn't bother me a bit that you're giving me this ticket. For some reason you have decided I'm gonna have this ticket to give you the money that you apparently need.' I said, 'it's one of the most unjust tickets I've ever had.' But, I said, 'the way I really feel about it deep down inside, is for the next three years I've got to pay the insurance company for this ticket. You're an unpaid insurance agent.' You know, you, you get a ticket out here, all right, the cop turns it into the state, the state sends it back to your state, your insurance company looks at it and says, 'Well, here's a dummy eight miles an hour over the speed limit.' Your insurance goes up 30 percent.

Ted was disgruntled that what began as a fifty dollar fine for a traffic violation cost him four times as much per year for the next three years in insurance premiums. For him, the situation was totally unjust, one in which there was a suspected conspiracy between the insurance company and the police force.

On this trip Ted and Lisa were transporting, among other goods, seventy-two pounds of hazardous materials – flammable substances. The disturbing part of the situation was not the existence of the material in the trailer but that Ted did not know the nature of the hazardous materials he was carrying. I asked Ted how he could effectively respond in an emergency if he is unaware of the substance. Ted explained that because he has less than five hundred pounds of flammable product he is not required to placard the trailer. If something unforeseen should happen, he would read the instructions on the top bill with a red tag on it, located in his folder.

Ted believed that the issue of hazardous materials and placarding can become unruly. He talked about a tunnel between Phoenix and Jacksonville, Florida, where no hazardous materials are allowed. On one trip Ted had fifteen pounds of car batteries. He had to take a forty-two mile detour because of the regulation. Ted reasoned:

> The tunnels in the country, it don't matter if it's one pound or 5,000 pounds, you don't go through it. I mean you can't take a five gallon bucket of paint through there, you know, but you can go through there with 300 gallons of fuel oil in your tank, you know. Does it make good sense? I can see me running here with my station wagon, going around it because I've got some paint in the back. You can't take a car battery through there. If I got a car battery in the back end of the trailer, as freight, I can't go through the tunnel, with a corrosive.

Ted knew that other truckers have little choice but to cheat. Drivers look at the law and think, "that's absolutely stupid, I can't take five gallons of paint through but I can fill up my tank with gas and go through." On this trip Ted intended to drive through. He is not going to lose an hour driving time detouring the tunnel for what he considered to be a light load and a ridiculous law.

As a passenger with some naivete, undefined hazardous materials scare me. Furthermore, Ted's lack of effort to become informed about the materials he was carrying made me more nervous. A clash of world view prevailed. To me, hazardous materials are special, demanding attention. To Ted, it all seemed routine – so taken-for-granted. For a trucker who routinely hauls bleach, detergent, and batteries, hazardous materials are "no big deal." I cannot criticize Ted for his of-course attitude about hazardous materials. There are too many commodities to worry about. As an outsider, I thought that to be informed in case of an accident is a reasonable compromise.

Goodbye

We arrived in Phoenix just before noon. It was choking hot – dry and immediate. Ted and Lisa dropped me off at the company truck yard, wished me all the best and ventured forth to Jacksonville, Florida. I took a picture of them holding hands in front of their tractor. They looked like newlyweds standing before their A-train.

References

Bem, S., and Bem, D.J. 1970. "Training the Woman to Know Her Place: The Power of a Nonconscious Ideology." In Bem, D. (ed.), **Behavior, Attitudes and Human Affairs**. NY: Wadsworth.

Berger, P., and Luckmann, T. 1967. **The Social Construction of Reality**. Middlesex, GB: Penguin Press.

Bureau of Census. 1987. **Statistical Abstract of the United States, 1987**. Washington, DC: U.S. Government Printing Office.

Cicourel, A. 1968. **The Social Organization of Juvenile Justice**. NY: John Wiley and Sons.

Goffman, E. 1963. **Stigma**. NJ: Englewood Cliffs.

Industry Report. 1987. **Truck World**, January, pg. 1f.

Laser, E.D. 1984. "The Relationship Between Obesity, Early Recollections, and Adult Life-Style." **Individual Psychology:Journal of Adlerian Theory, Research and Practice**, 40(1), pp. 29-35.

Ponzani, L. 1988. "L.A. Proposal To Restrict Trucks Draws Fire From Industry." **Transport Topics**, December 19, pg. 20.

Tevlin, H.E. 1980. A comparison of Daily Activity Patterns of Obese and Normal-Weight Women. Unpublished Ph.D. dissertation, University of Oregon, Eugene, OR, March.

9

SMOKIES STOPPING TRUCKERS

While I was in Phoenix, I travelled with Phil, an Arizona state trooper and also a member of the CVSA (Commercial Vehicle Safety Alliance)[1], who was charged with the investigation and enforcement of truck regulations. These experiences form the skeleton of my discussion, further fleshed out by interviews and observations with members of the California Highway Patrol, the Royal Canadian Mounted Police, a British Columbia city police team and many truckers.

Before documenting my observations, I would like to step back for a moment to discuss the stage for description. Truckers haul goods for economic needs. Police officers are on the highway to invoke state authority on truckers engaged in illegal or unlawful actions. They try to prevent actions considered to be contrary to public policy (Gusfield, 1981). To pursue their individual goals, police officers and truckers use all the resources they can find, whether they be material or symbolic.

The truckers use an equal amount of wit and energy to avoid being stopped by the police. If they are ordered to pull over by an officer, they use certain strategies to limit the penalty. The result is a game of one-upmanship between the police and truckers.

Phil Picks Out the Truckers

Phil picked me up at my hotel on Saturday, seven a.m. He drove a four-wheel drive Suburban that was packed with electronic equipment and inspection gear. Phil had a cellular phone, Citizen Band radio and a police radio. There were switches, dials and knobs throughout, looking more like the cockpit of an airplane than the inside of a police cruiser.

While we ate breakfast at a fast food restaurant, Phil described parts of his life. He was a former trucker, born into a trucking family. From trucking, Phil graduated to bus driving, where five years prior to his present position he owned two buses. The vehicles were on the road most of the time driving company employees on gambling excursions to Reno. While Phil was younger he did not mind driving a bus for fifteen to twenty hours from Reno to Phoenix. Now, as a forty-five year old, driving twelve hours consecutively wears on him.

Phil began considering selling his buses when he joined the police. Although he was still earning good money with hired drivers, he began to feel nervous about the passenger's safety whenever a driver arrived late in the middle of the night. He couldn't sleep at night and became anxious during the day. Finally, he sold the business to one of the hired drivers. Since that time he has felt much happier and content.

During breakfast, Phil advised me that in the United States the highway patrols are not allowed to stop and enter trucks without due cause. State troopers must, by virtue of the law, be selective about which truckers they can stop, for what reasons. The selection principles become the "trade knowledge" (Goffman, 1959) of the police, the "inside" lines for marking certain truckers. They serve as "official markers."

Based on his experiences, Phil uses several strategies to determine which truckers should be stopped for inspection at roadside. A popular opening frame he and other members of the Arizona Highway Patrol use is to check if mudflaps on trailers are out of place. By law, mudflaps must cover at least seventy percent of the tires. The top of the flaps must be parallel with the trailer's frame and they must be constructed of anti-soil material to retain stiffness in wind or drag. Any rip or shift in position represents a violation of the law. Because mudflaps experience wear and tear from normal driving, a state trooper searching for a reason to investigate a trucker, is generally assured of entry through a mudflap violation. The emphasis is on "looking for a reason" or for "due cause." Although a trucker may not be driving illegally, by hauling hazardous materials or by driving for a carrier with a bad safety record, he may make himself a candidate for police inspection. Although tattered mudflaps is the point of entry typically used by the police to hit upon suspicious drivers, there are others which are equally successful.

A strategy often used by members of the Arizona Highway Patrol is looking for yellow reflector lights. Typically a truck's lighting system includes red reflectorization for tail lights and back-up lights. Yellow reflectors are used for turning and/or braking. Any deviation from this structure can become a reason for police officers to stop the trucker.

Some truckers install a variation of the official rear lighting scheme. To be individualistic and unique they replace the red tail light with a yellow one, creating an unorthodox red-yellow glow. This unconforming practise tips off the police. As Phil explained:

> When they have a yellow and red light combination I stop them. I guarantee you, nine times out of ten, they'll either be over hours, gross falsification in the log book, or drugged. It never ceases to amaze me.

Phil is fascinated at the relationship between burning yellow lights and log book violations. As he said, "I cannot believe how often we put trucks out of service for log book violations when we find that light combination." According to Phil, yellow lights and broken reflectors gets his "foot in the door to do his log audit."

The process for picking out truckers to be inspected can also be direct. A moving traffic violation, like speeding, makes a trucker an immediate ~speeding~ target for a police stop. However, for Phil, serving truckers traffic citations is not an objective clean cut process. Phil considers his personal philosophy when he writes tickets. He discussed:

> We have officers, if we have a policy six miles per hour over, he'll write a ticket. The policy is a written guideline, and these guys weren't around – I was around when the speed limit was 75 and we didn't stop cars 'til 85; now it's 55 and we stop them at 61 and write them a ticket. I can't believe it . . . You have to add in everything. You're the only car on the road, you're doing ten over, I give you a warning.

Phil does not believe in blindly following a policy. He interprets it according to the conditions at the time. As a former trucker, Phil appreciates how truckers feel when they are "nickel and dimed" for charges like speeding.

The strategy most dear to Phil's heart is spotting trucks that are improperly placarded. In the last five years Phil has become the State expert on the transportation of dangerous goods. He is on twenty-four hour response call for hazardous materials related accidents that occur anywhere in Arizona. Although two of Phil's colleagues have already died of cancer, he feels that he takes sufficient precautions to avoid unnecessary risks.

The hazardous materials being transported through Arizona usually originate in Texas, destined for California. The vehicles must have placards appropriately displayed on their units, meaning they are easily seen from ~chemical~ the directions they face, their words or numbers are level and can be read ~trucks~ from left to right, and that each placard is at least three inches away from any other markings (State of Washington, 1989, pg. 9).

Whenever a placard does not meet the specifications Phil stops the trucker, because the nature of the load forces Phil to consider every infraction as important. Typically, "one out of every ten hazardous materials loads" Phil inspects is improperly packed. Some are so bad that they leak on the roadway. Whenever this occurs Phil will:

> Shut him down, make him either repack it or he can't leave until it stops leaking, and he has to hire a cleanup contractor to clean up the spill. Had one cost $3,500 and it took the cleanup contractor about two hours and 20 minutes.

On a more general note, Phil also looks towards "cosmetic trucks" as tip offs for possible violations. They are owner operator vehicles customized to perfection with paint and chrome sparklers, names written on the sides, professional signs on the side of the tractor, chromed smoke stacks, grills, bumper, etc., and other personalized adornments. In short, they are trucks that are in immaculate condition, worth in excess of a hundred and twenty thousand dollars. According to Phil these trucks are home to the drivers. For some, "everything they own is in that truck." To keep ahead of payments the truckers "drive long and hard," increasing the odds that these trucks are running over ten hours consecutive driving time.

At the opposite end of the trucking image spectrum is the dirty old "beater," which also serves as a tip-off for police officers to initiate a thorough search. Often there are visual signs such as bald tires, broken headlamps and cracked windshields that Phil uses to "get into the truck and muck around." According to Phil, if the truck is in rough shape, chances are good that the driver is also in poor condition. This kind of a vehicle is a reasonable indicator of drug usage by the driver.

Other reasons for stopping a trucker are not so much driver-specific as they are carrier or company specific. Bad experiences a police officer had with a commodity hauler, or a poor reputation a company shares among the trucking-police community, could initiate a roadside stop for a trucker. Phil provided an example. Furniture movers or "bed bugs" have a reputation for being notorious log book cheaters. They are "perfect" candidates for finding a cause to stop and interview them. By coincidence, when I was in Phoenix the carnival was in town. Based on his stereotypical view of carnival drivers, Phil was prepared to do the following:

> I'll stop a carney truck today, the carnival's moving through town, the worst trucks in the world. The lesser class truck driver drives a carnival truck. Most of them are loonies. Three of them the other day, two of them had warrants out on them for drugs.

As much as Phil employs certain core definitions to open the door for trucker inspections, he also uses personal rules to avoid certain trucks at all possible costs. Some loads are "built" for avoidance. For example, Phil hates to be peed on by cattle transported by livestock haulers:

> Please don't ever stop a bull hauler. I won't stop them. They stink too bad. I stopped one already and had a cow take a whiz. It whizzed and it shot out of the truck and could spray you, you don't crawl under and check their brakes – that's the last thing you do.

Phil's experiences and training are his major resources for selecting truckers most likely to be unsafe and illegal. Most times his hunches, suspicions or quick intuitions pay off. For example, a mudflap check once led to a trucker being charged with possession of drugs. The "due cause" strategies, although cheap at first glance, usually prove to be valuable police tactics.

The Truckers Avoid Selection

Phil had checked several trucks during the morning I was with him. One of the trucks was yellow tagged to be repaired while another trucker received a citation for bad brakes. As we sat on the side of the highway, Phil and I discussed measures truckers use to avoid him. Some strategies are more obvious than others. Phil remembered the time he was on the lookout for a specific hazardous material carrier who had an awful safety record. The drivers of this company knew that their vehicles were poorly maintained and unsafe. They also knew that Phil and his colleagues could not stop them for roadside inspection unless there was "probable cause." To limit the chance of being stopped, company drivers made sure that their trucks were in perfect running order from a distance. According to Phil, "they've done everything they can do to keep us from stopping them. They have even chained the mudflaps down." As a result, Phil, suspecting that the trucks have maladjusted brakes, could not pull them over. He was forced to "lay off them a little bit."

The approach typically used to avoid being singled out for traffic violations is direct communication over the CB. When a police officer has singularly stopped a trucker on the side of the road, or a major speed trap is in force, the CB airwaves come alive with warnings about the state troopers' actions. A bear is on the loose! Drivers approaching the "danger zone" make efforts to drive legally and safely.

When some truckers hear that Smoky is doing roadside checks, they may attempt to bypass him. To counter this move, Phil organizes "wolf packs," a squad of thirteen men working twenty-four hours a day for two to three days on a stretch of highway. Realizing that truckers will try to miss the check, Phil usually sends one or two officers to the bypass route and detour the escaping truckers back to the highway check. Because of the heavy police pressure being placed on truckers, they are more likely to pull into truck stops and wait it out. In Phil's words, "if they pull into the truck stops, we'll get the fatigued driver off the road. Our job's done."

An interesting version of truckers intentionally missing police roadside checks was told to me by two California Highway Patrolmen I met in Yreka. They informed me that logging trucks are often overloaded. To combat the situation the California Highway Patrol sets up portable scales. As truckers CB other truckers about the spot check, some drivers circumvent the roadside check by turning onto bush roads. Like Phil, the members of the California Highway Patrol are aware of the tactics truckers use to avoid roadside checks. So they employ "rovers," local people driving through the backroads, to identify the truckers who are detouring the scales.

Once the officer has been notified about a specific trucker, the patrolman may "go out of his way to coincidentally" check the accused trucker in "a lonely, isolated area" on a logging road where it is difficult for the driver to get help after the officer puts his truck out of service for mechanical failure. He tells the trucker, "Guess what, your brakes ain't so good. Guess you'll have to wait it out here."

A preventative strategy some truckers use to avoid possible come-ons by the highway patrol is the "getting to know you" method. Long distance truckers learn the name, general disposition and routine of an officer in a certain part of the country. They plan their driving schedule on the basis of the officer's itinerary. If a highway patrol member changes his usual pattern of action, truckers take note, warning each other over the CB about the change. Often they chat up the officer to determine why he changed plans. Some of the questions truckers ask of the officer are amusing. One that Phil has been asked when he changes his patrol times are, "Did you lose your watch? Did your wife kick you out of bed? Are you bucking for a promotion? Are you lost?"

If truckers cannot stop a meeting with the police they can still take measures that will cost them the least amount of trouble. They make sure that the intended log books are filled out, other log books are well hidden, or illicit materials are safely stored.

Truckers are fully aware of how they are perceived by the police and how this perception could lead them into a relationship with the law. At most truckers try to avoid the legal encounter. At the least they try to keep the inspection from getting out of hand. The highway patrol wants an encounter. Officers know that certain truckers are unsafe and/or illegal. Experience, anticipation, schooling and observation help the police officer determine which trucker is selected.

The Police Guide the Trucker

Once a state patrolman like Phil has chosen a trucker for intervention he flashes his emergency lights and gives chase. He reaches the trucker by CB, informing him that a "Smoky" or a "Bear" is "on his tail" and that he must pull over to the side of the road wherever it is safe. The trucker responds by giving a few words of acknowledgement like "Right," "Damn" or "Shit," then asking Phil where he should stop.

Once the truck stops in a prudently safe place, Phil walks to the truck, jumps on the step, opens the door, and greets the trucker with a "How're ya doing?" The greeting is a tactful opener followed by Phil's explanation of why the trucker was stopped. Surprise, disbelief, amazement and anger are responses often given by truckers if, for example, they were stopped for a mudflap violation. Several truckers who were stopped by Phil told me that being stopped for this reason was a "bunch of crap." It was "police harassment" or "a shakedown for quick cash" at the expense of truckers. Still they responded with reason and calmness. They interpreted Phil's actions as the "cost of trucking in Arizona."

After his opening remarks, Phil requests all pertinent papers from the trucker. He reviews the freight, insurance, registration and other legal forms pertaining to interstate commerce. If all is in order Phil does a visual overview of the rig, inspecting the tires, lights, and signal lights. If Phil suspects lapse in braking he checks the tractor and trailer brakes. Based on Phil's experiences, the odds of him discovering brakes that are out of adjustment are good. If Phil sees any signs of major problems, he retrieves a heavy blanket and tools, crawls underneath the trailer and carefully inspects the tractor and trailer's braking capabilities. When he does this, Phil depends on the trucker to cooperate by pushing on the brake pedal when Phil demands. For hazardous materials carriers Phil extends his checks to include the low-air warning device, a light or buzzer that comes on when the brakes hit fifty-five pounds of air pressure. The gauge warns the trucker that he has an air leak in the system. He must take note or, according to Phil, "they go to emergency system that just locks all the brakes and locks the trailer up too." The probable outcome is a serious crash with hazardous materials escaping into the environment.

On this particular day, Phil stopped a truck carrying chlorine because the oxidizer sign on the side of the trailer was only one and a half inches from commercial print rather than the regulation three inches. Phil discovered that the warning device did not work, making it impossible for the trucker to respond in case of brake lockup. Phil discussed the seriousness of the problem. He told the driver that if he does not repair the fault immediately, the trucker could, all of a sudden, "drag the trailer off the road."

Once Phil completed his inspection of the truck he requested the truck's log book.[2] He took the book to his police cruiser and in privacy engaged in a thorough review of all entries. Once Phil determined the entries, he asked a series of rapid fire questions.

He wanted to know if the trucker was running more than one log book and whether he was hiding one, whether he was hiding any receipts, liquor or drugs, whether the trucker had a drink of liquor or had taken illicit drugs. The final question was a clincher, "If I was to search the cab, would I find anything hidden?" Phil asks the last question to make the truckers realize that he knows about truck cabs and to "shake them up a bit."

The trucker answered all questions with a direct "no." Like other truckers, he has learned that although there is a possibility that Phil will inspect the cab, the likelihood is that he will not. Besides, if an officer is determined to check the truck, the driver's answers are really inconsequential. Hence, truckers have "nothing to lose" and everything to gain.

During this phase of the inspection, Phil was in full control. He structured the questions, demanded explanations and enforced his status as a police officer. He informed me that the only truck violation the driver could be charged with was the air system. The brakes were all brand new. However, the log book was problematic. Usually he investigates a trucker's receipts going back for three days, then matches the distance with the time. Phil is trained to spot frauds. If in the process of investigation he establishes that gas and/or hotel receipts, time of inspection and present location do not match, he builds the tempo of the interaction. All receipts are carefully scrutinized. Gas receipt codes, of which, according to Phil, truckers are unaware are decoded. To the police YNQK translates to 6:15 a.m. To the trucker the code represents little more than a company serial number.

Whenever the situation demands it, Phil uses a large Atlas to help him locate towns truckers use as their points of departure or destinations. In this way, Phil determines real highway miles between sites, which he translates into time, then compares with a trucker's log entries. Furthermore he can pinpoint little "out of the way places" truckers may write in their log book in the anticipation that an officer in Arizona would not know about a hamlet in northwest California. The result of an intensive review is usually different than one entered by the trucker in the log book. The trucker Phil was inspecting was a good example of one trying to cheat. He omitted four hours of driving and two hundred miles. According to Phil, "there's no way in the world you can do five hundred and seventy miles at an average of sixty mph in six hours."

Phil told the driver directly, "Well, you cheated me by about two hundred miles, which is about four hours driving." The truck driver agreed. But his cover story was that rather than purposefully hiding four hours driving time, he was physically exhausted at the time he was entering times in his log book. Consequently he forgot details. According to the driver it's a natural thing, one beyond his control. But now that Phil had outlined the discrepancy, the trucker said he learned his lesson and will, therefore, complete future logs when he's more energetic. At this time Phil stepped out of his enforcer role and told the trucker that he's going to save him four hundred dollars and a citation for a log book violation, if he tells me, the guest researcher, the "real reason" for the log book discrepancy. The trucker refused Phil's offer. He stuck to his original story that the log entry was an honest error, not an intentional cover-up. Phil was not impressed. He intended to exchange a major traffic charge for the "real story" behind the lost hours. The expected payoff did not materialize. Although Phil was disappointed, he kept his promise and did not charge the trucker.

According to Phil, he uncovered the trucker's cheating because of special training he and his members of the truck investigation team received. He described that the typical police officer jumps in and asks for the trucker's log book. If he sees a correct date and the time is judged to be reasonable, he lets the trucker proceed. Most police officers do not go back to reconstruct the trip and inspect the driver's load documents or receipts.

If Phil finds the trucker's eyes in "rough shape," he will tighten the control of the inspection. If he and his colleagues believe that illicit drugs are involved, they have the legal right to search the cab. Sometimes they get lucky. Phil highlighted a colleague's recent success:

> I have one officer, Bob, he stopped two trucks from the same company last week, the first driver handed him white crosses/bennies. He said, "Well, you got me now," and he reached in his pocket and pulled out a vial of cocaine, with a little spoon attached. They arrested the guy, called the company and the owner showed up, took the truck and said, "You're my best driver," – hauling gasoline, 8,000 gallons. Three days later Bob stopped another truck from the same company, gets the other driver. "Am I going to find any drugs in your truck?" He says, "You got me," – reaches in his pocket and pulls out marijuana and cocaine. When the owner comes out again, he says, "Is this going to be a daily occurrence or what, he was my second best driver?" Second best because he didn't have as much dope?

In Phil's view, a fatigued trucker taking drugs is the "scariest thing on the road. He is a loose cannon ready to kill some innocent people." Phil goes to extremes to put this type of trucker out of commission. He leaves little room for a trucker to talk his way out of such a serious charge.

The Truckers Try to Gain Informal Control of the Inspection

The trucker does not want the inspection to end with an "out of service" sticker, or a citation with a large fine. To help his cause, he uses techniques such as "letting things pass," "not ruffling feathers," "looking humble" or "glossing events." For example, glossing is often used in log book violations. Police officers and truckers share the assumption that log books are as close to the truth as "comic books" are to reality. Truckers, when caught, invariably invoke the gloss that "everybody rides with more than one log book," hoping that the police officers will re-think their intent.

If, or when, the police recognize log book falsification, truckers are well armed with excuses to lessen the damage. They are tired, forgot specific details, lost receipts somewhere on the trip, already submitted their receipts to the dispatcher or they were too busy earning a living and being a good citizen to attend to the log book. Through their identification of practical reasons such as poor memory, job pressures and support for company policy, truckers try to fashion the events according to occurrences that happen to the common man. Typically, Phil is not influenced by the trucker lines. He draws on a higher moral order, believing that truckers who hide hours place themselves in a no-win situation in an accident.

Once a trucker has an accident, Phil must collect all of the driver's receipts. If the log is up to date and accurate and the receipts are in order, the trucker may be charged for certain driving infractions but it is unlikely that an attorney can build a civil case on the basis of lying and cheating. To avoid possible libel suits over falsified log books, Phil wants truckers to be honest and thereby "help themselves."

Phil knows why truckers "rip off" log books. It is no secret to truckers or the police officers, nor is it a secret "that everybody does it." However, Phil expects truckers, when caught, to be responsible for their actions, and not try to outmaneuver him on-site. When they attempt to "hoodwink" the police and in the process possibly hurt themselves, Phil becomes upset refusing discretion and invoking formal sanctions.

Throughout Phil's truck inspections, I observed that truckers routinely furnished police officers with topics of conversation such as "events they experienced on the highway," "weaknesses in the transportation system," "brothers, cousins and uncles that are in police forces," "weather and road conditions," and/or "their appreciation of the difficulties experienced by a highway patrol officer." The truckers try to be sociable and friendly to influence the investigation through subtle but powerful "groupness" feelings.

To help their cause at a roadside inspection, some truckers suggested that they should look clean. It is probably the most influential tactic against the police. In my discussions with Phil, it became evident that he perceived clean truckers as ones engaged in the least number of driving problems.

When truckers employ all of their social skills, their chances of slipping out of an encounter unscathed are increased. Poise, or in Goffman's (1967) terms, coolness is the operative presentation.

A good example of coolness happened when Phil stopped a Mayflower Moving Truck for speeding early Sunday morning. The driver was traveling over sixty-five mph in a sixty mph zone. The trucker was in his mid-fifties, clean shaven, hair neatly combed, wearing clean clothes (jeans and plaid shirt).

In the opening sequence of events Phil introduced himself and prepared to explain the cause for stoppage. The driver interrupted him by wondering aloud, with a smile, why the highway patrol was active on a nice bright Sunday morning. He considered it to be unusual for the police to patrol on the Lord's day. Nevertheless, for the sake of safety, he felt that it was a good idea.

Phil immediately took a liking the driver. Despite the fact that he was clearly speeding, Phil was prepared to show discretion. During the inspection, the police officer told me:

> Sunday, and here it is, he's stopped. If everything's OK, if the log book works out, I'm going to let the old fellow go, without a warning and without a ticket . . . It's a pleasure stopping a guy like that . . . He is what's left of the old school.

Phil did not engage in a zealous truck inspection. It was a short two minute review, largely because of the driver's social tactfulness. This outcome was significant, because the police finger furniture movers as being overly involved in log book infractions. Highway patrol members search them out. For a driver to escape a citation after visible proof of speeding and avoid a rigorous review of his log book was an accomplishment worthy of mention.

Concluding the Inspection

Obviously, the trucker hopes to leave the inspection with minimal damage. The officer as an administrator of justice wants to be certain that the driver and his rig are operating as safe as is reasonably possible. So the encounter ends.

The worst way for the trucker to leave the inspection is by arrest for drug-related charges. Less severe, yet still major is when the tractor is sidelined for repair (out of service condition) or overloaded. In some states if a trailer is overloaded, or improperly loaded, the drivers correct the matter on-site. It is time consuming and may prove to be very expensive if heavy machinery is rented to shift the load.

Less intense, but still impactful, is when a trucker receives a "restrictive service condition" sticker. A trucker, who is tagged with this sticker, is allowed to drive twenty-five miles (forty-five kilometers), or to the nearest service repair shop and have a mechanical problem repaired. In addition to the sticker, a trucker receives a traffic citation for operating the vehicle in a state of disrepair.

When a trucker has been assigned an out-of-service or restrictive service condition sticker, it indicates the end of the encounter but not the event.

Other systems may become involved. For example, a liquid hazardous materials carrier operating out of Arizona operates thirty trucks. The Arizona highway patrol tagged twenty-eight of them out of service for violations as disconnected front axle brakes, missing parts and broken fifth wheels. A week later the same trucks were stopped without having undergone the repairs. To combat the situation, Phil red lined a truck, then drove the trucker to Flagstaff where he presented the company owner with a "ticket for unsafe operations." In response, the company owner wrote a letter to the governor claiming police harassment. Phil had to visit the governor's office and present all the violations the company had received and the business' lack of initiative in repairing the trucks. As a result, the governor dismissed the company's complaint.

Usually the trucker and officer part ways after the trucker receives a warning or a citation. The occurrence of single violation truck inspections in Arizona and California are rare. Most truckers that are stopped receive multiple citations. According to Phil, an average of thirteen citations per trucker stopped is the rule of thumb for the Arizona highway patrol.

The impact police officers have on truckers they stop is not lost on truckers. Numerous discussions with drivers proved that whenever they are stopped by the police they expect at least one violation. Their goal is to lessen the "damage," to limit the severity of the inspection. The truckers major goal is to negotiate the encounter in a way that minimizes the assignment of responsibility.

Once trucker and officer part their ways "goodbyes" are offered. Occasionally Phil uses the moment to remind the trucker of a mechanical problem and his duty to solve it quickly. Other times Phil wishes the trucker good luck. For, according to Phil, it makes little sense to upset a trucker needlessly. To keep rapport with truckers is a primary goal.

Truck Inspection at the Municipal Level in Canada[3]

Whereas highway patrols concentrate on all aspects of truck driving features, in a port city like Vancouver, which serves as a major destination and departure point for truckers, the usual reason truckers are pulled over by the police is for being "overweight" and having "bad brakes."

Sam, a Vancouver police officer, was a member of the two man accident truck investigation squad with whom I drove for a day. Between traffic accident investigations, the team checks trucks. Although their main focus is dump trucks, they also monitor long-haul vehicles on two major truck routes in the city.

On this particular day, the first item on Sam's itinerary was an accident on Marine Drive, a main city route. A twenty-seven year old owner operator, on his way to being loaded with lumber for Los Angeles, ran a light in heavy fog and hit a Honda Prelude proceeding on a green light. The driver's girlfriend, a future would-be trucker with a learner's permit, accompanied him. The truck damage was minimal, a few scratches on the rim and several bent bolts. However the car's front end was ripped apart.

The trucker conceded that he went through a red light but he quickly pointed out the other driver should have taken some precautions. The Honda driver was shaken. He assumed that the huge truck would stop. However, he said, "it kept coming right on without stopping." When asked, the trucker was in a hurry and wanted to make it through the intersection. Stopping was never a consideration for him.

For his actions the trucker received a seventy-five dollar citation and two demerit points on his driving record. The trucker was not especially concerned about the other driver, jokingly telling me, "Well, I guess he ain't gonna have such a good day." His concern was about the two demerit points. It translates into another driving suspension because he already had accumulated ten demerits for the year. Also, he anticipated an increase in insurance rates because he will lose his forty percent safe driver discount on his premium.

Sam completed his investigation. He reminded the trucker to get a green municipal sticker that allows him to carry goods in the city. However, Sam did not expect the driver to follow his orders. As we headed to a coffee shop where Sam could write a full accident report, the officer showed me the computer printout on the driver's history. Since 1985 in British Columbia alone, the trucker accumulated seventeen moving violations and he had a four month suspension the previous year.

The accident clearly illustrated the different motivations behind Canadian municipal police and American state police actions. For me the issues were two fold, why the trucker was only given a "running through a yellow light" citation, and why the trucker did not receive a ticket for failure to show a proper permit? In the United States the trucker would certainly have received multiple tickets.

The first issue revolved around the officer's interpretation of events. He felt that a ticket for driving through an amber light would stand up better in court than would running a red light. Also there is less likelihood that a yellow light infraction would be fought in court. Sam used the trade-off strategy of minimum charge for maximum chance of a guilty plea. The second issue of not possessing a municipal truck permit entailed a policing strategy worthy of note. Unlike the state highway patrol in the United States, municipal officers in British Columbia do not stack tickets on drivers. They consider it to be unfair to the drivers and they believe that it decreases police members' chances of receiving trucker cooperation in the future.

Rather than assign tickets and fines for each particular mechanical violation, the city police try to write one citation for general maintenance worth a hundred dollars. The police do not want to appear as crusaders against a trucker or company. Consequently Sam, having already presented the driver with a moving violation, did not believe that a ticket for an incidental fault such as lack of permit was warranted.

During the encounter the trucker misinformed Sam about the ownership of the truck. He told him that the vehicle was a fleet truck, while informing me that he was an owner operator. The misinformation was shrugged off by Sam as just another ploy the trucker used trying to look better in Sam's accident report, thereby influencing his insurance premiums. According to Sam, many encounters with truckers hinge on some form of misinformation. Sam takes it all in stride, realizing that his "official version" overrules any "informal description" of events.

Sam's rule is that any truck-related accident occurred because of driver behavior. As Sam said, "I always try to give a ticket. Somebody always blew it." Concerning this particular mishap, I asked Sam whether the real cause could have been the brakes rather than the driver running a yellow light. Sam dismissed the idea because of the lack of skid marks. I asked whether it was possible that the driver knew he had poor brakes and therefore did not bother applying them, choosing instead to run the red light. Sam's reason for placing little faith in this scenario was because the truck looked "pretty good." It was fairly new and clean. Sam alone could not engage in a thorough brake check even if the brakes were malfunctioning because his partner had court duty that day. The lack of time and needed teamwork negated any attempt at a comprehensive brake investigation.

Behind The Scenes Of Municipal Enforcement

Vancouver has several officers assigned to trucks. However, the team's primary role is accident investigation. While riding with Sam, accidents for investigation were stacked on the computer. According to Sam and other officers, there is a lack of manpower to handle truck safety properly.

Clark, Sam's partner with whom I spoke at the police station, indicated that truckers know of the manpower situation. As he reported:

What are their chances of getting stopped? You gotta figure there are 2 cars at the most on any given day out there on dayshift where police even remotely know anything about trucks. That's the accident investigation guys and the chance of these guys getting stopped for any of these things is really remote . . . Truckers are aware that they're practically never stopped by the average Joe policeman for things they know are wrong like brakes out of adjustment or a leaky air system.

Because the city lacks truck inspection officers and training for all police members, truckers have a good chance of driving illegally without being caught. If the "average policeman" does stop a truck, he knows so little about the truck that "the driver can easily snow him," unless it is something obvious like brake lights. The situation follows nicely Gusfield's (1981) observation, if something is not observed by the police, it is not acted upon.

The enforcement rules vis-a-vis available officers and time became clearly evident during the time I spent in a police cruiser. In one instance, traveling from one accident scene to the other we observed a heavy equipment hauler being obviously overweight, and a dump truck and a flatbed truck driving on residential streets. Sam could not tackle these obvious municipal violations. He was restricted as to which truckers he could stop at any given time.

However, there are violations and there are excessive violations, ones which go beyond reasonable avoidance of action. For example, while we were waiting at a red light a container truck drove through an amber light. Directly behind him was a loaded dump truck blasting his airhorn signalling his intent to speed through the intersection. Sam and I had front row seats to the drama. Witnessing the event, Sam flashed his emergency lights, and sped behind the dump truck. For this kind of flagrant violation Sam said:

> I would be amiss of duty to let it go. I mean the accident will just have to wait. Geez I hate that, that's so stupid and unsafe blasting your horn to the truck so you can run a red light.

Sam jumped up the truck's step and told the trucker that he had stopped him because he ran a yellow light. The trucker responded that he could not stop in time. Sam retaliated by suggesting that instead of a yellow light infraction, he should then give the trucker a speeding ticket. "No, no," replied the trucker. He now claimed that he could not stop in time because of his heavy load. Sam, becoming a little impatient, suggested to the trucker that if he did not stop making such excuses, he would present the trucker with a ticket for being overloaded and for an amber light infraction. The ploy was successful. The trucker shook his head in defiance but he stopped making excuses. As the driver left the site, he twice honked his airhorn in defiance.

Municipal police are concerned about three major forms of truck violations; moving vehicle, brakes and truck maintenance, and overweight. Although Vancouver is a long-haul destination, Sam told me that, "We never concern ourselves with how long the guy's been driving. The Mounties on the Trans-Canada Highway are more into that."

Once truckers arrive in Vancouver they are close to their point of unloading. It is considered futile to chase them because other infractions are easier to find and they have a higher priority. Similarly, drugs are a non-issue:

> Drugs don't concern us in relation to truck drivers. Never comes up. Most of the drivers around town, even tractor-trailers, are local guys. They don't use them.

Rule number one is overweight, and rule number two is brakes. All else becomes secondary.

Police and Truckers Teaming Up
Against a Third Party

The municipal situation often brings police officers and truckers together at close range. At times they become allies forming an informal contract in order to respond to an unsafe or lawbreaking affair. For example, owner operators lease their trucks to a construction contractor or a shipper, who decides to overload the trucks. Dump truck drivers will flag down police cars to inform officers that they are running heavy. Truckers may suggest that the officer return the next morning at a certain site to scale the loads. These drivers hate running heavy loads because the excess weight is hard on their equipment.

According to Sam, big rig drivers may also flag down a police officer if they are operating trucks that are not properly maintained. They want the maximum number of tickets written on the truck. As Sam explained:

> You know, inadequate brakes, maybe there's no brake lights, aah no mudflaps, bald tires, stuff like that. The fines add up pretty fast. It's about 50 bucks for each offense. And then he goes back to his boss and says look I got all these tickets for this thing and, and the boss generally, if it's a decent company, generally pays the fines. He gets the vehicle fixed if it's going to cost him a lot of money. That's the bottom line, if it's not going to cost him any money they're not going to fix it.

Truck drivers invite police involvement to help fulfill safety, economic and/or mechanical needs that they believe could not be met otherwise. There is a sense of desperation when the police and truckers become allies against a third party.

Phil and Sam, Representatives of Police Action

Phil, in the United States, and Sam, in Canada, are two police officers operating in different countries symbolizing what is occurring in North America. They patrol, chase and catch according to a set of contextual rules relevant to their jurisdiction fully understood by the truckers. Truckers risk, miss and escape the police according to their rules of participation. Each group is aware of the other's motives and behaviors. Hence each inspection between trucker and police officer becomes a situation whereby the police formally investigate the trucker while the latter tries his best to manipulate the investigation to his benefit.

Notes to Chapter Nine

1. In 1980, representatives from the states of California, Idaho, Oregon and Washington and from the Canadian provinces of Alberta and British Columbia met to discuss guiding principles for the Commercial Vehicle Safety Alliance. The four major principles were vehicle inspections, uniformity, compatibility and reciprocity (Henry, 1989).

   Because each state and/or province shared a common traffic stream, members were concerned that they were potentially reinspecting each other's work. So an original goal was to eliminate duplicity in the truck inspection process. To accomplish the latter would require uniformity as a minimum standard. Furthermore, the standards for inspection must meet and be compatible with the operational needs of the motor carrier industry and local government officials. Reciprocity for inspection work that would benefit each state/province and both the regulated and the regulators was defined as a major principle. Arising from these principles came the CVSA:

   > . . . an association of state and provincial officials responsible for the administration and enforcement of motor carrier safety laws in the United States and Canada, working together with the federal government and industry to improve commercial vehicle safety. CVSA . . . provides the basic framework for uniformity, compatibility, and reciprocity of inspections, and motor carrier safety enforcement activities of its member jurisdictions. The Alliance serves as the major focal point for enhancing motor carrier safety, bringing together state/federal and truck/bus industry interests in a one-of-a-kind discussion/problem solving interchange. It also provides an effective mechanism for expressing the consensus views of its member jurisdictions. (Henry, 1989; pp. 2-3)

   Members of 47 states, nine provinces and 200 trucking associations work to meet the following goals:

   - To bring about an overall improvement in commercial vehicle and hazardous materials transportation safety.
   - To improve the safety of equipment being operated on our highways.
   - To increase the number of on-highway inspections.
   - To avoid duplication of inspection efforts by the various jurisdictions.
   - To minimize inspection delays for the operating industry.
   - To improve commercial driver safety performance.

- To improve compliance with the Hazardous Materials Transportation Regulations.
- To bring about improvement of the collection, dissemination, and use of operational motor carrier safety data and research findings.

All government signatories agree to certain truck inspection procedures. For in the Memorandum of Agreement it states:

> Where state or provincial governments party to the Commercial Vehicle Safety Alliance (CVSA) Memorandum of Understanding whose political subdivisions, i.e., county deputy sheriffs and weighmasters, employ personnel for the purpose of inspecting commercial vehicles operating within their jurisdictions, they may allow such agencies and their personnel to issue and affix state or provincially owned CVSA decals to vehicles passing Alliance inspection standards providing:
>
> a. The CVSA member government has trained and certified such employees as passing the same inspection qualification standards as their own;
> b. The member government provides inspection forms, out of service documents and decals;
> c. Completed inspection documents are submitted to the member government for review and processing and,
> d. The Alliance member government assumes full and complete responsibility for their authorized political subdivisions' actions relating to the conduct of CVSA inspections and the quality control of all decals. (CVSA, pg. 1)

2. The highway patrols in the United States and, as of late, Royal Canadian Mounted Police detachments in Canada are signators of the CVSA. Consequently they abide by the rules, regulations and expectations of the CVSA, following one or more of the following procedures:

1. North American Standard–This is a thorough "get down and get under" driver/vehicle inspection. It includes examination of: driver's license, medical examiner's certificate and waiver if applicable, driver's record of duty status as required, hours of service, seat belt, vehicle inspection report, brake system, steering mechanism, wheels and rims, tires, coupling devices, suspension, frame, fuel and exhaust systems, windshield glazing and wipers, lighting devices, cargo securement, and hazardous materials requirements as applicable. A CVSA decal will be applied to each vehicle that passes this inspection.

2. Driver Only – This inspection covers the driver and its purpose is to insure that vehicle operators are properly licensed, medically qualified and observing statutory hours of service requirements. The inspector will also check seat belt installation and use, and the vehicle inspection report.

3. Walkaround Inspection – This inspection also covers the driver and includes a vehicle walkaround "audible and visual" check of the following key vehicle components: fire extinguisher, warning devices

for stopped vehicles, headlamps, turn signals, stop lamps, windshield and wipers, wheels, tires, fuel systems, exhaust systems, visible brake components, coupling devices, cargo securement, low air warning device and visible suspension components. Compliance with hazardous materials regulations will be checked if applicable.

The "driver only" and the "walkaround inspection" are intended to be brief, but each has a specific purpose and each is thorough for that purpose – to identify unqualified and unfit drivers and obviously unsafe vehicles. These can be expeditiously removed from service while allowing those in compliance to proceed with their business with minimum delay.

4. Special Road Inspections – These inspections include a one-time examination of a particular item and are normally made in support of a study or to verify or refute a suspected trend. (CVSA, 1989)

At times a Canada/American commercial truck/bus safety check is held in accordance with procedure number four. To illustrate the extent to which the CVSA penetrates truck-policing activities, a segment of a Highway and Vehicle Safety Inspection Report, June 5, 1989, is included:

U.S., Canada Coordinate Largest Truck, Bus Safety Check

The largest commercial truck/bus safety check ever held, involving 1,836 state police officers and trained inspectors in 47 states, six Canadian provinces, and Puerto Rico, was completed last month with impressive results.

Organized by the Federal Highway Administration's Office of Motor Carriers and officials of Transport Canada, the three-day roadside campaign inspected a total of 31,522 commercial vehicles. According to an FHWA spokesman, 32 percent of the vehicles that were checked, — some 10,134 trucks — were placed out of service until safety problems could be remedied.

Overall, 73,227 violations were issued. The defects ranged from common brake problems to more serious safety concerns, according to FHWA's final report. Transportation Secretary Samuel K. Skinner described the scope of the safety check, noting that it would have been difficult for any driver to avoid inspection with 150 sites and more than 1,600 police officers involved.

Inspections of driver's log books and records accounted for about 1,908 drivers being given out of service notices. However, last month's 32 percent vehicle out of service rate was an improvement over the 38 percent rate inspectors issued on the 1.2 million trucks inspected in 1988. The 6 percent violation rate for drivers remained close to the rate in past checks.

The inspection procedure was comprised of the Level I North American Standard Inspection, which covers safety belts, vehicle inspection report, brake system, steering mechanism, wheels, tires, coupling devices, suspension, frame, fuel and exhaust systems, windshield wipers, lighting devices, cargo securement, and hazardous material requirements as applicable. South Dakota, Texas, Wyoming and the District of Columbia did not participate in the campaign, which ran from May 15 to May 18, 1989.

State and provincial truck operations legislation meshes closely with the Commercial Vehicle Safety Alliance. Police officers are expected to follow CVSA rules and acknowledge the CVSA inspection sticker. As of the time of this writing the Arizona highway patrol was a signatory but municipal police forces in British Columbia were not.

2. The highway patrol enforces regulations 395.3 and 395.8 of the Federal Motor Carrier Safety Regulations pertaining to hours on duty and updatedness of log book:

#395.3 Maximum driving and on-duty time.

(a) Except as provided in paragraphs (c) and (e) of this section and in #395.10, no motor carrier shall permit or require any driver used by it to drive nor shall any such driver drive;

  (1) More than 10 hours following 8 consecutive hours off duty; or

  (2) For any period after having been on duty 15 hours following 8 consecutive hours off duty.

  (3) Exemption: Drivers using sleeper-berth equipment as defined in #395.2(f), or who are off duty at a natural gas or oil well location, may cumulate the required 8 consecutive hours off duty resting in a sleeper berth in two separate periods totalling 8 hours, neither period to be less than 2 hours, or resting while off duty in other sleeping accommodations at a natural gas or oil well location.

(b) No motor carrier shall permit or require a driver of a commercial motor vehicle, regardless of the number of motor carriers using the driver's services, to drive for any period after:–

  (1) Having been on duty 60 hours in any 7 consecutive days if the employing motor carrier does not operate every day in the week; or

  (2) Having been on duty 70 hours in any period of 8 consecutive days if the employing motor carrier operates motor vehicles every day of the week.

  (3) Exception: This paragraph shall not apply to any driver driving a motor vehicle in the State of Alaska, as provided in paragraph (e) of this section, or to any driver-salesperson whose total driving time does not exceed 40 hours in any period of 7 consecutive days.

(c) The provisions of paragraph (a) of this section shall not apply with respect to drivers of motor vehicles engaged solely in making local deliveries from retail stores and/or retail catalog businesses to the ultimate consumer, when driving solely within a 100-air mile radius of the driver's work-reporting location, during the period from December 10 to December 25, both inclusive, of each year.

#395.8 Driver's record of duty status.

(a) Every motor carrier shall require every driver used by the motor carrier to record his/her duty status for each 24-hour period using the methods prescribed in either paragraphs (a)(1) or (2) of this section.

    (1) Every driver who operates a commercial motor vehicle shall record his/her duty status, in duplicate, for each 24-hour period. The duty status time shall be recorded on a specified grid, as shown in paragraph (g) of this section. The grid and the requirements of paragraph (d) of this section may be combined with any company forms. The previously approved format of the Daily Log, Form MCS-59 or the Multi-day Log, MCS-139 and 139A, which meets the requirements of this section, may continue to be used.

    (2) Every driver who operates a commercial motor vehicle shall record his/her duty status by using an automatic on board recording device that meets the requirements of #395.15 of this part. The requirements of #395.8 shall not apply, except paragraphs (e) and (k)(1) and (2) of this section.

(b) The duty status shall be recorded as follows:

    (1) "Off duty" or "OFF."
    (2) "Sleeper berth" or "SB" (only if a sleeper berth used).
    (3) "Driving" or "D."
    (4) "On-duty not driving" or "ON." (1989; pp. 277-280)

3. In Canada, truckers and police officers must abide by the Motor Carrier Act administered by the provincial Ministries of Transportation and Highway. The Act speaks on operating requirements, licensing, duties and restrictions imposed on motor carriers and general supervision of motor carriers. If a police officer charges a trucker who is found guilty, the latter will be dealt with according to "Penalty 53":

> 53. Every person who commits an offence against this Act or who violates a provision of this Act or of any regulation or order of the commission, or who refuses or neglects to observe or perform any duty or obligation created or imposed by this Act or by any regulation or order of the commission is liable on conviction, for a first offence, to a penalty of not less than $250 and not more than $500, and for a subsequent offence to a penalty of not less than $500 and not more than $1000. Each day's continuance of any violation, refusal or neglect constitutes a new and distinct offence. (1989; pg. 13)

In major municipalities like Vancouver, the Motor Vehicle Act is the primary support document used for enforcement. However, local bylaws such as designated truck routes and gross weight allowance are standard enforcement keys.

The political will as to where local politicians and administrators spend their enforcement dollars appears to be at the root of the enforcement scenario. It leads to numbers of police officers in action, training, and availability of equipment. Although equally relevant in provincial and federal scenes, at the municipal level it seems more tangible, direct and immediate.

References

B.C. Ministry of Highways. 1989. **Motor Carriers Act**. Victoria, BC: Quickscribe Services.

CVSA. 1989. "Alliance."

CVSA. "Memorandum of Understanding Between Those Government Agencies Whose Signatures Appear Thereon." (Undated)

Agar, M.H. 1986. **Independents Declared**. Washington, DC: Smithsonian Institute Press.

Cooley, H.C. 1964. **Human Nature and the Social Order**. New York: Schocken.

Ditton, J. 1977. **Part-Time Crime: An Ethnography of Fiddling and Pilferage**. New York: MacMillan Press.

Goffman, I. 1959. **The Presentation of Self in Everyday Life**. Hammonds-Worth: Penguin.

Goffman, I. 1961. **Encounters**. New York: Bobbs-Merrill Company.

Goffman, I. 1967. **Interaction Ritual**. Garden City, NY: Anchor Books.

Gusfield, J.R. 1981. **The Culture of Public Problems**. Chicago: University of Chicago Press.

Henry, Paul R. 1989. "Comments of Paul R. Henry, Deputy Administrator, Transportation Safety Division, Oregon Public Utility Commission – May 3, 1989." Presented to the Society of Automotive Engineers Government/Industry Meeting, Washington, DC.

Highway and Vehicle Safety Report. 1989. Vol. 15/No. 19, June 15, Branford, CT.

Lyman, Stanford M., and Scott, Marvin B. 1970. **A Sociology of the Absurd**. New York: Meredith Corporation.

Mead, G.H. 1934. **Mind, Self and Society**. Chicago: University of Chicago Press.

Simmel, Georg. 1950. **The Sociology of Georg Simmel**. Translated by K.H. Wolff, Glencoe: Free Press.

Strauss, A. (Ed.) 1956. **George Herbert Mead on Social Psychology**. Chicago: University of Chicago Press.

Turner, J.H. 1988. **A Theory of Social Interaction**. Stanford Cal.: Stanford University Press.

U.S. Department of Transport. 1988. How Do You Know . . . How to Achieve A Satisfactory DOT Safety Rating.

U.S. Department of Transportation, F.H.A. 1988. **Federal Motor Carrier Safety Regulations**. Alexandria, VT: American Trucking Associations.

Washington, The State of. 1989. **Commercial Driver's License**. Olympia WA: Department of Licensing.

10

GIDDYUP QUICK FREIGHT AND THE COURIER TEAM

I traveled with the Arizona state trooper for a period of two and a half days, after which time I decided to leave. For my ride out of Phoenix, I was assigned to Giddyup Quick Freight, whom I met early Monday morning, shortly after he exchanged trailers at the airport. His real name was Richard, a senior driver for P Courier.

Giddyup always made an effort to be the last driver leaving Phoenix heading north so that he could handle any parcels that were forgotten, or any last minute items that required immediate attention and quick response. His conscious efforts to make sure that every parcel gets out led to his colleagues nicknaming him Giddyup Quick Freight.

Giddyup prepared to leave for his Phoenix to Flagstaff run at six-thirty a.m. His anticipated arrival time in Flagstaff, Arizona, was ten-thirty in the morning. P Courier was adamant that time schedules be respected for reliable customer service.

Giddyup's company prides itself on uniformity. All tractors are basic units and all trailers are painted the same color with identical lettering. According to Giddyup, P Courier drivers cannot give their trucks any personality by adding a few touches such as chrome exhaust pipes. The company policy states that the vehicles remain standard.

At six-thirty precisely, Giddyup maneuvered the truck to the gate. A security officer examined the papers, questioned my presence and, with a clipboard in hand, inspected the appearance of the truck to make sure no damage is evident without it having been reported. His last deed was to check the locks on the trailers to make sure they are secure. Security was tighter here than any other trucking company I visited.

After the five minute inspection, Giddyup and I left the marshaling yard heading towards Interstate 17. We never exceeded fifty-five miles per hour because, according to Giddyup, that is P Courier's speed limit policy, one that demands full driver support.

Because it was the early morning, there was little traffic, allowing us to approach Interstate 17 with ease. The entrance ramp to the freeway provided little difficulty. Once we were on the freeway, Giddyup spoke about P Courier Service as an employer. According to the driver, P Courier is a "great company . . ., the benefits and pay are good, the equipment is well maintained and no equipment moves on Saturdays and Sundays." The entire operation is smooth. Giddyup always drives his own unit. At a destination point he exchanges loaded trailers with another driver. The entire process is built on efficiency and tight scheduling.

Giddyup is a line driver, one who travels from point A to point B at a scheduled time during the day. Unlike the over-the-road truckers, line drivers usually spend their nights and weekends at home. Giddyup does not experience the strain on family life as do other truckers who drive around the country on weekends, holidays and nights. For him, the P Courier driver position is like an eight to five office job.

Sixteen years ago Giddyup was a barber cutting hair at a university barber shop. Because he became dissatisfied with his life, and desired more excitement, better retirement benefits and a proper medical plan, he applied to P Courier as a local delivery driver. The company offered him these advantages as incentives for getting qualified drivers. Over the years Arizona experienced rapid growth which necessitated the company to expand its operations as a state-wide courier service. After nine months of local delivery, Giddyup applied for line duty, which he has now driven for fifteen years. In courier jargon, Giddyup is a "feeder driver," who brings loads to the sorting terminals.

The P Courier Service Image

P Courier Service has a visual image that is easy to identify. The dull color, clean step vans, standard tractor trailer units and recognizable logos signal P Courier Service to the ordinary person. The look is enhanced through mass media advertising.

The police, however, pay scant attention to the visual imagery of company trucks. They define P Courier according to the truck maintenance the company practises and the driver behavior they consider to be appropriate. Occasionally members of the Arizona state patrol visit P Courier terminals, checking the equipment, observing drivers-in-action and reviewing company records and driver files. On the basis of their company inspections, officers like Phil judged P Courier as a company "running good equipment" and using professional drivers. Because of this pre-determined assessment, Giddyup is seldom stopped by state troopers for a roadside inspection.

P Courier has another advantage which helps their truckers avoid police involvement. Some of the state's police truck inspectors working with Phil are also P Courier drivers. On their days off they become truckers, gaining firsthand knowledge about the operation while earning extra money. For Phil, the matter is not a conflict of interest, rather it helps the state troopers keep abreast with their trucking knowledge and it keeps them in the trucker's social grapevine. They gather information about Arizona truckers that as police officers on the sideline they would not be privy to.

At weigh scales and check points, P Courier drivers are usually given the green light. Attendants are aware that Giddyup drives with only one log book that is generally kept up to date, the bills of lading are in order and the truck is properly maintained.

P Courier is diligent about retaining its image of employing safe, competent drivers. Thorough screening, training and safety surveillance is the operational norm. For example, to become a P Courier driver, Giddyup had forty hours of company training, at the end of which he passed a written examination. In the classroom, future P Courier employees become familiar with coupling systems, truck units and safety measures. After the classroom comes apprenticeship driving on the freeway and in the city. For a week a supervisor accompanies the new driver at all times. If, after the probation period, the driver still lacks confidence, the supervisor will ride along for a few more days before the driver is "turned loose" on his own.

The Company and Safety

As we drove through the desert, Giddyup kept telling me of little things he does that are safe. For example, he keeps checking his mirrors to keep a proper check on the driving environment. He positions his hands on the steering wheel at three and nine o'clock because it maximizes his control of the vehicle. He scans the roadway to anticipate possible problems. On the basis of these actions, Giddyup considered himself to be a model driver, one P Courier demands of its senior truckers.

Inside the tractor, the cab was sparse. There was no sleeper, room was tight, and there were no electronic or mechanical extras except for a CB and tachograph, the latter of which is installed in every P Courier truck so that management can monitor the truckers' driving behaviors. Giddyup considers the tachograph to be a good friend, a handy data reference if he should ever get into an accident and get sued. Because he is committed to safe driving practices at all times, Giddyup has no fear of the electronic equipment's presence. According to Giddyup, the tachograph chart:

> . . . shows the miles per hour, the time and everything. Our runs are set up on a pretty close meet schedule, so at night my log book, my time card, my tach chart are all audited. They can sit there and look at the times I put down

on my time card, my departure, arrival, my break time, my turnaround time
and then they can look at my tachograph chart and see what speed I was driving,
and what times I said I was stopped. That shows the engine shutdown and
everything.

Giddyup reasoned that the company has a right to monitor drivers. By
auditing the chart, the safety supervisor can tell, "if a driver gets a little
ragged or messed up." If the supervisor becomes aware that a driver is
experiencing problems, such as losing time, he will ride along with the
trucker for a short time to pinpoint possible problems. For Giddyup, the
supervisor's involvement is a positive strategy designed to help the driver
and company. According to the trucker, P Courier only has top-rated
drivers. There is no question of inability, alcohol/drugs, or bad attitude.
Rather, there are temporary factors, such as a marriage breakdown, that
will cause even the best driver to waiver a little. He needs help, and gets
it from the safety supervisor.

As a policy, P Courier demands that managers ride along with every
driver four times a year to familiarize themselves with the daily operation
of hauling freight. Occasionally the district manager may decide to
participate. In his fifteen years experience, Giddyup twice had the privilege
of having a district manager ride with him. The possibility of a high level
administrator spending a full day with a trucker is, according to Giddyup,
"mind boggling." He finds it enjoyable because, "they share a lot of
interesting information as to what the company is doing, its future plans
and the operations." Other company VIPs he entertained over the years
were the personnel manager and shop manager for the entire state.
According to Giddyup:

> And that's nice, it's always good to get him out in one of his tractors so you
> know, if I feel that my power's down a little I could really, first hand, bring
> it to his attention because I'm one driver who does go through the mountains
> you know.

Giddyup considers managers to be people like himself, former drivers
who decided to move on to bigger and better things. According to Giddyup,
P Courier is owned by the management, and, therefore, there is a greater
appreciation for the welfare of the drivers and safety. A happy, safe driver
is a good company driver who is great with the customers, works hard to
be promoted and tries to make the company profitable. Several years ago
Giddyup considered moving into management, but after careful reflection
he decided against it because he did not want to "wreck" a good thing.
He was totally satisfied being a trucker. Everything was perfect for him,
so why take a chance and "wreck it."

Concerning log books, hours of consecutive driving and fatigue, P Courier implemented a series of policies that reflected the safety image of the company. P Courier's motto is, "Safety brings in customers, safety sells." To practicalize the slogan, P Courier demands that their drivers always run legal speeds, run logs and timecards. The driver's paperwork is audited every night. To assure that drivers do not break the speed limit, each truck has a governor installed, preventing drivers from exceeding sixty-two mph.

Giddyup feels no need to cheat on his log book because his schedule is set up on a sixty-hour work week, twelve hours per day for five days. The company's feeder department constantly checks a driver's available hours, particularly around Christmas time when, due to heavy demand, drivers work overtime, close to their maximum hours. Giddyup had personally been stopped fifty to sixty miles from his destination because he did not have enough hours to reach the terminal. Because the feeder department knew ahead of time that Giddyup was running short of hours, they sent another driver to complete the trip.

Giddyup consistently interrelated his image as a professional, safe driver with the company image of reliable, safe service. He reasoned that the better he drives, the more the company benefits, which in turn translates into more perks for him. His uniform represented the dignity of the company. He did not want to dishonor it in any way.

I should report, that permission for me to ride as a passenger on a P Courier truck hinged on me wearing a company shirt, standard fare for passengers traveling in company vehicles. Because P Courier does not permit passengers, a driver observed to be carrying a rider not dressed in P Courier clothes may be reported by the police, another P Courier driver or some curious trucker. If a driver is detected with an unauthorized passenger, he is immediately dismissed without compensation. Giddyup refuses to take any riders because, as he said, "we got good jobs and we know our job's on the line." It is company policy that any passenger must be cleared through the central office. Once a rider receives formal permission, he must wear P Courier shirts. According to Giddyup:

> You never know when there's going to be some management person or someone going down the road and look in the cab and see you driving with someone wearing this, that or the other.

Although Giddyup is not permitted to pick up hitchhikers or other drivers on his trip, he is allowed to help a fellow trucker who is broken down. The aid, however, is limited. For insurance reasons, Giddyup cannot drive a stranded driver farther than the next telephone.

Giddyup believed that because P Courier drivers get paid well, the truckers do not look for other jobs, or moonlight in the evenings. According to the driver:

> We get paid good so, therefore, when I get home and punch off the clock, I've got a little free time to go to my family, to do a few things at home, to go to bed and get my rest in time to be rested and come back on the job the next day – and I have more than eight hours off.

Giddyup suggested that good pay helps fight fatigue. Truckers are well off and, therefore, they can start each shift well rested. If a driver has an accident because of fatigue, he will be fired.

I continued to quiz Giddyup on the concept of safety and company image by bringing up the topic of daytime running lights. During the trip, I noticed that Giddyup did not have his lights turned on. Yet he was wearing a safety belt and appeared to apply all common sense and technical rules for increased safety. I became interested in his reasoning.

In town, where traffic is heavy, Giddyup usually turns on his lights to "bring more attention to his truck." On the highway he behaves like other drivers, seldom bothering to turn on his lights. He does not feel compelled to use daytime running lights on the highway because the company does not have a policy mandating their use. Because the the "company likes uniformity," managers prefer non-use of headlights. Giddyup grimaced, saying that the company "didn't know I run with mine (lights) on in town."

Giddyup wants to avoid a company supervisor coming up to him and telling him, "This is not company policy. Hey, you forgot to turn your headlights off. What's the idea of running with your headlights on?" Giddyup fears being singled out in a company built on uniformity. According to Giddyup:

> The company is really uniform, right down to where, you notice we wear one antenna, it's a white antenna. They don't let us put on other antennas, a lot of stuff like that. They like uniformity, so and really nationwide, I don't think you'll see that many, at least here in the west, running with headlights on.

Giddyup was a company man, a proud member of the P Courier Service. To drive a P Courier truck meant obeying company policies. Personal negotiation of company routine or regulation was not warranted even if it meant increasing safety. For example, P Courier, although a safety conscious company, had no policy on daytime running lights. Giddyup believed that lights-on during the day should not be practised, reflecting compliance with a non-policy rather than a company policy. Nevertheless, Giddyup refused to use daytime running lights unless company mandarins demanded it. After this discussion, there was a short period of silence as I looked around the countryside, admiring its many unique features.

The Desert Ride

I was held captive by the contours of the land. As a northerner, my only experiences with scenes of desert and cactus came from movies. At times I surveyed the countryside half expecting Clint Eastwood in a ruffled trench coat, and wearing a bullet-ridden cowboy hat galloping his horse alongside us to the music of "The Good, The Bad and The Ugly."

We journeyed through a desert spotted with Saguaro cactus and Palo Verde trees. Some of these forty foot high cactus began growing buds which in a short while will cover the tops of the cactus with beautiful white blossoms and yellow centers. Because the scenery was so impressive, I asked Giddyup about the countryside and Saguaro cactus around Black Canyon City. According to the trucker, this was Apache Indian Country where cacti are prominent. The cacti only grow a half inch per year, making a ten foot plant at least two hundred and forty years old.

To the right of us was a river bed dried up because northern Arizona received little rain during the winter and the distant mountains did not have their usual snow cover. Around the river bed were cliff dwellings, which years ago were occupied by Indians. To preserve them, Arizona has placed the entire area under Park system protection.

The Arizona desert was Giddyup's life. As a line driver he knew every "square inch" of the road and countryside. This knowledge, Giddyup believed, made him a safer driver. He could anticipate problems before they arose because he knew all the hills, valleys, turns and blind spots.

On the Phoenix to Flagstaff run Giddyup was the P Courier representative. He picked up the CB and wished other drivers good morning, whether it was a woman driving a half ton truck, a man operating an old single axle gravel truck, another P Courier driver or a line driver for another company. He knew many people, much like the familiar figure of a postman walking down the street waving at neighbors and passers-by.

We approached Flagstaff. The cacti were behind us. Before us stood the Ponderosa Pine, evidence that we approached higher elevation – from one thousand feet in Phoenix to seven thousand feet in Flagstaff. Shortly after we pulled into the Flagstaff terminal, where I teamed up with George, a P Courier trucker who drove me to Gallup, New Mexico. From there I proceeded with a P Courier driver named Mike who took me to Albuquerque.

From Flagstaff to Albequerque

Much of what Giddyup said was echoed by George and Mike. Like Giddyup, they were proud to be P Courier drivers. They would not consider changing jobs, instead they saw themselves as retiring with P Courier Service. For them driving for this company was like a "regular job" where you worked for eight hours and went home. All three men were comfortable and felt dignified to be driving a truck with a company of P Courier's reputation and status. They liked the idea that there was always uniformity and no surprises.

While I drove with George, we traveled through the valley of the painted rocks, a popular backdrop for western movies. George's fascination for this environmental beauty began to wane after driving through the area every day for the last eight years. The drive from Flagstaff to Gallup was described by George as "absolutely boring." Every day he drives the same distance according to schedule. Trucking was not his love, it was a job, and a boring one at that. But the pay was good and the hours were terrific. The truck had no special meaning. It was a standard piece of equipment without personality. Company policy dictated that it remain that way.

Gallup, New Mexico, was a small roadside city with a Mexican transient look. Dusty gravel roads ran beside rundown trailers and leaning old houses. The town looked sleepy under the ninety-five degree Fahrenheit heat. At first Mike hated Gallup, but now that he lived here, he has become used to it. "You gotta live somewhere," he told me. "It may as well be Gallup."

In Gallup I hitched up with Mike, a grizzled driver who had two years left before retirement. He drove me to Albequerque. On the way he discussed how trucking had changed for the worse. At one time there was honor in owning and driving your own truck. Today, according to Mike, "people look at you like you're shit." He sold his truck nearly twenty years ago to become a company driver with P Courier.

Mike spoke highly of the company. He has benefited from it and now cannot wait to retire, because trucking has lost its magic. On the way to Albequerque, Mike stopped at the side of the road so I could admire the adobes still being used by Indians and protected by the New Mexico state.

At six p.m., we arrived in Albequerque. Just before we entered the city, a panorama of lights could be seen from the top of the mountain where the highway began to descend towards the city. This view was Mike's favorite. It was not only sensational but it reminded him that he was home, his trip was finished for another day. He dropped me off at the truck stop and bade me farewell.

Conclusion

Truck graphics and general cleanliness do not go unobserved in public. The image of driver and company are portrayed for all in the vicinity to see. Giddyup Quick Freight was fully aware of the relationship between his driving and the image of P Courier Service. He considered his driving style to be enmeshed with the company image.

More than George and Mike, Giddyup Quick Freight went to great lengths to be a company ambassador through his driving tact. His speed was constant. He would not enter the passing lane unless he knew he had the horsepower to pass a vehicle comfortably. He did not want a complaint lodged against him or his company. He would rather place his face beside a compliment.

Notes to Chapter Ten

1. Some companies and lease operators promote their firm or certain products through dramatic graphics whereby they turn the truck and trailer into an advertising tool. According to Fuochi (1988), nearly 75 percent of all pedestrians exposed to fleet graphics develop an immediate impression of the company represented in the graphics. Based on 1968 and 1977 studies sponsored by the American Trucking Association, Fuochi concluded that not only do 75 percent of pedestrians develop an impression of a company but, more significantly:

   > . . . almost a third of the market will make a purchasing decision based on their initial impression of a company vehicle. (Fuochi, 1988; pg. 13)

   According to the president of Autograph Trim, a high-tech graphics firm, companies like Levi Strauss believe that a truck driver with a smart looking truck takes greater pride in his job and in the company for which he is hauling.

   Like the P Courier Service drivers, any operator of a well advertised rig can be identified if he takes liberties on the road. According to Harle (1987; pg. 10), truck imagery is strong enough that it can become a powerful marketing strategy. He writes:

   > With increased competition in obtaining long-term shipping contracts, graphics and signwriting can be used as a valuable negotiating tool.
   >
   > Fleet owners should remember too, that 29 percent of the public said they would – or would not – make a purchasing decision based on the impression gained from a company truck.

References

American Trucking Association Foundation. 1982. **The Influence of Truck Appearance On Driver Attitudes.** A Research Report Under a Grant from 3M.

Bradley, E. 1979. **Trucks and Trucking.** London: Octopus Books.

Fuochi, A. 1988. "Marketing Through Graphics." **Truck Fleet,** July, pp. 12-16.

Harle, Martin Stuart. 1987. "Graphic Impact Pays." **Truck Fleet,** July, pp. 10-12.

Harper, Brian. 1989. "An Exercise In Truck Painting: Multi Striping." **Body Shop,** June.

McQuail, Denis. 1987. **Mass Communication Theory: An Introduction.** Beverly Hills: Sage Publications Inc.

Nase, Eileen. 1987. "Commercial Vehicle Safety – Graphics Contest, 1986 Winners." **CCJ – Commercial Carrier Journal,** June.

Wyckoff, Daryl. 1979. **Truck Drivers in America.** Lexington, MA: Lexington Books.

11

ON FAMILY

Natchos and tortillas were ordered at a local restaurant in Albuquerque, New Mexico. The Manager of Operations, Safety Supervisor and Controller of one of the largest American trucking companies invited me to have lunch before commencing my journey from Albuquerque, New Mexico, to Denver, Colorado. While we were eating, mechanics at the maintenance shop were installing a passenger seat in the truck I was scheduled to take. Like P Courier, X Freightlines had a policy, no passengers unless authorized by the management. I took this time to interview the managers and later the dispatchers.

When I met Tim, my next driver, he was sipping a soft drink in the coffee room, waiting for some last minute repairs on his truck to be completed. The unexpected delay pleased Tim because X Freightlines pays fourteen dollars per hour for any driver who, regardless of departure time, has arrived upon the request of the dispatcher. While Tim quenched his thirst, I wandered around the huge truck compound chatting with other truckers. A grizzled old driver from Texas approached me quoting the bible, preaching "fire and brimstone," hell and condemnation about drivers and drugs. For fifteen minutes he talked while I listened. Shortly after the sermon I broke away and helped Tim load his gear for Denver. Our departure time was quarter after three in the afternoon. Our anticipated arrival time in Denver was eleven thirty at night.

Tim was a young man, twenty-five years old, who had six days left on his six-month probationary driving period. Once his trial time is up, Tim will be promoted to a full-time driver with his seniority date posted and his pay increased. Although Tim was on a probationary driving program for X Freightlines, he had extensive trucking experience, the most noteworthy of which was the last three years he drove for an owner operator hauling shingles between Albequerque and Dallas.

According to Tim, the name of the game for transporting shingles was "push, push, push." He drove a 1986 Kenworth with a four hundred cc motor and a fifteen gear overdrive transmission. He ran the six hundred and thirty-five mile trip in eleven and a half hours which meant driving a hundred and fifteen mph. During his three year tenure driving for the owner operator, Tim received five speeding tickets in Texas, and several more in Arkansas. Because Tim's driver's license is from New Mexico, and the Texas/Arkansas governments do not communicate the citations to New Mexico, Tim's driving record is clean.

During those days, Tim drove with three licenses, one each from New Mexico, Texas and Arkansas. His boss had "seven to eight licenses." However, things are changing with the new federally regulated commercial drivers license (CDL). According to Tim, before the advent of computers a state would have to call your home state's Department of Motor Vehicles to find out if he had a license or if it was turned into the department. "Now," Tim explained, "they just punch it in the computer and they get it in thirty seconds."

While we were talking, Tim was busy burying wads of chewing tobacco in his lower lip and when the time was right, he spit it into an empty coffee cup. Before us was an over-the-road direction sign that read "North 25, Las Vegas, New Mexico." The drive was pleasant as we were cruising around sixty mph, windows down with a breeze to help us stay cool. Visible to the North were the Sangre de Cristo Mountains, a range through which we were destined to pass before we reached Las Vegas, New Mexico.

Tim always drove within the posted highway speed limit because like P Courier Service, X Freightlines' executives had governors installed on all company trucks. The technological innovation removes the option for truckers to drive faster than sixty-two mph. According to Tim, the move was generally applauded by the company drivers because they work on assigned mileage per ten hour trips. Also, the installation of governors on trucks frees the trucker from worrying about speeding violations.

Our discussion on speed and company policy shifted to appreciation of the countryside. In the field were two roadrunners, a state protected bird. I was astonished to learn that these birds are able to kill rattlesnakes. Then a silence overcame us. Tim stopped speaking. He pointed to the east:

> Right over there is where my wife's at. See those two pine trees about halfway up to the mausoleum, she's right there in between 'em. Part of life.

Tim's wife and two-year-old daughter were buried in a small, hidden cemetery about a hundred feet from the side of the road near a small grove of pine trees. They lay in marked graves, their deaths caused by a car crash.

Tim's Former Family

Tim was a widower, mourning the deaths of his wife and two-year-old daughter. He spoke emotionally about life before their deaths, producing a dramatic context that was stirring and tense. Throughout the trip Tim was reminded of his family's plight. It was the foremost thing on his mind. It helped me better understand truckers' emotions and home life.

Tim's life has always revolved around trucking. As a youngster, he wanted to be a trucker like his father, who at the time owned fifteen trucks. He was a member of a trucking family that included older brother and sister drivers. He developed into a trucker within a family context where trucking was a way of life. For Tim the road was all he had ever known for making a living. While being a trucker he married and started a family. The change in lifestyle created a counter theme to trucking.

Tim's trucking and family life "weren't coming together." Both he and his wife were lonely. During his times away from home, Tim's wife had to take charge. An example fresh in Tim's mind was the night the water heater froze. Tim explained that, "She had to go out there at midnight up to her knees in mud trying to figure out how to get the water heater going again." Things became so tough before his daughter was born that he asked his wife to ride along with him. As Tim said, "I had company and we had a good life together on the road." Eventually Tim taught his reluctant wife to drive. According to Tim, "I taught her how to drive. She could. She didn't like it, but she could do it. She never felt confident."

As a team, Tim and his wife became "commercial tourists." Unlike Lisa and Ted who drove together for income and family union, Tim and his wife combined to actively share life through travel. Tim liked the idea of making a living while his wife was vacationing. As a tourist team, they visited the Smithsonian Institute, the New Orleans Mardi Gras, Mount Rushmore and Disneyworld. According to Tim, he and his wife would:

> . . . get laid over into a town where we couldn't unload until Monday morning; we would drop our trailer and take the tractor and go see the museums and see the sights of the town.

Tim loved the experiences of being a commercial tourist with his wife. He commented:

> When I was on my own, if I had to be laid over in a town I would probably be sitting at the truck stop unless there was a movie house close or something like that that I could walk to. But with her, we got to see everything. We went down into Juarez, go down to El Paso, down in Tijuana, you know, we'd take the tractor and just go over there. That's a lot of fun. We don't have to pay to go on vacations because you're already there, you just do it, and it's okay.

Once his wife became pregnant, Tim drove solo again. He did this until his daughter was two years old. In Tim's view, because his daughter was special he decided to quit driving and join the police. As a trucker, he was missing a big part of his little girl's life, not knowing what she was doing. At the same time, Tim was disturbed that his daughter did not know, "where daddy is or what daddy's doing."

When Tim "had the wreck" everything changed. He returned to trucking because, according to Tim, "It's what I like and what I do the best." He looked at me, smiled and, for the next minute, remained silent.

We neared the town of Sangre de Cristo, locally referred to as the "Blood of Christ." In the near distance we could see the mountains. As a unit, the town and mountains held special meaning for Tim. It was here that the Spanish looked for the Seven Cities of Gold. In the process, they colonized the area and "murdered a lot of the Indians." Tim's wife was part Indian. He understood the mixture of Spanish and Indian as it reflected in his wife's religion. She was a strong Catholic with "a lot of Indian in it."

A Blowout

We were cruising along confidently when, without warning, a loud bang was heard. Tim immediately checked his rearview mirror, noticing that his trailer was listing. We were struck by a tire blowout while traveling at fifty-five mph, in the isolated hinterland of New Mexico. Tim steered the truck to the shoulder of the road, to stop and analyze the damage. A tire had exploded! Tim theorized that heat affected the walls of the tire, causing it to "disintegrate." Because the unit was a Double Trailer, the chance of the trailer going out of control was remote.

Although Tim brought a high-powered portable CB on board, he did not connect it. However, had the CB been operational, it would have been of little use because the Albuquerque to Denver route was not a major truck thoroughfare. Tim had few possible trucker recipients for a CB call. The problem was compounded by the fact that we were too far from X Freightlines office in Albuquerque to make radio contact. Also, the cellular telephone I was carrying did not work because there were no commercial cells in the New Mexico backlands.

Having a blowout going north of Albuquerque was a new experience for this young trucker. He had no idea of who could exchange the flat tire. Whenever he travels west to Arizona, there are tire banks all along the route where repairmen "come out and fix your tire." In our case, Tim felt that the best strategy was to drive to Las Vegas, call the company dispatcher on the telephone and "see what he says."

After the damage was assessed, Tim and I hopped back into the truck and continued on traveling at a maximum speed of thirty mph. Our immediate destination was Las Vegas, New Mexico, a town sixty miles away.

According to Tim, blowing a tire is not an unusual experience when you pull trailers running on recap tires. A difficult part of having blowouts is finding help fast and cheap. The average cost for changing a trailer recap is three hundred dollars, plus traveling time for the repairman, who may conceivably drive two hours to provide help. What scares Tim most about a blowout are the drivers behind the truck. They are at risk when an emergency occurs. This is especially true for tailgaters who fail to understand that blowouts happen. When tires blow the trailers begin to jerk making it difficult for the driver to maneuver his rig. Tim's experience hit at the crux of his family life. A trucker he was passing had a blowout and smashed into Tim's half ton. His wife and child were killed immediately. Now Tim wanted to be stoic. He does not want to cry anymore. He described:

> Like, her relatives and stuff would come into my hospital room, and they would be crying and all upset and it just tears their life up. You know, I mean it hurt me, yes, it hurts me deeply, still does and it always will, but to break down and cry and to get that emotional where it tears your own life up, it doesn't make sense to me. Because your crying and upsetting your life is not going to help them any and it's just going to hurt you. So I always considered myself very practical.

On his daughter's birthday Tim's coolness broke down. Doctors had to give him a high dosage of morphine to ease his physical and mental pain. Other than that, the young man prided himself on his sense of practicality and level-headedness. According to Tim, "You can't blame anyone, you have to forget. It was just that, that the driver blew his tire."

We continued driving on the shoulder at thirty miles per hour maximum. Tim kept checking his mirrors to make sure all is well with the trailer. Technically, the police could restrict Tim from driving with a blown tire. However, whether an officer would actually do so was doubtful:

> You know, as of right now, if a cop saw me, legally, he could shut me down. Tell me to park it right here until I got that tire fixed. I don't think it's necessary, but he could do it.

Near Seratina around an "S" turn was a crudely built cross on the side of the road. It was about four feet high, and quite weathered, standing in front of a small barb wired patch of semi-desert just over a bridge spanning a creek. I looked with curiosity and asked Tim about the significance of the cross. He did not speak for a short while, repacking his lip with Skoal chewing tobacco, the spittle of which began to stink. He looked at the road for a few seconds, then at me.

"In many parts of New Mexico," he responded, "country families just come out here to put up a cross." The placement of the cross marks the location where a family member died because of a car accident. Although road construction crews take them down, many families return to resurrect their's. Tim personalized the cross:

> Like, there's the one out there with my wife and daughter's name on it right there on the way to my house. That's good and it's bad 'cause it sure is a big reminder. Every time I go there I see that cross. I guess it wouldn't really matter; I know where it happened anyhow.

A trend was becoming evident. Whenever Tim touched on his wife and child he would briefly describe the issue, become silent, then change the topic of conversation. It was a tactic he used to remain calm. This time Tim pointed out Wolf Creek Pass to me. According to him, the pass is the highest pass in the United States, surrounded by twenty miles of beautiful greenery. Tim estimated that we would reach the pass just before we crossed the Colorado border. In the meantime Tim explained the construction and cultural significance of the adobes in the distance.

The Decision To Continue With A Flat Tire

We arrived in Las Vegas at seven p.m. where Tim telephoned his dispatcher from a pit stop service station. He received the order to drive to Raton, a town located a few miles south of the Colorado border, and to contact the company repair contractor. Tim was told to drive one hundred and ten miles at thirty miles per hour, with a flat tire. Tim conceded that it was now impossible to estimate our time of arrival in Denver. The late start in Albuquerque and the blowout made timing at best an optimistic projection.

As we left the outskirts of Las Vegas, Tim discussed the difficulties of managing a personal life while being a widowed trucker. He does not date, partly because he "can't bring himself to do it yet" and partly because the company's schedules can change at a moment's notice, forcing him to cancel pre-arranged plans. More than once his dispatcher called Tim unexpectedly, "Hey, you're going to work tonight?"

Driving on the shoulder of the highway at about thirty mph requires a patient driver. Tim fit the bill. If it was his call, he wouldn't mind driving all the way to Denver with a flat tire as long as he was paid for it. The fact that such a trip would take a long time made little impact on Tim since he had no future plans anyways. The only thing that made Tim a little wary is becoming fatigued late at night. He had already been awake since eight in the morning, doing chores around his house.

Thirty miles north of Las Vegas, the road began to straighten out, helping Tim maintain proper control of the unit and motivating him to speed up a little. At times we chanced forty mph, but the trial speed was quickly cancelled when the trailer began to wander. To the north we saw massive rainclouds approaching us. Tim appreciated the oncoming rain because it would cool the road thereby reducing the chance of another blowout. In the back of Tim's mind was the thought that if one tire blew, why can't another one go. If that happened we would be stranded for a long time because few motorists traveled the highway at this time of year and at this time of day.

In the distance we had our first glimpse of the Raton lights. My impression that we would soon arrive was quickly squashed when Tim informed me that we were still a hundred miles away from the town. According to Tim, the nearness of town lights is an illusion that can play tricks on truckers' minds, especially if they are tired. The time from first seeing the lights to final arrival is one of frustration and anticipation. "You just want to get there," said Tim.

Up to this point of the trip I realized that Tim had his four-way flashers working, but up to the oncoming darkness caused by the rainclouds, he did not have his headlights turned on. There was no sense in it explained Tim, we were driving on the shoulder with little oncoming traffic. The chance of a head-on collision was zero. As to daytime running lights policy, X Freightlines had none and Tim could "care less if they never do." There are enough things for a trucker to worry about than a "fuckin' drained battery" caused by lights still on after the motor was switched off.

Half way to Raton the rains came down. Tim was a little concerned about the possibility of trucks approaching from behind whose drivers assume that he is driving at regular speed. The chance of such a serious mishap was real, especially when at times the shoulders narrowed and Tim was forced to drive on the highway proper at thirty mph. The trucker felt uneasy during these stretches of roadway.

During the rain storm I asked Tim about the trucker's plight and his own future. Tim was aware that government deregulation of transportation hurt the trucker. He experienced the pressures of an owner operator trying to make it in a deregulated industry. As a company driver, Tim does not feel the pressure of deregulation as much. Echoing the feelings of other truckers, he is suspicious of all politicians. In fact, he was not certain whether Ronald Reagan and George Bush were Democrats or Republicans. Tim refused to vote, feeling that it is a waste of time and it would, "only encourage them on."

As far as Tim was concerned, governments "don't give a shit about truckers." Talk about safety is only a smokescreen to hit the trucker even harder. The benefits go to the consumers who can "buy stuff cheaper" and to large corporations who "get a deal shipping their stuff." Tim's observation was that trucking was always pretty wild but it was never really dangerous. Most truck accidents are unavoidable due to other drivers and equipment failure.

Near Raton we traveled around a long arching curve at the end of which stood a man and a woman, rucksacks on their backs, hitchhiking to Colorado. Tim's compassion for the couple's plight was moderate. He did not think a great deal of a man taking a woman to the side of the highway to hitchhike. It was too degrading for the woman. As he spoke about his feelings, Tim again spoke about his deceased child and his decision to join the police. It was sad talk:

> Megan looks, from the day she was born I talked to her every day on the phone. I mean, just, every day, 7:30, 8:00 o'clock. When it hit me was the day I was sitting at home. She was playing with her pictures. She was ten months old. The phone rang and I was holding her. It was 8:00 o'clock when I usually called (from the truck trip), and she looked up to the phone and said, "Dad." Even though I was holding her, she didn't identify me as Dad. She identified the telephone as Dad. And I couldn't see my daughter growing up in that, so that's why I decided that I wanted time to quit driving.

Tim wanted his daughter to know him, to watch her grow and experience her changes. Because he could not do this as a trucker, he quit driving, waiting to start his formal training program at the police academy.

By giving up truck driving, Tim was able to spend quality time with his daughter – time that has come to be the most precious thing in his life. He felt sorry for truckers who cannot see their children grow, who cannot be with their families in times of need or times of joy. According to Tim, the lack of family intimacy leaves a huge hole in truckers' lives. It is a vital ingredient in how they drive.

On more than one occasion Tim has left Phoenix, Arizona, early in the morning to hasten his arrival in Albuquerque. He would not stop anywhere as he sped along. Before long he realized that "there was nobody waitin' " for him. So he slowed down, taking his time, trying to delay his arrival time. He still hates entering his empty house which was once filled with the sounds of a young family.

The Family Choice

Tim and I agreed that families occupy a central position in truckers' lives. However a caveat must be introduced. The trucker's marriage is built, to a large extent, on separation by distance. The wife and children have a location, an address of residence. Over-the-road truckers only share the domiciles for a few days each month. The family residence at times represents little more than an overnight pit stop on a long haul. As Tim described with his daughter, whenever he came home as a driver for an owner operator he was a homecomer who, temporarily, enters the front door as a stranger.

Whenever Tim and other long haul truckers come home they must re-establish their relationships with their wives and children. In some cases, they only have a few hours or one to two days to spend at home. During this time they have to accommodate the family if they wish to once again become an intimate part of it – even for a short period of time. During the time between the last visit and the recent one, the trucker and his wife had separate experiences. Each one has become a little more individualistic. The wife, according to Tim, had to become the "man of the house." She has learned to "wear the pants in the family."

As a result, truckers I met often spoke of their families along maternal rather than paternal lines. Because of the driver absence the woman, out of necessity, takes full control over the household, business and child rearing. She becomes independent in the day-to-day affairs.

As a general rule, married drivers, especially owner operators, want time at home. They consent to the dispatcher's wishes so that they may get a trip through or near their home town and take one or two days off. Drivers like Giddyup Quick Freight and Tim who work for line carriers are at an advantage. They can be home nearly every night and on weekends. They reflect more closely the broad definition of traditional family.

Based on my interviews with truckers, a definite risk factor became evident. Married drivers are prepared to take driving risks such as fatigue, running over hours, or speeding to gain time with the family. Being home is special, or as Tim said, "It is something worth fighting for."

However the anticipation of getting home was often different from being at home. Whereas most drivers wish to spend time with their wives and children, once they get home they are inclined to lay around. They like to sleep and watch videos. Often they fall asleep during the movie, at which time understanding wives do not wake them.

The scenario of watching television and/or videos and sleep was defined regularly. For some truckers the former activities are not enough. They go beyond and entertain themselves by going fishing, or boating, working around the house or thrillseeking through skidooing, motorcycling, and four wheeling. Women are usually not part of the recreation plans. Truckers want to be by themselves within the security of a family.

This desire may be ideal for the trucker, but it is less than acceptable to spouses. After being alone for weeks, they do not appreciate their husbands coming home and entertaining only themselves. They desire affection and confirmation of their individual worth. According to Tim, while he worked hard to do this, most truckers do not. As a result, divorce is the typical outcome of a first-time marriage. If I were to collect all the reasons truckers gave me for creating marital difficulties, I could summarize them by arguing that wives have difficulties staying faithful, are jealous when the men stop at truck stops, become sexually "cold" or "aloof," become overly independent or they are afraid of the physical risks their husbands take on their jobs. But truckers are a resilient group. They tend to seek out new partners and marry again or they live common law.

The implicit and explicit meaning of family, whether by choice or birth, is a major factor in trucker's driving lives. Tim's extreme, yet real family circumstances, symbolize the truckers desire for rootedness.

The Family of Birth

Not only is the trucker's immediate family important to his driving career, equally relevant is his family of birth. It is here that the trucker developed his attitudes, roles and impressions about work, family and trucking.

Most often a trucker like Tim comes from a conjugal family that was fully involved in trucking. As he stated, "Everybody in my family can drive a truck except for my little sister." If we recall, Victor, Dale, Simon, Danny, BJ, Mike and Ted all came from truck driving families. It seems that in families where trucking is practised by one or more members, there is a sharing of values and beliefs about trucking that influence youngsters to become full-time truck drivers. According to Tim, "The children begin to feel the same way as their father, the very same way."

On my research trip I only met Giddyup Quick Freight and Danny whose families were not involved in transportation. They quit school at an early age to earn quick money. One became a barber, then a trucker. Danny became a trucker at seventeen, much to the dismay of his parents. To this day Danny's parents wished he would change careers.

Heading Toward Denver

We finally arrived at Raton. From a diner, Tim telephoned the company repair contractor, who changed the tire while we ate dinner. The full charge for the tire replacement was three hundred and sixty-five dollars. While we were munching on french fries and slurping oil can coffee, Tim conceded that he was looking forward to getting sleep in Denver. He has been up since nine in the morning and has been at work since two p.m. It would probably be three in the morning before we arrived in Denver. A twelve to sixteen hour trip was in the making, meaning that Tim will be tampering with his log book entries.

After a quick meal, we jumped into the truck and headed towards Colorado at a normal pace of sixty mph. According to Tim, "Colorado is a tough state on truckers." He expected to be weighed twice; once at Strakvill, which we were quickly approaching, and then again at the scales north of Trinidad, Colorado. In comparison to Colorado, New Mexico was an easy state. Tim told me that officials in his home state seldom weigh trucks. The majority of time he gets waved through at the scales. I observed the non event when we approached the last weigh scale in New Mexico. It was past midnight and the scales were officially closed. An old fellow opened the front window of a small, isolated, run-down building and sleepily waved us along. He decided not to review Tim's documents. Tim declared that this occurs about "ninety percent of the time."

Tim credits the attendant's wave to proceed to the X Freightline truck. According to Tim, "They know you're pretty well legal and that I have my permits." Weight is not an issue. Tim suspected that, "the scale probably doesn't even work. It's probably been coated with snow and ice so many times that it can't work." Whether Tim's assertion was correct remained to be tested. From the looks of it, the image of a small, aging, weathered building with a fading fence surrounded by overgrown weeds did not leave an image of efficiency and heavy use.

The young driver believed that New Mexico relied on its neighbouring states to assure that interstate truckers met the safety standards and regulations. For example, if a trucker is cleared according to Arizona or Colorado's rigorous standards, then surely it must be within New Mexico's guidelines. Tim assured me that we would not have such an easy time of it in Colorado:

> At Colorado we will probably be weighed and we will probably have to go inside and take my permit. They will punch it, then give you a little trip ticket, and you have it punched at Monument again. At Monument they will weigh me again and make me go back in and get that little ticket punched.

Like Arizona, Colorado registers the trucks as they enter and proceed through the state to check on fuel use and time of driving. "In Texas," Tim said, "they don't even know what a set of scales are. I bet they have three or four for the whole state and they don't use them." As I discussed in Chapter Two, each state has its own regulations on weight and procedures of policing truck regulations. Truckers are fully aware of the discrepancies.

Near Colorado Springs I found the night air becoming rather cool, so I closed the window. Tim reacted immediately, requesting that I reopen the window slightly. He was claustrophobic, suffering vertigo in close quarters. Whenever vertigo comes on Tim has major problems telling direction and judging speed. To compensate, he keeps his window open.

Before us was a sign that read Strakvill Weigh Scales. We drove through it without any of the troubles Tim expected. The attendant did not bother weighing Tim's truck and he decided not to check his papers. He waved us along. Farther up the highway came another surprise. The Trinidad Weigh Scales were closed for the night allowing us clear sailing to Denver, now visible on the horizon.

Arrival in Denver

Tim and I arrived at the X Freightlines' marshaling yards in Denver at four a.m. We were both subdued. The trip was exhausting, both from a mental and physical point of view. The all-night dispatcher called the motel and asked for a van to transport us to the Traveler's Lodge, a chain contracted by X Freightlines to accommodate its drivers at special rates.

The next morning I caught a plane back to British Columbia to continue my voyage in Canada.

References

British Columbia Trucking Association. 1989. **A Survey of Truck Drivers in British Columbia**. Vancouver: BCTA.
Carter, B. 1973. "Reform-School Families." Society Magazine, 11, November-December, pp. 36-43.
Niederhoffer, A. 1976. "Learning An Occupation On The Job." In Nash, J. and Spradeley, J. (eds.) **Sociology: A Descriptive Approach**. Chicago: Rand McNally College Publishing Co.
Schutz, Alfred. 1971. Collected Papers II. **Studies in Social Theory**. The Hague: Martinus Nijhoff.
Statistics Canada. 1988. **Profiles**. Ottawa: Statistics Canada.

12

GIVING MOTORISTS A BRAKE

A few days of rest at home and I was off, venturing with a trucker traveling from Vancouver to Lillooet. Outside of Vancouver on the Upper Levels Highway we stopped just southeast of Horseshoe Bay, British Columbia, preparing to check the brakes as mandated by the law. At a government brake checkpoint located just before a treacherous mountain highway and steep slope before a ferry terminal, truckers must stop and check the brakes before continuing downhill to the ferry or to drive along Highway 99 North to Squamish, Whistler, Pemberton and finally Lillooet, British Columbia.

Hugging the left side of the highway is Howe Sound, an arm of the Pacific Ocean that winds its way to Squamish. On the right hand side are the Coast Mountains, perpendicular granite walls sealing off the roadway. In the event of an emergency, Karl, the trucker with whom I am riding, had three choices; hit the embankment, smash into the other vehicle or roll into the ocean. Good brakes are an absolute necessity for driving Highway 99, nicknamed the "Killer Highway."

At the check point Karl, a sixty-three year old driver, investigated the brakes by pumping the pedal at intervals, checked the tires for wear and cuts, reviewed the headlights for cracks and he cleaned the windshield with an old rag he had underneath the seat. He enjoyed doing these things because as a company driver for short haul trips Karl willingly takes the time to complete safety checks. He gets paid by the hour, regardless of whether he is stopped or on the go.[1]

Similar to BJ in Chapter Seven, Karl was a sixty-three year old driver who had been an owner operator for forty-five years, during most of which he hauled furniture across Canada. As he became older, he lost much of his energy and ambition needed to succeed as an owner operator. Also, he was losing blood circulation in his right foot which makes it hard for him to drive long distances. The answer for him was to become a local line driver, one whose working day ends at seven p.m.

At the brake check, George, the attendant, came over and chatted with Karl. Because Karl stops here daily, they have come to know each other well. In fact, Karl boasted, there are times he passes the brake check because George knows that his truck is in good condition from the previous day's check stop.

George's authority is to ensure that all truckers stop at the brake check. The extent to which Karl and other drivers undertake the formal or government expected inspection procedures described in this chapter's "Notes" is left to the truckers. George's only concern is for the trucks to come to a dead stop before they hit the steep grade, avoiding possible runaways.

After a twenty minute stop we prepared to exit. Re-entry onto the Upper Levels Highway from the brake stop is tricky. Although the speed limit on the downhill part of the highway around the wide bend where the truckers must enter is sixty km/hr, most vehicles travel at eighty and ninety. With the excess speed of vehicles and the difficulty in seeing coming traffic, Karl became a little tense. Finally his patience ran out as he entered the highway, "What the hell, it's now or never, anything goes."

Cars whipped around him to avoid driving behind a slow moving heavily loaded semi trailer. About two thousand feet ahead of the brake check highway entry point is a major division in the roadway. The left lane goes to the ferries and the right one continues through the mountains to Squamish. Some of the cars that passed us had to re-enter the right-hand lane at high speed to make the cut off for Squamish. For Karl, the event happens all the time. The police agree. Ed, a local constable, loves using his radar around the bend because, "the cars just keep coming and I just keep giving tickets."

From the beginning of the trip, it became apparent that Karl emphasized the rights of truckers at the expense of other motorists. According to Karl, he was a professional driver "out there day and night making a living." Other drivers are "four wheeling it" at their convenience. They are not under the same pressure as are truckers. They are not responsible for the safety of huge pieces of equipment that can go out of control at any time. Karl's feelings are not unique. Other drivers I described, like Vic, Simon and Giddyup Quick Freight, shared similar views. Amongst them was a criticism that motorists are unaware about the trucker's problems when he operates an eighteen wheeler. They should understand a truck's limitations of braking and acceleration, the danger of shifting loads, the threat of jackknifing on slippery roads and the difficulty of making right-hand turns from the centre lane at intersections. Karl told me that he becomes especially frustrated in Vancouver trying to make a right-hand turn. To achieve a smooth turn, he waits in the inside lane, and signals his intentions. According to Karl, "Sure enough, the bastards crowd you in the right lane. They got to know what you're doing. Nobody's that stupid."

Cars don't understand

As Karl sees it, the intersection episodes are perfect examples of motorists violating his rights. On the highway, Karl's sense of priority becomes especially pronounced. For example, as we approached a steep incline Karl stepped on the gas, coming dangerously close to the station wagon ahead of us. When the highway widened to a double passing lane Karl swung to the left intending to pass the vehicle. With a load of lumber he matched the car's speed for a short distance, but he lacked the power to pass it. So we drove alongside the other vehicle for about one-half mile.

When Karl originally encroached the station wagon's territory or safety cushion, the couple sitting in the back seat of the car glanced back, looking disturbed, wondering, I believe, about Karl's intent. They looked back several times, talking animatedly and pointing to us. Karl routinized the scenario by suggesting that he needed maximum speed to challenge the steep grade. According to Karl, people must understand the trucker's plight. Without the extra push the trucker would be shifting gears forever, trying to make it up the mountain at a reasonable speed. To Karl, the people in the station wagon obviously did not know anything about driving trucks. But, he legitimized, that is their problem, not his.

As we crawled up the incline in the passing lane a row of cars began to collect behind us. Karl's speed was beginning to slip from seventy, fifty, to forty kilometers per hour. It appeared that the elderly driver in the station wagon beside us was unsure of his next move. Should he speed up and pass the truck on the inside lane? or should he slow down and let the truck pass? He took a third option continuing to drive at an equal speed beside the truck.

Whenever I drive my car in mountainous terrain and experience lineups created by slow moving trucks in the passing lane, I usually become irritated. When I asked Karl about this irritation he shrugged his shoulders and answered, "Well, what can I do? If the driver doesn't realize that forty km is as fast as this truck can go, that's his problem." According to Karl there should be a shared understanding between trucker and other drivers of what a trucker can do and what he's allowed to do, and how a truck performs compared to a car. Once this is achieved, four wheelers and truckers can better cooperate on the nation's highways.

The station wagon driver finally sped up, passing us in the right lane. Other cars passed us the same way, upsetting Karl because he was now unable to re-enter the slow lane. Our speed now hit twenty kilometers per hour. Karl, still in the passing lane, was restricted from entering the slow lane because of the many cars passing us here at about eighty kilometers per hour. Karl commented:

> There you go. I see it just about every day. Guys passing on the inside lane. They don't give a damn ya know. Then when you want to get over it's dangerous. What's a guy to do?

We continued to drive in the fast lane all the way to the merge point, located a mile before Britannia Beach, a tiny mountain hamlet. The approach to the village consists of a tight right turn at the end of a long steep downhill run. It necessitates heavy braking. Although the speed limit through the small historical mining village is fifty km per hour, Karl rumbled through at seventy. Then another steep mountain grade! A passing lane provided the uphill traffic with an advantage.

The long steep climb towards Murrin Lake again forced Karl to creep along at twenty km per hour. Because of the tight turn at the foot of the mountain, Karl could not take his customary speed-up strategies for the oncoming climb. He had barely enough power to travel a consistent twenty to thirty km per hour up the two mile long mountain incline.

Twenty minutes later we approached Shannon Falls. A dotted center line greeted us. Karl became excited as he passed a jeep. While passing, the truck was laboring. Karl had little choice but to pull back into his lane before achieving a safe distance with the vehicle behind him. The jeep driver slowed down to allow Karl the privilege, flashing his headlights for acknowledgment. Karl interpreted the act as positive, a courtesy or sign of camaraderie, friendship, and intimate approval of Karl the truck driver.

On the approach to Squamish, I became fully aware of the need to have perfect brakes. The twisting steep mountain grade is not amenable to negotiated braking. One of the real issues in trucking and brakes is front axle brakes. When I asked Karl about them I discovered that he was seriously committed to the belief that front-axle brakes are a hindrance and not an asset for safe driving. All of his life as an owner operator he drove without front-axle brakes and never experienced negative effects.

Karl's point was that if you drive on icy roads, the trucker's chance of losing control is greater with front-axle brakes than it is without them. He prefers to drive without front-axle brakes in emergencies because when they are needed they pull the truck to the right. Phil, the Arizona Highway Patrolman I described in Chapter Nine, told me that the truckers he catches without front-axle brakes tend to be "old hard-liners" who believe "those front brakes are going to cause them to lose control." With the new technology, the likelihood of front-axle brakes locking up on a trucker is remote.

I mentioned Phil's judgements to Karl. He snickered and told me, "Look, I've been driving for forty-five years, I know." According to Karl, there is little weight in the front. It is all in the back. So, he asked rhetorically, "Doesn't it make sense that in an emergency the brakes on which the weight is located will grab the best?" He continued to tell me that for gradual braking, front-axle brakes are adequate. But, he reasoned, truckers don't use front-axle brakes for this purpose. Instead they rely on their engine brakes. In forty years of driving, Karl has never experienced his truck going out of control because of only using his rear brakes. Karl shrugged his shoulders, indicating end of discussion.

Peter, a member of the Royal Canadian Mounted Police, gave me a visual description of Karl's dependence on rear-axle brakes in an emergency. He suggested that I take my car to a parking lot, hit a speed of about fifty km/hr (thirty mph) and hammer on the emergency brake. The back wheels stop as the car turns around. You cannot hold the car straight. However, if you travel the same speed and stomp on the foot brake, the car will come to a controlled stop. The reason, Peter explained, is that the main brake is attached to the front wheel.

The police officer's imagery is not shared by all truckers, particularly some older veterans who steadfastly maintain that ever since front-axle brakes have been mandated on trucks there has been a steady increase in jackknifes. It is this belief shared by Karl and other truckers that calls for redress through research.

For example, in 1986, the American Bureau of Motor Carrier Safety selected twelve truckers who shared Karl's point of view and requested them to participate in front wheel brake tests. All the candidates expressed grave reservations about front wheel axle brakes. The chosen truckers were representative of the drivers Dunigan, Kirkpatrick and Smith (1986) observed to have removed, disconnected or disabled these brakes.

The Bureau of Motor Carriers used five three-axle tractors, of which three were with trailers and two were used as bobtails. After all the brakes were properly adjusted in accordance with manufacturer expectations, the drivers engaged their vehicles in stops on wet and dry asphalt, wet jennite on a curve and lane change. The truckers drove their vehicles at controlled speeds. They applied their brakes at designated locations. All the while they were expected to retain control of the vehicle in a cone line course.

When full use of front brakes was compared with no front brakes it was established that in all cases stopping distances increased when front brakes were disconnected. On a performance curve the increase in distance ranged from five percent (for combinations) to one hundred and four percent (for bobtails), depending on the driver and vehicle configuration and from sixteen to eighty-five percent in lane changes, again from empty combinations to bobtails (Radlinski and Flick, 1986). Stopping distances without front brakes ranged from forty-four to fifty feet. With front brakes, the stopping range decreased from twenty-two to twenty-four feet.

Following the tests, nearly all the drivers were convinced that front wheel axle brakes are effective. They work well by shortening stopping distances and preventing loss of control. Only one driver could see no difference and one had mixed comments. He was still left unconvinced.

I related the experiment to Karl. He listened attentively, then shook his head. According to him, there is a major difference between experiments and real life. As a betting man, he would place his money on trucks without front wheel axle brakes. But, because his rig was owned by a company, and it was driven by more than one operator, Karl could not tamper with the brakes the way he did in his owner operator days running a 1972 Kenworth. Begrudgingly he adhered to company policy.

A review of the literature illustrates even greater disagreement with Karl's belief. In February 1986, Transport Canada decided to test the hypothesis that front-axle brakes increase the likelihood of jackknifing. Based on a variety of steering and braking modulations on ice, Transport Canada (1986) concluded that use of front-axle brakes eliminated jackknifing and subsequent spin outs that occurred on runs without these brakes. Also, stopping distances were considerably shortened with the use of front-axle brakes.

A more rigorous study was undertaken in British Columbia.[1] A professional truck driving instructor test drove a conventional and cabover bobtail under wet and dry road conditions at speeds of fifty and eighty km/hr. Two conclusions were outlined by McInnis et al., 1986. Front-axle brakes are more likely to increase the stability of trucks in wet conditions and bobtail tractors without front-axle brakes are a hazard on the road, particularly at high speeds in wet conditions. I must point out that these conclusions are not as generalizeable as McInnis et al. pointed out. The study was done only in experimental conditions. There were no on-road tests to validate highway driving reality.

To a driver like Karl, proof is not necessarily dependent on scientific research. Proof is in the person, his experiences and his street smarts. Furthermore, Karl asked rhetorically if the safety of front-axle brakes was so well proven, why has the Canadian government not legislated front-axle brakes? My answer that the United States has done so, was treated by Karl with suspicion and a slight sneer. "Yeah," he answered, "but don't we live in Canada?" The entire issue left Karl unmoved.

We finally hit Squamish, the end of the line for me. The trip with Karl was a short one but it was certainly a memorable one. The man was a proud trucker who believed in the old days when truckers were knights of the road. They hauled the freight, but they did it their way.

Conclusion

Karl's driving duties kept him on Highway 99. He knew every "nook and cranny, every turn and mountainside." He felt confident that he had the skills to maneuver around any emergency situation. This confidence was a little unsettling to me because it led to him taking chances I considered to be risky and unsafe.

The taken-for-granted nature of trips and the total faith truckers like Karl have in their brakes tends to place them in unwary states of driving. They may tailgate downhill to pick up momentum for the next steep climb. They may speed more because they can anticipate the twists and turns of the highway. Through experience and habit, they judge a turn according to optimal speed not safe or suggested speed. And, as Karl suggested, the optimal may increase every time the trucker is on the road. Having navigated Windy Point at sixty km/hr one time may encourage the driver to try it at sixty-five km/hr or even seventy km/hr. Such gamesmanship may have serious repercussions.

I disembarked in Squamish, a little shaken. Karl's taken-for-granted rule that everything-will-be-ok was not shared by me. Although I felt safe sitting high in a cab, I felt uncomfortable knowing about the risks Karl takes, the possibility of him creating a crash and the possibility of victimizing a motorist, all because he wants to drive his way.

Notes to Chapter Twelve

1. According to the Province of British Columbia Professional Drivers' Manual, at any time a sign is posted in the advance to a down grade, warning drivers of trucks to stop in the pull-out area and inspect their brakes, the driver must comply.

   Drivers of trucks equipped with air operated braking systems will check:

   > Compressor is maintaining full reservoir pressure.
   > Pressure drop on full application is within limitations.
   > Slack adjusters for push rod travel and take up slack.
   > Audible air leaks.
   > Security of glad hands and lines.
   > Drums for overheating.
   > Emergency valve operation.

   . . . before proceeding down the grade.

   Trucks equipped with hydraulic brake system check:

   > Pedal reserve.
   > Vacuum booster operating.
   > Drums for over-heating.
   > Visual inspection for hydraulic fluid leaks.

2. The brake tests were performed on July 16-18, 1986, at Boundary Bay Airport, Vancouver, British Columbia. Testing was performed with two bobtail tractors, and control tests were performed as required with the

full-sized passenger car. Immediately prior to the test program, the emergency (spring) brake system was tested for effectiveness.

Prior to each series of tests, or as road surface conditions changed, a control test was run using a passenger car to establish the control "drag factor" of the test surface. The specific test number and description was communicated to all persons responsible for data collection. The runway was checked for surface condition; either wet or dry, or for any possible changes that would indicate that a control test or lane washing was required.

The tractor moved to the launch point, and the operator armed the shot marker. If used, the fifth wheel controller would also be reset at this point. Once these steps were performed, the brake pedal was not touched (because the systems were armed) until the actual test. The tractor operator, in radio contact with the radar operator, signaled his start verbally as well as by headlight and horn signal.

A professional truck driving instructor test drove a conventional and cabover bobtail under wet and dry road conditions at speeds of 50 and 80 km/hr. Five traffic accident analysts of the Royal Canadian Mounted Police participated in the lane delineation using cones, radar usage, skid factor control measurement, axle weight measurement and grade measurement. Three engineers from Trantech Engineering, two members from the Insurance Corporation of British Columbia, a civil engineering professor from the University of British Columbia, two faculty members from the British Columbia Justice Institute and four individuals from trucking manufacturing companies contributed to the test event.

Based on the test procedures, the following conclusions were presented:

1. The passenger car used as a control vehicle achieved, on the average, an overall deceleration of 0.65G on wet pavement and 0.78G on dry pavement. The overall deceleration was never below 0.6G.
2. The overall deceleration obtained by the short wheelbase cabover tractor was, on average, 16 percent lower than those achieved by the conventional cab tractor in comparable tests.
3. With 100 percent front brake pressure, the conventional cab tractor achieved an average of 82 percent of the control vehicle deceleration. The cabover engine tractor similarly tested was only able to achieve 62 percent of the control vehicle deceleration.
4. Overall braking deceleration increased substantially, almost doubling, as front brake pressure was increased to its maximum.
5. There was no appreciable difference in stopping distance between 75 percent and 100 percent front brake pressure.
6. The short wheelbase cabover engine tractor experienced greater braking instability, as demonstrated by final yaw angle (and associated lane breach), than the longer wheelbase conventional cab tractor.

7. Wet road conditions increased the vehicle braking instability.
8. Higher speeds markedly increased the vehicle braking instability.
9. Changes in front brake pressure had little effect on the stability of the cabover engine tractor.
10. The conventional tractor demonstrated less instability with front brake pressure settings of 75 percent or greater. The conventional tractor achieved large yaw angles (and associated lane breach) with front brake pressure setting at 50 percent.
11. The cabover engine tractor demonstrated marked instability at higher speeds, and at higher steering axle brake pressures. The planned 80 km/hr speed tests on the wet road were conducted at 65 km/hr because of safety concerns.
12. There is little evidence to support the contention that the use of 100 percent steering axle brakes in wet conditions decreases the stability of bobtail tractors.
13. Bobtail tractors operated without steering axle brakes are a hazard to other roadway traffic, particularly at higher speeds in wet conditions, a finding more implied than proven.
14. In real-world conditions, an operator may be able to maintain control of a tractor by careful steering, minimizing both the yaw angle and associated lane breach. This corrective effort would place additional demands over those otherwise presented to him by the driving task, as he is obliged to correct for vehicle-induced instability. The driver cannot, of course, reduce the stopping distance (McInnis et al., 1986; pp. 16-17).

When all the test results were combined, it became evident that the difference between the 0 to 100 percent front axle brake pressure created an approximate 1:2 stopping distance ratio. Whereas at 80 km/hr at 100 percent brake pressure the stopping distance was 45 meters, at 0 percent brake pressure it increased to 93 meters. A similar ratio was evident for 50 km/hr.

More exacting was the difference in stopping distances under different levels of legal brake adjustment. When the truck was driven at 35 km/hr according to industry standards as a semitrailer combination it had a full-braking stopping distance of 10 meters. If the same truck was operated at MINIMUM British Columbia legal brake limits it had a stopping distance of about 50 meters, five times that of a well-kept truck.

References

Cunagin, W. 1986. "Observational Study of Southwest U.S. Heavy Truck Safety Components." Letter Report, U.S. DOT NHTSA Contract Number DTNH 22-85-D-37259.

Hargadine, E.O., and Klein, T. 1984. "Brake Performance Levels of Trucks." Report, U.S. DOT/FHWA/BMCS Contract Number DTFH 61-83-C-00082.

Kirkpatrick, P. 1986. "Observational Study of East Coast U.S. Heavy Truck Safety Components." Letter Report, U.S. DOT NHTSA Contract Number DTNH 22-84-D-67080, February.

McInnis, D.; Bigg, G.; and Moebes, T. 1986. "Highway Tractor Steering Axle Braking and Stability Performance Tests." An ICBC Project Number 60505MT, September.

Navin, F.D. 1986. "Truck Braking Distance and Speed Estimates." Canadian Journal of Civil Engineering, Vol. 13, No. 4, pp. 412-422.

Radlinski, R., and Flick, M.A. 1986. "A Demonstration of the Safety Benefits of Front Brakes on Heavy Trucks." Report, U.S. DOT Number HS 807061, December.

Smith, R. 1986. "Observational Study of West Coast U.S. Heavy Truck Safety Components." Letter Report, U.S. DOT NHTSA Contract Number DTNH 22-84-D-57080, April.

Transport Canada. 1986. Demonstration of Heavy Duty Vehicle Braking on Ice and Snow Covered Surfaces. Unpublished Technical Memoranda, Standards and Regulations Division, March 15.

13

THIRTY HOURS ON THE ROAD,
NO BIG DEAL

Time and speed, when paired, are a theme, a litany in the lives of owner operators running between Vancouver, British Columbia and Edmonton, Alberta. The distance between Vancouver and Edmonton is about one thousand, three hundred kilometers (eight hundred miles), and from Vancouver to Calgary it is about one thousand and forty kilometers (six hundred and fifty miles). To the trucker the distance is like a see-touch or imagine-do range. One trip, right through, carrying produce or meat products for the market! The project is not especially courageous or creative, rather it is usual or typical. To make the dollars, truckers hauling produce or meat from Vancouver to Edmonton accept the job as a sixteen hour trip with little if any scheduled sleep time. Randy was one of those truckers whose body chemistry and economic thinking were set on maximum driving hours, and not on the legal limit of thirteen hours consecutive driving time.

Randy was a twenty-eight year old owner operator on contract to a freight carrier that runs a fleet of reefers within British Columbia, across the Canadian Prairies and to some western states in the United States. He has been with L Company for four months, pulling himself out of a financial hole created by his last experience, driving for a friend. When he quit driving for his friend, he owed twelve thousand dollars in fuel bills, four thousand dollars on his Visa card and two months rent. Witness Randy's remark:

> Yeah, we were hauling for people and they were slow paying. The stuff we were doing didn't pay that good to begin with and it just snowballed. The money kept coming in slower and slower and slower and I kept getting further and further behind. It was ugly. And then I was driving an old truck, I had a couple of breakdowns and the next thing you know I was really behind. It was a bad year.

Now Randy was collecting regular checks based on an eighty to twenty percent split. He pockets eighty percent of the freight cost while the company receives the remainder.

Over the last three months Randy's gross revenue was "about sixteen thousand dollars a month." His payments for his new Peterbilt tractor are two thousand, four hundred dollars a month and for his trailer they are a thousand dollars a month. Also, once he subtracts insurance, fuel, depreciation, wear and tear, and "fifteen million other things" from the gross, Randy's take home income shrinks considerably.

Because of his high payments, Randy hates to take time off his job. Missing trip from Vancouver to Edmonton return can cost him upwards to four thousand dollars. The loss is heavy for a trucker with a child and expectant wife. The extent to which Randy and his wife are prepared to go to keep downtime at a minimum can be illustrated by his wife's pregnancy. Rather than wait for the due date, Randy and his wife decided on a Cesarean scheduled for a specific date. This way, he minimizes his hospital time and he controls his time-off days.

It was three thirty, Wednesday afternoon, mid-August. I sat around L Company chatting with the manager and dispatcher. Fifteen minutes later Sonny, the dispatcher, introduced me to Randy. While several items were still loaded on the truck, Randy and I walked to a corner coffee shop and had a cup of coffee. His cargo was a mixture of mangos, red and yellow peppers, tomatoes, lettuce and, still being loaded, processed meats and sausages, the latter of which had to arrive in Edmonton by ten Thursday morning. The dispatcher based the company's reputation on being able to deliver on time.

Randy's Work Schedule

Randy's work day began at ten in the morning with his first pick up in Vancouver. This early start is standard whenever he makes an LTL (Less Than Load) trip to Edmonton or Calgary. The time now was about quarter to four. Randy has already put in nearly six hours of driving time, picking up loads at different warehouses throughout British Columbia's Lower Mainland. Once we add the additional hour it took for Randy to drive his truck from his home in Aldergrove to Vancouver, we approach close to seven hours on-duty. To reach Edmonton, Randy's consecutive work time was expected to climb over twenty hours.

Does Randy get tired during these marathon hours? "Yep, what can you do. They want the freight, the pay is good, so away you go." The twenty plus hour days for Randy were routine. To accomplish his tasks, Randy cheats on his log books. According to the trucker, "It sort of makes it more fun. We run two or three all the time in the States." In Canada it is easier. Witness Randy's description:

We run one all year round, all the time. Most of the time I can get away with just the one 'cause up here they don't check it so it doesn't matter what it says. Just as long as it is filled out nice and neat and says more or less that you were here and there, everybody is happy. It will get stricter and in a way I hope it does because I would like to work less. And hopefully everybody says if it does come the rates will come up and nobody will have to work so hard.

Danny's time on the job is a direct reflection on the low rates and expense. If the rates were higher, he would not consider driving over twenty hours a day. He would try and get eight hours sleep every night.

The highway from Vancouver to Edmonton is mountainous and, at times, treacherous through the Fraser Canyon. Randy believed that such terrain is a definite advantage for long haul driving. It forces the driver to stay alert at all times. To make it through the terrain, Randy sometimes rests for one or two hours on the side of the road, after which he goes straight through.

Some truckers take even less time for a rest. A popular maneuver is to "nap" about ten minutes to "shake the cobwebs." The trucker stops at the side of the highway, opens all the windows, lights a cigarette, and holds it by the filter between two fingers. The trucker then places his head on the steering wheel and naps. When the cigarette burns to the end it nips the trucker's fingers. Like an alarm clock, the trucker wakes up, goes outside for a brief walk, has a cup of coffee, if available, and drives off. The next stop, most likely, is his destination point.

Through our easygoing discussion Randy provided me with a few guideposts for the oncoming trip. Few stops! Average speed of a hundred km/hr (sixty-five mph)! No sleep or, if any, one to two hours! Supper around midnight! As I stored my backpack in the luggage compartment, I knew it would be difficult for me to stay awake for the entire trip. Yet, I assumed Randy would be able to successfully do it.

Precautions Against the Police

A few minutes after our departure, we entered the Surrey weigh scales for a routine weigh-in. When we left the government facility Randy switched on the radar detector. He likes to travel between a hundred and a hundred and ten km/hr (sixty-five to seventy mph) speeds that exceed the legal limit. Randy believed that to arrive in Edmonton on time, high speeds are necessary. For the last two years Randy had used the radar detector to warn him if the police are using radar speed checks. The gadget has paid off. On nearly every trip Randy had been tipped off on police activity around Princeton and Lytton, British Columbia.

Having switched off the radar detector during our fuel stop in Chilliwack, Randy once again turned it on near the town of Hope. Although Randy routinely drives in different provinces and states, he was unaware of the radar detector legal status in the different jurisdictions. For example, he did not know that, although they are legal in British Columbia, they are illegal in Alberta. The difference in status did not bother Randy because Alberta's speed limit is one hundred km/hr compared to British Columbia's ninety km/hr limit. Randy suggested that he seldom exceeds the hundred km/hr speed and if so, the speed is not high enough to warrant a speeding ticket.

Around Spuzzum we became the third truck in a convoy of ten trucks. It was not a conscious strategy orchestrated by truckers. It was a routine event, truckers leaving Vancouver, intending to hit the Prairie Provinces in the morning. Ahead of us was the Fraser Canyon, a winding highway riddled with dangerous turns and curves. One wrong move could spell disaster.

We were winding our way around Boston Bar with daylight slowly leaving us. To the left was a gravel parking lot which reminded Randy of an interesting experience that happened here with a dispatcher five years ago. The company for which he was hauling was judged by Randy to have been an unsafe one. As Randy said, "Like they stressed safety, but if it cost any money, there was no safety."

Randy, along with another trucker, was told to haul two truck loads of acid north to Quesnel. At eleven p.m. his buddy's tank sprung a leak. Randy drove on to quickly find a mechanic who could repair the leak immediately. A garage owner came with "some bolts and stuff" and tried to repair the hole. According to Randy, the men "got muriatic acid all over, breathing fumes."

Randy's partner telephoned the dispatcher and told him that the tank can't go on. The load has to be transferred to another tanker. The dispatcher replied, "Oh no, just go with it. It's dark and you'll be there before daylight . . . Whatever you do, don't call the environmental people because they'll be really upset."

Randy and his partner decided to call the police and Department of Environment. The parking lot was beginning to look "awfully messy." The outcome of the scary episode was that the company had to pay for removing the parking lot gravel. Randy and his colleague had their hours cut in half by the dispatcher. Randy wrapped up the story, "That's the thanks we got for our efforts."

As Randy finished speaking, the radar detector began to beep and the first of a series of five red lights began to flash. The trucker's immediate reaction was to glance at the speedometer and determine the speed. It was a hundred and five km/hr (sixty-six mph). Randy stepped on the brake to slow down. The beeping continued. Then two lights lit up. Several seconds later all was quiet. What happened? Randy suspected that the policeman was sitting in the cafe parking lot we just passed. For Randy, it could not have been otherwise:

> He had to be there at the cafe having supper or something at the truck stop. If the signal is going across your path it won't light up until you are right on it. If he is coming towards you, it will light right up before he is right on you. They do what they are supposed to do.

Like a suspense thriller, the detector again beeped and lit up. Randy found the answer. Rather than the police waiting somewhere in hiding or on the side of the highway, this RCMP officer was probably following the truck, aiming his radar gun at oncoming traffic. Randy's detector picked up the intermittent beam. According to the trucker, the police turn off the radar until somebody is close to them. They then turn it on. By doing it this way, the police try to thwart radar detectors.

Randy bought his detector on the black market for a hundred dollars. It is a Fox model, typically selling for upwards of five hundred dollars new. It was considered to be a good one, proof of which was that it picked up a signal behind the truck through a forty-six foot trailer.

The police action produced excitement on Randy's CB. Truckers were warning each other of the police cruiser behind Randy's trailer. It was not a "Smoky" or a "Bear" as police officers are colloquially called in the United States. For Randy, it was a "cop." It appeared to me that it mattered little whether the police are called "bears" or "cops" and whether they operated in the United States or Canada, they like to play games with truckers.

Randy told me of a situation that happened to his trucking buddy. "He was wasting down the road, just giving her." On the way he saw a policeman giving a driver a ticket. As I described in Chapter Three, when truckers witness police activity they are expected to warn other truckers. Randy's friend warned oncoming drivers to slow down because "there was a cop working." After several miles a user hit the CB and told Randy's friend "No, no, that cop isn't busy now, better tell everybody to take it easy." His buddy answered, "No, no, he was busy. I seen him there, he was out of his car and writing that guy up." After a little more chatter, Randy's friend finally said, "Look, you're full of shit, he's writing that guy a ticket." The guy then said, "As a matter of fact, I'm right here." So the cop pulled out into the centre lane and turned on all of his lights. Although his buddy was travelling seventy mph, the cop never pulled him over. Instead, they drove down the road a ways and talked.

All the way from Vancouver to Edmonton, to Calgary, and then back to Vancouver, Randy had his radar detector activated. For the entire trip the gadget signaled police radar activity three times. Of the three times, Randy was speeding twice.

Dusk fully enveloped us. It was now quarter to eight. We were twenty-two kilometers (fourteen miles) from Spences Bridge, a small town twenty-nine kilometers from Cache Creek. We were driving through the Fraser Canyon. To the right were rolling hills almost like small mountains. Hundreds of feet below us was the raging Fraser River winding alongside the highway. The sides of the mountains were made up of sand and rock with little vegetation, a burnt color of brown with some mixture of green. The highway was treacherous with incredibly steep inclines, and equally steep downhill runs. There were many passing opportunities and some very tight corners where – as was pointed out by Randy – a number of serious accidents happened. Alongside the road I saw ample yellow grass and small areas of low lying shrubs and trees. Few clouds were in the sky. It seemed like every tree was an individual sitting up on the mountainside to be counted, to be noticed. We drove on at a steady pace discussing where we should eat. Randy wanted to drive as far as possible in daylight. Since I was the passenger-researcher, anything Randy intended was fine with me. I did not wish to influence Randy's driving decisions.

Randy's View on Speed

Randy recognized that speed was a major cause of accidents, but he was not prepared to sacrifice his speeding behavior regardless of its danger. Economics was the determining factor. In fact, while we were driving, Randy was travelling a hundred km/hr, which was ten km/hr over the posted speed limit.

Just ahead of us a flatdeck truck crept along at about ten km/hr, signaled left, then turned onto a gravel road off the major artery. Randy gave him a blast of his air horn – a disciplinary measure used by truckers. Randy thought that on a straightaway with wide shoulders the trucker should have stopped on the shoulder, waited till the traffic was clear, then turned.

It was eight-thirty p.m. when we approached Cache Creek. The skies were nearly dark as town-related traffic and business signs were starting to greet us. Breakfast for $1.99 at the 88 Restaurant. Further up the valley was the lit up town. We drove part way through town, then turned onto Highway 97 destined for Kamloops, eighty-four kilometers away.

When we were eight kilometers (five miles) out of Cache Creek, Randy looked over and remarked that whenever he drives along this stretch of the road he gets a "weird feeling." It had to do with speeding, the topic we discussed fifteen minutes earlier. The reason for his strange feeling was that a few days ago around a corner was an oncoming truck halfway in his lane, because, according to Randy, the trucker was pulling one of the longer trailers. He lost control. Both Randy and the other trucker managed to come to a complete stop. Fortunately, neither one was speeding. They had time to take preventive measures.

According to Randy, speed is to blame for most accidents. As he said, "Everybody is in such a hurry. Cars get impatient following big trucks. Big trucks get impatient following the cars." Truckers also compete with themselves at one time "taking a corner at fifty mph," then at sixty. Finally "you get the odd guys that say, geez, I can make it at eighty. Lumber everywhere."

In a Peterbilt with a CAT 425 engine, Randy had the truck cruising along at a hundred and twenty km/hr (seventy-five mph). He was apologetic that he was not driving faster explaining to me that the truck "is not geared as fast" as many other trucks. Whenever he can, he tries to stay within eight km/hr (five mph) of the posted speed limit. Randy knew a police officer who once told him that officers allow between "five and seven kilometer error for the gun (radar)." To drive twenty-two thousand kilometers (fourteen thousand miles) a month and make it pay, Randy felt that it was necessary to stretch the speed limit and take advantage of the police tolerance. Whenever he runs a little late, he drives a little faster.

On the way from Cache Creek to Kamloops we kept a steady pace of a hundred km/hr (sixty-two mph) pace in a ninety km/hr speed zone. At times Randy crawled up to a hundred and ten km/hr (sixty-seven mph) because we were in the "middle of nowhere." By "speeding a bit," Randy said, he "wasn't hurting anything." There was nobody around.

Fatigue: First Discussion

In the dark with a partially clouded moon shining, the trees reminded me of a picture composed of painted ghosts against a hazy countryside. Randy was fully concentrating on the road. I broke the silence, ready to catch his thoughts on fatigue. For him the first signs of fatigue are burning eyes and the tendency to forget where he is. He has a difficult time staying awake, wanting badly to go to bed. Whenever these sensations hit him and Randy has a deadline he will stop at the nearest coffee shop and have a cup of coffee. If he has time, he looks for somewhere to stop. A one hour nap is sufficient for Randy to get the edge off fatigue.

Agar (1986:119) described the following signs of fatigue that were echoed by Randy and other tuckers I met:

Subtle signs of fatigue first appear, such as variations in motor rpm's, indicating a decline in attention to pressure on the foot pedal; or slight drifting of the vehicle within its lane, signaling lapses in monitoring the tractor; or the body movements that accompany the two indicators mentioned above, such as rubbing the head and face with the hand.

Randy always tries to have complete control over his actions, trying to keep his reaction time to nearly zero. To make sure he is always ahead of early fatigue signs he scans the roadway, waves to other truckers, uses the CB, focuses on steering and shifting, and repeatedly checks the mirrors. Randy's rule is that by increasing his activities while driving, he counters fatigue.

The time approached nine fifteen. While oncoming vehicle lights kept hitting us, I asked Randy whether glare constitutes a problem for truckers. Randy's response was that glare "plays you out a bit. It tires your eyes." I learned that glare is a major reason Randy prefers to drive around midnight. He likes night driving because there are fewer vehicles on the road resulting in less headlight glare.

While Randy spoke about driving in the dark, he enjoyed a ten second luxuriant stretch. He took both hands off the steering wheel, clenched his fists, strained his elbows towards his back and rotated his neck. For a few seconds the truck steered itself. According to Randy, he stretched to relieve a stiffening body and not to counter or hold off fatigue. Although he has worked for eleven hours, he felt in good shape.

At half past ten we reached the weigh scales located a few kilometers before Kamloops. For Randy it brought back memories of a time when he tried to beat the scale while he was overloaded and tired. He stopped two kilometers before the scales and slept until two a.m., the time when these scales are often closed. Without bothering to radio other truckers about the scales' status, Randy drove towards them fully believing that the government facilities were closed for the night. To his surprise, the scales were open and he was caught.

Randy's oversight cost him three hundred dollars in fines. He knew he was responsible and had to pay. When we drove through the scales on this trip, Randy did not bother stopping. He rolled across them. The attendant looked up sleepily and waved Randy along. Randy's hunch that the operator was half asleep and would not bother asking him to stop or back up proved to be correct.

Ten minutes later we arrived at the Kamloops truck stop for dinner. Greasy french fries seemed to be on everybody's plate. The salad bar was already dismantled, giving us little choice but french fries and hamburger or deep fried fish.

While waiting for our food I looked outside and saw more trucks than were drivers in the restaurant. According to Randy, there are probably truckers sleeping already. I wondered why drivers would sleep in Kamloops when Vancouver, as a destination point is only about two hundred and fifty miles away.

Randy explained it this way:

A lot of the guys there are from further east in Alberta and it's 11:00 o'clock now. If their home is Manitoba it is 1:00 o'clock to them right now. They are probably out of hours, you know, tired. So if they go to bed now and get up at 5:00 in the morning and be in Vancouver at 8:00 or 9:00 o'clock and not be late.

Truckers typically stop for sleeps according to a strategy based on fatigue, available driving hours and distance from the destination. However, if they drive reefers (refrigeration units on trailers) that must be turned on at all times, the truckers receive little sleep. According to Randy, he spends more time awake than sleeping when he lays in his bunk with the reefer running.

We pulled out of Kamloops at quarter past eleven p.m. As we gathered speed I was becoming sleepy, having been awake and active since six a.m. I put my head against the window, trying to catch a few winks. At the same time I did not want to miss important data while sleeping. So I kept talking.

Midnight Driving

A few miles out of Kamloops brought us to the Yellowhead Highway. Around Heffley Creek, twenty-nine kilometers (eighteen miles) from Kamloops, the highway began to narrow, with rough surface, broken-pavement shoulders and numerous tight curves. Despite the conditions, we were clipping along at a hundred km/hr (sixty-two mph).

When the highway began to widen and the pavement smoothed out, Randy passed a black truck that was "holding us up." Our running speed fluctuated between a hundred to a hundred and ten km/hr (sixty-two to sixty-eight mph). Randy was fulfilling his pretrip plans to average a hundred km/hr all the way.

Before us shone a half moon that seemed to move with the changing direction of the highway. Hugging the moon were several small clouds. A roadway sign read, Barriere fourteen km, Jasper, four hundred km.

This leg of the journey was very calm. There was no traffic and the night was clear but for a few clouds lazing around the moon. As we hummed along I asked Randy about L Freight Lines.

When he applied to haul for this broker company, Randy was never asked about his driving history or credentials. The interviewers were only

interested in his equipment and in telling Randy, "what the job is all about
. . . (and) how the company is run." Randy said:

> They just gave me a trailer and a load and that was it. He explained how to
> do the bills and stuff. You know, all that is basic. Once you have learned to
> do it at one place it is just slightly different variations of the same thing.

Randy summarized that L Freight Lines made it easy for him to get
on. They were not especially concerned about safety, only expecting him
to do his best.

The half moon began to hide behind a mass of clouds that now appeared.
You could only see tinges of light peeking out. Finally, the moon was
covered entirely by one large cloud as we passed Barriere and headed
towards Little Fort, about thirty km (nineteen miles) away. An oncoming
furniture truck approached us with a single headlight, traveling at a pretty
fast clip.

I was becoming increasingly drowsy. Randy removed his jean shirt,
continuing to drive in a t-shirt. While he claimed to be getting hot, I began
to get chilly. My eyelids became heavy. My eyes slowly shut as I dozed off.
I forced them to open again, trying to stay awake. Each time I began to
fade I caught myself, only to doze off again a few minutes later.

To shake off the oncoming fatigue I asked Randy about his opinions
of owner operators and company drivers. According to the trucker, the
major difference is attitude. Owner operators take more pride in their job
and truck. Randy reconfirmed Dale's views in Chapter Four that the image
of owner operators depended on the pride they take in the looks of their
trucks. Randy told me that in his opinion owner operators are more
professional. He explained his assessment this way:

> Most company drivers really don't give a shit. You know, they carry their quarter
> for a phone call when they run into trouble and that is it. No commitment to
> the job in a lot of cases, more so than the independents. That is the one thing
> that really bugs me about the industry is the whining.

Are the owner operators safer drivers than company drivers? Randy
answered:

> I wouldn't say they were any less safer. They might take more chances because
> they seem to rush more. I would say I would rather drive a truck an independent
> owned than a company truck.

As an owner operator, Randy knows every part of his truck. He has
set the brakes himself and, therefore, trusts what the vehicle can do in an

emergency. He is aware of the power the truck has and he can immediately tell by the sound of the motor if a mechanical problem is starting. Company drivers, according to Randy, do not appreciate subtle changes in a truck's performance. Because the vehicle is owned by someone else, they don't appreciate the unique character or personality of the truck.

At one a.m. I could not fight the sleep anymore. Randy offered me his bunk and pillow, which I gratefully accepted. Although I was tired, Randy appeared cool, not showing any obvious signs of fatigue. The truck drove steady. There was little evidence of oversteering. Randy scanned the mirror, the conversation was precise, and his eyes did not appear as heavy as mine. Randy reasoned that the difference between he and I was conditioning. He has trained himself to stay awake. On the average, he drives twenty plus consecutive hours at least twice a week. He is used to it.

I woke up as we drove through Valemount at quarter to three. We were a hundred and thirty kilometers (eighty-two miles) from Jasper National Park. From Jasper, it was a straight three hundred and twenty kilometers (two hundred miles) to Edmonton. This part of the trip scares Randy a little because of the straight highway and boring landscape invites boredom. Nevertheless, up to this point of the trip Randy assessed, "I feel fine, no problems."

We arrived at the Tete Jaune Junction weigh scales at quarter past three. The facility was built at a tricky location because trucks going east and west had to be weighed at this station – located for eastbound traffic. Since there was no overpass for westbound trucks, operators have to drive across a hundred km/hr traffic flow to visit the scales.

The weigh-in was routine. As we pulled out of the weigh scales and started to speed up I noticed that Randy began to hug the center line. Also I observed that Randy often changed his hand placement on the steering wheel. Earlier he had his hands placed consistently at the nine and three o'clock positions. Now he alternated, sometimes steering with one hand, then with two hands, at various positions. At three thirty a.m. we entered Robson National Park.

From National Parks to Edmonton

Alberta and British Columbia's mountain national parks contain ample varieties of flora and fauna. For the tourist to see wildlife on the side of the road is an environmental treat. For the truck driver, animals on the side of the road can mean danger, especially at night. Particularily dangerous are the elk who at first light wander on the highway. Further north, the moose create a problem walking on the sides of the road. When the trucker hits the horn the moose get spooked, scatter to the side of the road. They then run back on the highway, directly in front of the truck.

A trucker who hits a moose can suffer significant damage. However, more serious is a truck colliding with a bear. Upon impact, the bear gets under the axle jamming the steering. When this happens, the truck is out of control with a bear lodged solidly under the vehicle. Truckers may be forced to drive and drag the bear for an hour before he becomes dislodged.

Hitting a deer can cause a trucker to lose his radiator. Randy told me about the time he hit a deer:

> The deer must have slipped just as I hit it. I hit it right where the bumper bolts to the frame, right into the absolute strongest point on the bumper. I just sent it spinning off the road. I got out of my truck and all you could see was where it polished my bumper a little bit and that was it, no damage. A little bit of fur.

Randy followed the deer down the hill, but eventually gave up because the animal was probably a "mile away." Even if Randy had caught up to the deer, there was little he could do. The driver grimaced, telling me, "I don't have the jam to hit him over the head until he's dead."

Randy's working rule is that he will not "wipe out (his) truck to avoid an animal." For the trucker, it is considered better to hit an animal and have proof of the accident than it is to avoid the collision and thereby drive off the road. If the latter happened, the police tend to blame the driver for falling asleep. To the police no skid marks, no witnesses, just a plain trail off the road means a fatigued driver. According to Randy:

> I would just close my eyes and hit the animal. If you are going to wreck your truck, you my as well hit him and have your proof. Blood all over the place.

It was a chilling argument. I could tell that Randy was sympathetic to the animals, but, in a worst case scenario the animal dies, often a brutal death. Although Randy loves animals, in a close highway encounter the animal will fall.

While we drove through the national parks, Randy became more attentive to the road, driving close to the center line. This strategy is designed to give him the option of going around animals standing at the side of the road. He held the steering wheel more loosely to provide himself greater flexibility and maneuverability.

Nearing the Destination

Our first stop since Kamloops, six hours ago, was in Hinton. We ordered coffees to go. Randy did not want to waste time sitting around. Instead we hit the washroom, paid for the coffee and hit the road.

Daylight was now upon us. This was a time when Randy normally catches his second wind. His adjustment to the new conditions usually keeps him alert until he reaches his destination. Still Randy expected fatigue to catch up to him later in the afternoon.

As I stated previously, the last leg of the trip, from Hinton to Edmonton, was considered by Randy to be the most boring. It was on this part of the journey that he felt vulnerable. According to Randy, when you have a straight highway and scenery composed of bush, you lose your driving edge. Trucking becomes monotonous. To counteract the monotony, Randy likes to greet every trucker he meets. This strategy became especially visible when we passed Alberta Beach, and the highway widened to four lanes. Because the center of the road was served by a wide divider of greenery, I could hardly make out the drivers coming in the opposite direction. Still, Randy waved! It helped keep him sharp.

From Hinton we passed through Edson and stopped for a phone call in Entwistle. The time was seven thirty a.m., and Randy had not yet assessed himself as being tired. But he was bored! And, seriously speaking, so was I!

We stopped at Entwistle for five minutes so that Randy could call his dispatcher in Calgary. He was informed that he could stay in Edmonton overnight and that he did not have worry about a return trip until Saturday. Randy was pleased with the news because he could visit relatives and perhaps do a little shopping at the West Edmonton Mall. We left the town at eight a.m.

The highway was almost clear of all Edmonton-bound traffic. For one stretch we traveled for fifteen minutes without meeting another vehicle going in our direction. Once in Edmonton we headed for the south side. The time was nine a.m. Mountain Standard Time.

I jumped off the truck at the Convention Inn, bade Randy farewell and wished him well. I later discovered that Randy worked until two thirty p.m. Edmonton time, delivering products. He then showered, enjoyed a two hour nap, had dinner with friends, and drank a few beer. The next morning, at seven a.m., Randy received a call from the dispatcher. He was asked to drive again. So he traveled around Edmonton loading up, preparing for the haul back to Vancouver.

For the Vancouver to Edmonton trip Randy logged the following hours without sleep:

1. From home to Vancouver area   –   8:30 a.m.–10:00 a.m.   =   1.5 hrs.
2. Vancouver area loading   – 10:00 a.m.– 4:00 p.m.   =   6.0 hrs.
3. Vancouver to Edmonton trip   –   4:00 p.m.– 8:00 a.m.   = 16.0 hrs.
4. Edmonton area unloading   –   8:00 a.m.– 1:30 p.m.   =   5.5 hrs.
5. Return to truck stop   –   1:30 p.m.– 2:30 p.m.   =   1.0 hr.

Total hours   30.0 hrs.

Our only break was a one hour stop in Kamloops.[4] In the log book, dated August 23rd, Randy marked that he began driving at four p.m. He did not include the time from ten in the morning to three in the afternoon that it took him to drive around Vancouver loading his trailer. We arrived in Edmonton at ten a.m. August 24th. Randy logged the time as seven a.m. Whereas his real time driving was thirty consecutive hours, his logged time was fourteen hours. Are log books considered to be comic books? Perhaps!

Notes to Chapter 13

1. Fatigue is an important theme in psychology. A review of the literature brings forth the problem of definition. Psychologists disagree on the meaning of fatigue as a singular concept and on methodologies required for accurate measurement. Does fatigue result from hours of work or hours on duty? Can fatigue effects occur irrespective of the amount of work accomplished (Holding, 1983)? Can fatigue be isolated? Is fatigue related to boredom, monotony, exhaustion, biorhythm, and motivation (Hulin and Blood, 1968; McBain, 1970; Thackery, 1981; Tilley and Andrew, 1988)?

Tsaneva and Markov (1971) reduced the definition of fatigue to the accumulation of lactic acid in the muscles. Fatigue is determined by the production of metabolite which raises the synoptic threshold between a nerve and the organ it controls. Scott already dispelled the lactic acid definition in 1970 when his research showed that a symptom of fatigue is not relaxed muscles but overactive muscles.

Bartley and Chute (1947) developed a definition of fatigue which in some psychological circles is still predominant, although empirically difficult to prove. Fatigue is a process, a form of conflict between the demands of the task situation and the person's aversion to effort. Yet Chiles (1955), among others, found that fatigue cannot be measured by output because fatigued people may still have the will to complete central tasks successfully, and most of the time people do so.

In 1914, Ash experimented on physical decrement/ability and fatigue by selecting a group of random subjects and having them press a finger ergograph. After numerous applications over an extended period of time he found a decrement in the contractions. However, when the subjects were made to believe that the weight on the finger had been reduced, the subjects began contractions again which were impossible before. Ash concluded that the psychological aspect was more important than the physical.

Caldwell and Lyddan (1971) had trainees pull repeatedly on a dynamometer handle during trials separated by brief rest periods. The authors concluded that the longer the rest period the greater was the recovery. However, subjects who were told of the oncoming hundred second rest periods performed better, even on first trial, than the subjects who were scheduled for 25 second rest pauses. Like Ash (1914), the researchers concluded that central factors like expectancy influence the performance exhibited.

Caldwell and Lyddan (1971) rejected a strictly mechanistic interpretation of fatigue data. They stressed the importance of motivation, instructional set and pain tolerance. The first limit encountered during physical exertion over an extended period of time is more often psychological than physiological. Equally important is the distinction between fatigue and exhaustion, which has not yet been properly addressed.

A second type of fatigue is perceptual fatigue outlined by Volle et al as declines in alertness not sensitivity. Results are steady fixations, which fatigue a part of the retina and enhance sensitivity in adjacent areas, desaturation of objects, frequency of flicker fusion, irregular pupillary contractions and increased rate of blinking are observable decrements. They are "short term effects" based on experiments in which other components may predominate. For example, flicker fusion reflects an arousal component provoked by the task and a depression component resulting from fatigue on the task.

Cameron (1973) conceived of fatigue as a generalized response to stress over a period of time. Holding (1983) pointed out that noise is a primary stress factor causing certain responses, regardless of fatigue.

Welford (1965) proposed a definition of fatigue that still finds favor with modern psychologists. It is a state of being that results from the chronic overloading of the sensory, central response mechanisms involved in task performance. Yet concerning task performance over time, we cannot overlook confounding variables such as boredom and monotony. Hulin and Blood (1968) explained that the perception of the sameness of the job from minute to minute, perception of the unchanging characteristic of the job may bring about physical and/or mental decrements.

McBain (1970) selected twenty line drivers to perform a highly repetitive 42 minute paced task in a laboratory, and to complete questionnaires on boredom susceptibility. The researcher concluded that boredom, or repetition over a period of time, was the greatest predictor of highway crashes (Davies et al., 1983). McBain believed that experienced drivers were not as susceptible to boredom because they had the ability to engage in behaviors that made their driving tasks more varied. He wrote:

> . . . Drivers spotlighted deer by the side of the road with practised accuracy, signalled to other drivers, observed and commented on the idiosyncracies of other drivers, pointed out changes in road and other construction projects visible since they had last been seen and in these and many other ways kept themselves almost constantly occupied. (1970; pp. 517-518)

The question becomes, is it exposure to a monotonous environment that exerts adverse effects on task performance or is it fatigue? or Is it both? If it is the latter, how can we proportion each in terms of causality? Smith's (1981) review of the literature concluded that boredom, regardless of fatigue, is a complex response pattern consisting of a variety of changes that have not yet been properly analyzed.

Arousal theories on fatigue were judged by Parasuraman and Davies (1977) to be too general to yield detailed prediction in vigilance tasks – visual and auditory. They argued that tasks showing declines in sensitivity are those that present a high even rate, with stimuli occurring every two or three seconds and which demand an ability to make rapid perceptual comparisons involving memory.

2. Several important experiments have been engaged to measure tasks fatigue. One of the most important was the post World War II study entitled the Cambridge Cockpit Studies (Bartlett, 1943). Random air force subjects sat for a long time in a cockpit responding to aircraft controls and changes in a variety of instruments.

Bartlett discovered that as alertness decreased over time, progressively larger deviations of the instrument readings came to be tolerated before any corrective action was taken. This resulted from a shift in standards of performance because operators felt they were as efficient as at the outset. As operators became more tired their lapses in attention increased. They became more easily distracted. They tended to reserve their attention for items of central importance such as course heading and speed, and neglect peripheral items such as fuel gauges. Operators tended to take correct actions but execute them at wrong times. Their skill, although still evident, lost cohesion.

Bartlett's benchmark study poignantly illustrated Holding's (1983) theme that subjects often transfer fatigue to subsequent or peripheral tasks where effects are either not expected, or if they are, they are difficult to observe.

Chiles' studied this theme with a group of subjects who performed continuously in an aircraft simulator without rest for 56 hours. The only relief for operators was periodic testing and tracking. Chiles concluded that although the operators were so tired that they had to be carried to the testing apparatus, once there, no decrement in mental or motor tests was observed. Similar findings were reported by Warren and Clark (1937), and Hammerston and Tickner (1968). Some further description on sleep and fatigue research, outstanding in its description of central and peripheral task abilities, appeared in **Psychology Today:**

> We don't find that the capacity for things like math or playing chess suffers. What's lost is willingness; you would prefer to be asleep. You don't make

errors of commission, but omission. Take an example from the war games
they do in the Israeli army. One of the prime rules of desert warfare is that
you take every opportunity to top off your water supply, whether you're a
tank commander or a soldier with a canteen. Whenever you find water, check
your supply and fill it up. Now, as the war games go on over several days
and the soldiers miss out on their sleep, following that rule is one of the
first things to go – not the ability to shoot or command well.

Take another case – from war games in England. Up north it's cold, and
a soldier is supposed to change to dry socks if his feet get wet. Otherwise
your feet are going to go out on you, get frostbitten. But as the games go
on, they forget, they just don't bother. They can still hit a target as well as
ever. It's the low-level, boring routines they skip. You see the same thing with
nurses working the night shift: They give all the correct drugs, but they skip
walking down the hall to check on a patient.

Low-demand, self-motivated tasks fail. There's a lovely old prayer in the
Episcopal Church: "Dear Lord, preserve me, keep me from leaving undone
those things that I ought to have done." And that's what goes first: You leave
undone those things you ought to have done. If you've got enough inner
motivation and drive, you can go that last mile. If not, when you're so sleepy,
you just give up. It's not your thinking or memory that goes – it's your will
to go on. (Goleman, 1982; pg. 27)

In 1972, Duseman and Boden engaged subjects in a simulated car driving
experience. They established that during four hours of simulated driving
there were changes in the subjective ratings of fatigue accompanied by
changes in performance measures such as steering errors and brake
reactions and in physiological measures including pulse-rate and skin
resistance. The difficulty with Duseman and Boden's study is that people
can feel tired but work efficiently, or they can suffer impairment without
recognizing fatigue. In addition, the power of suggestion and motivation
of people being involved in an experiment create further confounding
influences.

3. Nevertheless some post-fatigue effects were noted by researchers. Shinar
   (1978) and Hulbert (1972) provided reviews of research on the effects
   of fatigue on driving performance. Shinar's review expressed that fatigue
   decreases eye movements employed in information acquisition and results
   in poorer road-sign perception and decreased ability to maintain an
   appropriate lane position. Hulbert, describing research on sleep
   deprivation, fatigue and driving performance, noted that after 24 hours
   without sleep, drivers in his study began to doze off within one hour
   of beginning to drive. Immediately preceding the onset of sleep (while
   driving), Hulbert found that these drivers exhibited evidence of
   dangerous decreases in driving performance that included: longer
   duration, delayed decelerations to changing road conditions; fewer
   steering corrections; reduced galvanic skin response (GSR) to emerging
   traffic events; and more non-driving body movements such as face

rubbing, eye closing and stretching. Furthermore, Lisper Laurell and van Loon (1986) established that reaction time measures taken from their subjects while driving could be employed to predict the time subjects use to fall asleep during subsequent driving endurance experiments. The detection of drowsy drivers on the highway was discussed by Skipper and Wierwille (1986) and the effects of fatigue on commercial driver performance, brought on through shift duration and sequence, was discussed by Pokorny, Blom, van Leeuwen and van Hooten (1987).

4. At a public meeting held by the United States Department of Transport (November 29-30, 1988) invited speakers from Europe and North America reviewed the latest research on fatigue and truck driving. Two issues arose. First, it was nearly impossible to obtain "hard data" that measure fatigue and trucking. Second, the concept of fatigue is difficult to define. A proper measurement of driver fatigue should include off-duty-hours physical and mental exertion that affects on-duty drivers as well as simply dozing at the wheel and inattention due to "microsleep" (Beilock, 1988). Fatigue effects must be considered in terms of the total exposure of the individual (Crawford, 1961). If this is not done, the researcher is not likely to distinguish between fatigue which resulted from prior exposure to fatiguing conditions other than driving.

Wyckoff (1979) reported that truckers responding to questions on fatigue or hours on duty tend to focus on the ten hour mark for on-duty time. The focus, however, does not necessarily reflect accuracy, rather it may suggest that drivers accommodate a ten hour limitation benchmark. Having accommodated a ten hour regulation for some time, drivers could easily have made it their lense on viewing hours of driving and fatigue.

A relevant example of Wyckoff's critical reminder occurred in Beilock's (1988) report for the American Regular Common Carrier Conference. After analyzing 878 interviews, Beilock reported that the average trucker claims that he/she "normally can drive 10.6 hours before requiring sleep." The following appropriate footnote was added:

> However, a half a century of Federal regulations infusing drivers with the ten hour figure may affect the conveniently corroboratory result. (1988; pg. 35)

In a 1987 study by Transport Canada of 1,509 drivers, 85 percent stated that they never had difficulty staying alert while driving a truck, while 15 percent experienced difficulty very seldom or occasionally. The confidence truckers have in their ability is obviously not shared by legislators who, in the United States, have implemented the ten hour rule and who, in Canada, mandated a 15 hour on-the-job restriction.

Although optimism about scientific proof and ten hour-on-duty legislation should be tempered, the mandatory rule has benefits. It operates within the generally accepted eight to ten hour workday covered in Canadian and American labor codes. It sets a standard which, if not overly scientific, is certainly conservatively safe. On the side of liberal and conservative work hours, the American government has taken the conservative side, the side of industrial work hours and safety. In Canada, the rule is more liberal. Fifteen hour workdays were implemented in part to accommodate the geography of Canada which is vast and wide with few urban centers.

References

Agar, M.H. 1986. **Independents Declared**. Washington, DC: Smithsonian Institute Press.

Ash, I.E. 1914. "Fatigue and Its Effects Upon Control." **Archives of Psychology**, 4, pp. 1-61.

Bartlett, F.C. 1943. "Fatigue Following Highly Skilled Work." **Journal of Experimental Psychology**, 25, pp. 109-115.

Bartley, S.H., and Chute, E. 1947. **Fatigue and Impairment In Man**. New York: McGraw Hill.

Beilock, Richard. 1988. **1988 RCCC Motor Carrier Safety Survey**. Alexandria, VA: Regular Common Carrier Conference.

Bensman, J., and Lilienfeld, R. 1973. **Craft and Consciousness: Occupational Technique and the Development of World Images**. New York: John Wiley and Sons.

British Columbia Ministry of Transportation. 1979. **Commercial Transport Act**. Victoria, BC: Quickscribe Services.

Broughton, R. 1975. "Biorhythmic Fluctuations In Consciousness and Psychological Functions." **Canadian Psychological Review**, 16, pp. 217-239.

Browne, R.C. 1953. "Fatigue – Fact or Fiction?" In Floyd, W.F. and Wilford, A.T., **Symposium On Fatigue**. London: H.K. Lewis.

Buchegger, J., and Meier-Koll, A. 1988. "Motor Learning and Ultradian Sleep Cycle: An Electroencephalographic Study of Trampoliners." **Perceptual and Motor Skills**, 67, pp. 635-645.

Bureau of Motor Carrier Safety. 1982. "Accidents of Motor Carriers of Property 1980-1981." Federal Highway Administration, Washington, DC, August 21.

Caldwell, L.S., and Lyddan, M. 1971. "Serial Isometric Fatigue Functions With Variable Intertrial Intervals." **Journal of Motor Behavior**, 3, pp. 17-30.

Cameron, C. 1973. "Fatigue and Driving – A Theoretical Analysis." **Australian Road Research**, Vol. 5, No. 2, pp. 37-44.

Cameron, C. 1973. "A Theory of Fatigue." Occupational Psychology, 35, pp. 44-47.

Carskaden, M.A., and Dement, W.C. 1979. "Effect of Total Sleep Loss on Sleep Tendency." Perceptual and Motor Skills, 48, pp. 495-506.

Chiles, W.D. 1955. Experimental Studies in Prolonged Wakefulness. Dayton, OH: W.A.D.C. Tech. Report No. 55, p. 395.

Coleman, Richard M. 1986. **Wide Awake At 3:00 A.M.** New York: W.H. Freeman and Company.

Crawford, A. 1961. "Fatigue and Driving." **Ergonomics**, 4, pp. 143-154.

Davies, R.; Shaldeton, V.J.; and Parasuraman, R. 1983. "Monotony and Boredom." In Hockey, R. (ed.), **Stress and Fatigue in Human Performance**. New York: John Wiley.

Duseman, E.I., and Boden, C. 1972. "Fatigue in Simulated Car Driving." **Ergonomics**, 15, pp. 299-308.

Folkard, S. 1983. "Diurnal Variation in Human Performance." In Hockey, R. (ed.), **Stress and Fatigue in Human Performance**. New York: John Wiley.

Goleman, D. 1982. "Staying Up." **Pyschology Today**, March.

Hammerston, M., and Tickner, A.H. 1968. "Physical Fitness and Skilled Work After Exercise." **Ergonomics**, 11, pp. 41-45.

Herd, D.R.; Agent, K.R.; and Rizenbergs, R.L. 1980. "Traffic Accidents: Day Versus Night." Kentucky Department of Transportation, **Transportation Research Record 753**, Transportation Research Board, Washington, DC, pp. 25-30.

Hockey, R. (ed.). 1983. **Stress and Fatigue in Human Performance**. New York: John Wiley.

Holding, D. 1983. "Fatigue." In Hockey, R. (ed.), **Stress and Fatigue in Human Performance**. New York: John Wiley.

Hulbert, S. 1972. Effects of Driver Fatigue. In Forbes, T.W. (ed.), **Human Factors in Highway Traffic Safety Research**. New York: Wiley-Interscience.

Hulin, C.L., and Blood, M.R. 1968. "Job Enlargement, Individual Differences, and Worker Responses." **Psychological Bulletin**, 69, pp. 41-55.

Klein, R.H.; Allen, R.W.; and Miller, J.C. 1980. **Relationship Between Truck Ride Quality and Safety of Operations: Methodology Development**. Hawthorne, CA: Systems Technology, Inc. (NTIS: DOT HS 805 494).

Lisper, H.-O.; Laurell, H.; and van Loon, J.C. 1986. Relation between time to falling asleep behind the wheel on a closed track and changes in subsidiary reaction time during prolonged driving on a motorway. **Ergonomics**, Vol. 29(3), pp. 445-453.

McBain, W.N. 1970. "Arousal, Monotony and Accidents in 'Line Driving'." Journal of Applied Psychology, 54, pp. 509-519.

Muscio, B. 1921. "Is a Fatigue Test Possible?" **British Journal of Psychology**, 12, pp. 31-46.

Parasuraman, R., and Davies, D.R. 1977. "A Taxonomic Analysis of Vigilance Performance." In Mackie, R.R. (ed.), **Vigilance: Theory, Operational Performance Physiological Correlates**. New York: Plenum Press.

Pokorny, M.L.I.; Blom, D.H.J.; van Leeuwen, P.; and van Nooten, W.N. 1987. Shift Sequences, Duration of Rest Periods, and Accident Risk of Bus Drivers. **Human Factors**, 29(1), pp. 73-81.

Scott, D. 1970. **The Psychology of Work**. London: Duckworth.

Shinar, D. 1978. **Psychology on the Road**. New York: John Wiley and Sons.

Skipper, J.H., and Wierwille, W.W. 1986. Drowsy Driver Detection Using Discriminant Analysis. **Human Factors**, 28(5), pp. 527-540.

Smith, R.P. 1981. "Boredom: A Review." **Human Factors**, 23, pp. 329-340.

Thackery, R.I. 1981. "The Stress of Boredom and Monotony: A Consideration of the Evidence." **Psychosomatic Medicine**, 43, pp. 165-176.

Thomas, J.H. 1979. **The Long Haul**. Memphis: Memphis State University Press.

Tilley, Andrew, and Dalton, Louise. 1988. "Sleep Cycle Influences On Retrieval From Semantic Memory At Different Times Of Day." **Perceptual and Motor Skills**, 66, pp. 120-122.

Transport Canada. 1987. **Driving Behaviour and Characteristics of Heavy Duty Truck Operators in Canada**. Ottawa: Road Safety.

Tsaneva, M., and Markov, S. 1971. "A Model of Fatigue." **Ergonomics**, 14, pp. 11-16.

Volle, M.A.; Brisson, G.R.; Dion, M.; and Tanaka, M. 1978. Travail, Fatigue et frequence de fusion critique visuelle. **Ergonomics**, 21, pp. 551-558.

Warren, W., and Clark, D. 1937. "Blocking in Mental and Motor Tasks During a 65 Hour Vigil." **Journal of Experimental Psychology**, 21, pp. 97-105.

Webb, W.B., and Agnew, H.W. 1977. "Analysis of Sleep Stages in Sleep Wakefulness Regimes of Varied Length." **Psychophysiology**, 19, pp. 445-450.

Welford, W. 1965. "Fatigue and Monotony." In Edholm, O.G. and Bacharach, A.L. (eds.), **The Physiology of Survival**. London: Academic Press.

Wolkowicz, M.E., and Billing, A.M., 1982. **Commercial Vehicle Accident Survey**. Downsview, ON: Ontario Ministry of Transportation and Communications.

Wyckoff, Daryl D. 1979. **Truck Drivers In America**. Lexington, MA: Lexington Books.

14

NO TIME FOR CRASHES

Although Randy completed a thirty hour work stint on Thursday, he was telephoned by his dispatcher to prepare for a return trip to Vancouver Friday. His scheduled departure time was five p.m. The trip's itinerary included a detour to Calgary where he was expected to pick up pallets of goods. The additional cargo in Calgary pleased Randy because it gave him a bigger payload, making the trip back to the West Coast more financially lucrative. Without the Calgary cargo, his assigned load in Edmonton barely covered his fuel costs. To help Randy realize a profit, the company dispatcher made a special effort to arrange for a back-up load.

Randy's work day began at six a.m when he drove to different warehouses building his cargo. It was not strenuous work, but nevertheless, time-on-the-job. I caught up with Randy at two in the afternoon while he was waiting for his final load at a sandwich factory. The trucker was happy to see me again.

While we waited to load, Randy told me that although he had been on the job since six in the morning, he did little work. He took an hour for lunch, and played video games for another hour while waiting at a warehouse in south Edmonton. Because the loading procedure was a last minute assignment, there was little he could organize beforehand.

We lazed around in the truck in front of the sandwich factory until three thirty p.m. at which time Randy was called to back-up his truck to the loading dock. During the loading, Randy closely monitored the action, studiously counting each box to make sure the official count on the shipping form was correct. He double-checked the numbers, because if any items are missing at destination he is financially penalized. The predominant assumption is that the trucker lost, stole, or ruined pieces of cargo. It is seldom assumed that the shipper erred, miscounted, or cheated.

We finally left Edmonton at four thirty in the afternoon. The sandwiches and other goods were so light that the charge-out rate for the shippers was for space rather than weight, an option some companies pass on to the owner operators to increase their income for loads.

The rush-hour traffic did not unfold as expected, allowing us to breeze along the Yellowhead Road to the city's south side where we connected onto Highway Two otherwise called the Calgary Trail. This stretch of freeway is a four lane one hundred and fifty mile straightaway commuter highway between Edmonton and Calgary. The layout of the road is classic for inducing trucker boredom. To the left and right are flatlands, wheat fields, grazing pastures and an odd clump of trees. There are few demanding turns or uphill climbs.

Our entry onto the Calgary Trail was greeted by a heavy rain shower. The southbound side of the six lane highway was freshly paved, without painted lane markers making it difficult for a driver to determine exact location on the road. The deluge of water formed pools of shallow water on the road's surface. Randy was unfazed, stuck to the outer part of the roadway and drove a hundred kilometers per hour (sixty-five mph). That was, in a nutshell, the highlight or, from another perspective, the lowlight of the trip. Twenty kilometers (twelve miles) later the clouds passed over us and the rains ceased, leaving two rainbows, one bright and a second one hazy to bear witness of the downpour.

As I already implied, truckers regard the Calgary Trail as a boring stretch of highway. To keep their mind from wandering and/or to stop fatigue from setting in, truckers deploy a series of strategies. Randy's first line of defense is liberal use of the radio. His ultra-modern, powerful six hundred dollar AM/FM radio/cassette player can pick up Edmonton's rock 'n roll station up to one hundred kilometers (sixty-five miles) from Calgary, where Randy switches stations to Calgary's country and western station, and lets the music blare. At the point of station change, Randy can feel Calgary coming near. It is no longer the distant goal he had in Edmonton.

On this trip, I again witnessed inter-trucker communication for "collegiality" and for holding back boredom. Although the Calgary Trail has a wide median between north and south bound traffic, Randy waved to nearly every truck traveling north to Edmonton. During the storm Randy waved. At times the median widened so much that it was nearly impossible to distinguish drivers. Randy continued to wave. His hand movements represented an ongoing greeting ritual with anonymous colleagues. It was like a reflex action Randy uses to fight boredom.

About forty kilometers (twenty-five miles) south of Edmonton we passed a highway sign announcing that the Royal Canadian Mounted Police monitors truckers' CB radios on channel nineteen. This was the first time I witnessed the police advertising their CB monitoring procedures. Randy informed me that the intent for the signs is to inform truckers on how to reach the police in emergencies.

Near the Red Deer turn-off Randy pointed to a north bound flatbed with a double sleeper. He loved the look of the double bunk bed units, intending to buy one someday. His wife had already telephoned Kansas and inquired about costs. In addition to Randy's trade-in, the new sleeper would be seven thousand dollars American. According to Randy, the same sleeper in Canada would cost about twenty-two thousand dollars. It was a big price to pay for the image of owning luxury. For Randy it was worth it. As an owner operator, his image depended on the looks of his truck. To run a sharp unit with a classy looking sleeper costs money. Randy's discussion about the sleeper never featured practicality. It only focussed on looks.

Image has always been important to Randy. He purchased a red Peterbilt tractor because it "looked great." He refuses to haul for companies whose uncool colors are green or robin egg blue. An anteater design truck does not equate with Randy's visions of a "real truck," one that owner operators drive. Headlights have to make a statement – round and visible, not square and retracted. Before we left Edmonton Randy increased the distance between the trailer and cab for the simple reason that, "It looks good on the highway!"

The Edmonton to Calgary run involved an average speed of a hundred and ten to a hundred and fifteen km/hr (seventy to seventy-five mph) for a highway whose posted speed limit is a hundred km/hr (sixty-five mph). Occasionally, we were passed by other big rigs whose speed exceeded a hundred and thirty km/hr (eighty mph). Because of the light load, Randy was prepared to drive fast, although this particular trip required little incentive for increased speed. He did not have to make a warehouse delivery in Vancouver until ten a.m. Sunday morning.

At twenty minutes to nine we arrived at L Transport's Calgary warehouse. The shipper stayed late so Randy could load immediately and would not have to wait until Saturday morning. Five pallets of processed meat were loaded.

Once the pallets were stowed away in the trailer, the warehouse worker asked us if we needed anything else – cassette players, Reebock runners, CBs. Top quality for a few dollars! If we want it, his friend can deliver it. No questions please, was the bottom line. Randy expressed interest in a new radar detector. He desired the same cheap price he paid for his first one. The shipper promised to look into it and to have an answer the next time Randy arrived. Knowing that I would likely never see this man again I asked about car radios. "No problem," he said. "What kind? With or without speakers?" He would check into it for me. It surprised me that the shipper would make this offer to a stranger. With such up-frontness I doubt that it will be long before he is corralled for selling "stolen goods."

We left Calgary at nine thirty p.m. Randy turned on his radar detector and concentrated on driving. It was dark and few words were spoken. Around twelve midnight I crawled into the sleeper for a nap. At two thirty a.m. Randy turned into the Golden truck stop. The noise of the engine brake and change in direction and speed woke me. Randy was tired and wanted to sleep. He could afford to rest on this trip because there was no immediate time demand for his arrival. While Randy lay in his sleeper, I sat in the restaurant interviewing waitresses and analyzing field notes.

At the Truck Stop

At the Golden restaurant there were no telephones for the trucker's convenience. Also there was no jukebox blaring or gregarious waitress waiting to hit on truckers for a tip. Instead, it was quiet. A few truckers were eating and three young ladies, low-key, quiet and business-like serviced the restaurant. I spoke with them whenever a slack time appeared. Yes, truckers were real characters. They were fun and for the most part harmless. Several issues the waitresses mentioned were presented in the form of jokes.

Do truckers complain? All the time! A popular joke shared by waitresses was:

Q.   What do you call a basement full of truckers?
A.   A wine cellar.

Q.   What is the difference between a baby and a trucker?
A.   A baby knows when to quit whining.

According to a waitress named Cindy, truckers complain about everything; government, the police, wives, traffic, weather, companies, loads, other truckers. Most truckers who come to this truck stop are regular line drivers who sit together when they arrive and "bitch."

Truckers commonly invite Cindy for a date. However, an informal pact or a policy among the ladies at the restaurant is that they never leave for home with a customer. When overtures are made, the waitresses try to answer with a joke or a laugh. Cindy acknowledged that this kind of response "is not very nice," but it is effective. According to the waitress, truckers "don't get too far here."

A creative approach recently used by a trucker to familiarize himself with Cindy focused on income tax. He asked Cindy to write her home address and telephone number on the back of his meal receipt, in case he needed proof of his meal expenditure marked on the receipt. Cindy did not fall for the ploy. She refused to sign. Instead she did the customary thing by initialing the trucker's receipt. Although there was some original persistence, eventually the driver smiled and conceded defeat.

By five a.m. I consumed upwards of ten cups of coffee and visited the washroom at least as many times. Needing to stretch my legs, I went for a walk around the parking lot. Randy just woke up. With the reefer running Randy managed to get three hours of broken sleep.

He showered and had a quick breakfast, appearing relaxed and refreshed. On this trip Randy's time was his own. By not hauling sausages or other meats with a deadline, Randy had the luxury of easing his driving pace. We left Golden, British Columbia, at six a.m.

Toward the Canyon: Toward Accidents

Just outside of Golden Randy hit the hundred km/hr (sixty-two mph) mark again. Daylight was upon us. Two cars were ahead. Randy stepped on the gas and passed the first one – re-entered his lane – pulled up within a couple of yards of the next car driven by a lady, veered out and passed. The car driver looked like she was in shock. A semitrailer approaching quickly, tailgating and passing – all within a few seconds, can indeed be a scary episode. Randy recognized that he may have "freaked her out," however, it was a preventative strategy. He did not want to trail a car driving thirty-five km/hr (twenty-two mph) through the canyon several miles ahead. Randy considered it to be a hazard for truckers. To compensate, he tries to pass every car he can before he reaches the Fraser Canyon.

He has a particular dislike for retired people. According to Randy, they are tourists driving slow and enjoying the scenery. Similar to Karl in Chapter Twelve, Randy criticized them for not appreciating truckers. They forget that truckers "are in a hurry and have seen the scenery a million times."

True to his word, Randy passed two more vehicles on the way to Revelstoke, a distance of about seventy-one kilometers (forty-four miles). In the process, he tailgated a sedan and a recreational vehicle, something he does with a truck but hates when other drivers do it while he drives his family car. It was further proof of my description in chapter four that for truckers operating a semitrailer entails different rules of behavior than driving the family sedan. In a truck Randy feels omnipotent:

> No sense in worrying about what the guy behind you is going to do because whatever he does, it's his fault. He runs into the back of you, it is no fault of yours. He is going to get the worst of it anyway. Just drive your road. We are out here making a living. They got all the time in the world to get where they are going . . . I got a nice big bumper back there. It is hard enough to cope with all the people behind you.

We were about six hundred kilometers (three hundred and seventy miles) from Vancouver. I felt exhausted, having slept very little during the night.

Randy's eyes were beginning to burn, defined by him as a normal irritation. We were approaching Sicamous, heading towards Kamloops. Shuswap Lake, a resort for houseboaters, lay quietly on our right. Because the weather was dreary, few boats could be seen breaking the waves.

In Sicamous the speed limit was sixty km/hr (thirty-seven mph). Randy continued traveling at a hundred km/hr (sixty-five mph). Downhill around a bend was a slow moving motor home that forced Randy to slow down. Randy used the engine brakes, then the foot pedal. He was frank about his braking. He is the only person who set the brakes on his truck so he knows exactly what is happening. To see if there is an air leak, he keeps a close eye on his gauge and he applies the brakes whenever he is stopped.

Randy considered the government roadside brake checks to be a waste of time, a total nuisance. He set his brakes "the other day" and, according to Randy, "They're going to be good for a minimum of two weeks before they even remotely need adjustments." Randy believed that after two weeks of use, his brakes will still pass any roadside check because he "know(s) how to drive." By using the engine brakes most of the time, Randy asserted he is, "Barely using ten pounds of air." Also, whenever he "hits a hill" he grabs the gears and "goes down properly."

Akin to Simon, who called owner operators non professional, on the subject of brakes Randy labeled the company drivers "a bunch of assholes." He describes his feelings:

> They come to work all nice and clean and spiffed up. They got their uniform and their truck is sitting there. It is supposed to be serviced, safe, ready to go and they get their trailer number and off they go and hook up and off they go. They should be climbing under and checking every single brake on that trailer because they don't know who drove it last. They don't know if the guy before them used the brakes heavily or even checked them to see if they were set up.

According to Randy, once company drivers get to the top of a hill they go down with their foot on the brakes. While Randy claims to get four hundred thousand miles on a set of brakes, company drivers barely get half.

We were about twenty miles from Cache Creek, traveling about a hundred km/hr an hour when a Suzuki Samurai, approached us from the opposite direction passing both a car and camper. He experienced difficulty returning into his lane. The jeep came towards us head-on. Fortunately, the driver of the recreational vehicle saw the potential for danger. He drove on the shoulder to allow the Suzuki back into the lane. Randy laughed at the events. Close calls such as this are facts of life for truckers. If worse came to worse the four-wheel driver would have been forced to ditch the vehicle because Randy was not prepared to jeopardize his cargo for the safety of such a driver.

The Accident

A half hour later we were driving through the Fraser Canyon, a stretch of highway that invites crashes. We were around Boston Bar heading towards Hell's Gate when before us a lady suddenly slowed down. By keeping up his speed Randy was quickly upon her. For a moment she appeared to be puzzled, not being sure of what to do. Finally she drove off the road on to the shoulders. As she slowed down we sped beside her.

The woman then made an unexpected move to re-enter the highway, but quickly changed her mind when she saw the speeding semitrailer beside her. So she drove into a gravel parking lot and jammed on the brakes. The gravel flew as she slid toward the canyon embankment. She missed the approaching ravine by about a foot.

As this was happening a police cruiser whipped by, lights flashing, sirens blaring. Randy was totally surprised that a squad car was following us. He figured that the lady might have seen the police car and reacted to the flashing lights and siren. She may have become frightened and hit the shoulder. Whether it was the police car or Randy's truck that led to the dangerous situation is a question to which we have no answer.

About two miles ahead we saw the object of the police officer's attention. Cars and trucks were lined up on both sides of the highway. No less than four police cars were on the scene with people milling around. There was a kind of black excitement among them. A macabre expectation of a driver's misfortune. But, there was no sign of a crash. Somebody drove over the cliff – down the Fraser Canyon. The scenario was a scary one. We slowed down, but did not stop. According to Randy, the whole series of events was normal. We had experienced "just" another close call with the lady driver and "just" another accident, similar to the one he witnessed "last Monday." He sees crashes every week. The ones that stand out in his mind are those that involve trucks. For a complete description of trucker involvement in crashes, please refer to the Appendices.

On August 30, 1989, the "Hope Standard," a local newspaper, reported the event accordingly:

Crash Kills Woman

A New Westminster woman was killed Saturday morning when the car in which she was riding crashed down a 50 meter embankment, off Highway 1. Two other people were injured.

Dead is May Roberge, 92, a passenger in the 1979 Mercury Zephyr driven by her son Louis Campbell, 64 of 100 Mile House. The incident occurred 16 kilometers south of Boston Bar.

Boston Bar RCMP are doing a mechanical check on the car to see if anything had gone wrong with the vehicle. Police believe Campbell may have pulled over to the shoulder and in an attempt to turn around on the highway backed up too far, sending the car off the edge of the road down the embankment.

Campbell's wife, Angeline, 57 was sent to Fraser Canyon Hospital with a broken rib, but has since been released.

Campbell is still in hospital with a fractured wrist and a few other cuts.

Sgt. Dave Holmes of Boston Bar's RCMP detachment said the car was found upside down at the bottom of the embankment, where police, two ambulances, Hope Search and Rescue, and a traffic analyst attended the scene.

The investigation is continuing.

Gabrielle Werner
Hope Standard
August 30, 1989

Continuing to Vancouver

Regardless of his personal observations of severe crashes on the highway, Randy was determined to speed up, because he suddenly remembered that he had to reach his bank before three p.m. and deposit his cheque. His wife's shopping plans for Saturday depended on it.

We drove straight through from Golden to Yale, a distance of about six hundred kilometers (three hundred and sixty-five miles). At Yale we stopped at a restaurant to use the washroom but, as luck would have it, it was closed for repairs. I hurried to the hotel next door and relieved myself. Randy did not want to take the time, although he needed to. Instead he bought some popcorn, something of a tradition for him. We then sped off to Vancouver with Randy tailgating any vehicle he intended to pass. He was driving very fast, trying to reach the bank before closing time.

Around two thirty p.m. we arrived at the bank in the heart of Langley's business section. To get there Randy drove through tight streets not intended or allowed for semitrailer trucks. Randy was so near to his destination that he cared little about driving an eighteen wheeler through a residential part of the city, a bylaw violation that would cost him fifty dollars and earn him two demerit points on his driver record. Randy's wife and daughter, were waiting for him at the bank. They greeted him excitedly.

Once the banking business was completed, Randy, with his family aboard, drove to an outlying area near Langley where he parked and unhooked his trailer, reefer going full bore. He joked about a neighbor who complained bitterly that the reefer kept his family awake at night. Randy shrugged his shoulders. What could he do?

Randy drove me to North Vancouver, a special trip that took him and his family two hours out of their way. I thanked everyone and jumped out. A quick wave and Randy was off.

I tried to telephone Randy on Monday. No luck. His wife answered. Randy was already in Edmonton. He left Sunday evening for another trip.

References

Bowman, B.L., and Hummer, J. 1988. **Literature Review Summary Examination of Truck Accidents on Urban Freeways.** Federal Highway Administration Report No. RD-88-167. McLean, VA.

British Columbia Ministry of Solicitor General. 1988. **1987 Traffic Accident Statistics.** Victoria: Motor Vehicle Branch.

Golob, T.; Recker, W.; and Leonard, J.D. 1987. "An Analysis of the Severity and Accident Duration of Truck-Involved Freeway Accidents." Presented at the 66th Annual Meeting of the Transportation Research Board, January.

Oregon Public Utility Commission. 1987. Truck Driver Profiles in Traffic Offense Conviction Rates. Salem, OR: Public Utility Commission.

Oregon Public Utility Commissioner. 1985. Truck Inspections and Truck Association of Oregon: Statistics and Summary. Salem, OR: Public Utility Commissioner.

Sparks, G.; Bielka, J.; Smith, A.; Marzolf, D.; and Neudorf, R. 1987. **The Safety Experience of Large Trucks in Saskatchewan.** A report submitted to Saskatchewan Highways and Transportation, Regina, Saskatchewan.

15

A LOOK BACK AND AHEAD

In the 1978 movie, "Convoy," we witness trucking figures as Rubber Duck, the Michelangelo of Truckology, Lyle "Cottonmouth" Wallace, the sneaky snakey ole bear, Love Machine, a queenless driver, Dangerous Curves, and Widow Woman, the lady trucker enough to take on four husbands. The movie was about "men and women who fought the Great War of the Open Road." (Norton, 1978)

The characters in the movie, although still alive in many people's minds as the "real truckers of the day" have been surpassed by modern day truckers, who are less bent on sensation and violence and more concerned about challenging the system in a rational and peaceful manner. On a daily basis, they negotiate or manipulate safety rules and regulations not to make a social statement, but to enhance their earning potential.

Drivers described in the foregoing chapters represent trucker ideal types in North America. In calm desperation, these drivers cheat on their log books, take drugs, drive over the legal limit of consecutive driving hours, drink beer, disobey road signs, escape police activities, skirt weigh scales, and/or operate vehicles that are poorly maintained and mechanically unsafe. Their behaviors are not sensational unless they result in major crashes where one or more of the factors are featured as cause for the accident.

Challenging the laws and regulations are common everyday occurrences, fully known by truckers and police alike. They are part of the recipe knowledge truckers use to achieve their goals. For example, because freight rates are low, over-the-road truckers maximize their driving hours to compensate for reduced hauling rates per mile. Owner operators, like Dale in Chapter Four and Randy in Chapter Thirteen, and company drivers, like Danny in Chapter Six and Tim in Chapter Eleven, are prepared to drive from two to fifteen hours over the legal limit if they believe circumstances warrant it. To cover their actions, they enter false hours on their log books, or they employ two or more log books. Such practices do not represent an ethical dilemma for the drivers. They do not employ them to destroy the system or make a statement. Rather they are practised to help truckers make a living.

In the movie, Convoy, the Rubber Duck's basic issue was the fifty-five mph speed limit and high rise in fuel costs. Today, the specific point of contention is declining freight rates, increasing costs of truck maintenance and an increasing encroachment of government safety regulations.

American government deregulation of the transportation industry was considered by all truckers I met as the linchpin for today's problems. Although it made it easier for would-be truckers to enter the field and it provided a streamlined process for truckers to haul goods between states, the final fallout was perceived by truckers to be negative. According to drivers, deregulation led to increased competition for loads, declining rates, increased monopolization of the industry through corporate mergers and growth, and finally, increased government involvement in regulations.

In my observations and conversations with truckers, it has become apparent that deregulation led to a political/economic reality that contributed to the formation of a two tiered trucking system. The first tier is composed of company drivers, who are paid a flat rate per mile, social and health benefits, in addition to reimbursement for loading/unloading and show-up time. In this class are the line drivers, like Giddyup Quick Freight and Tim, whose trips are rigidly defined by time and distance and over-the-road drivers, like Danny and BJ, whose hauls can take them anywhere in North America. These drivers are not responsible for vehicle maintenance, and depending on the company, they earn enough money to make a decent living. Line drivers have the additional advantage of being at home at regular times.

Some of the large national and international companies for which these truckers drive pride themselves on their emphasis on safety, regulations and driving professionalism. Yet on an individual basis, each company is prepared to negotiate its commitment to safety on the basis of economic intensity. For example, Tim's company wanted him to continue driving a truck with a flat tire to reduce the cost of repairs. P Courier had no daytime running light policy despite research proving it to be successful. Danny's company expected him to drive beyond the legal driving hours to finish a haul. Still, these drivers and their companies consider themselves to be the upper class of trucking.

At the bottom of the trucker class system are the owner operators who shoulder the burden of economic intensity and government regulations. They drive for rates that barely keep them financially afloat once they deduct expensive vehicle maintenance and operating costs from their gross pay. With the transportation industry increasingly pressured by large company interests, owner operators are finding it more and more difficult to stay profitable. So they cut corners often at the expense of safety. For example, Dale in Chapter Four drove all night without headlights and engine brakes, Ted in Chapter Eight drove through a tunnel restricted to hazardous materials free trucks with dangerous goods on board and Randy drove for thirty-plus hours consecutively, actively speeding and tailgating. Risks are continuously taken by owner operators not so much to receive gains but to avoid taking losses.

The Controlling Variable

In most cases, whether drivers are employed by companies or they are contracted as owner operators by leasing divisions, the main controllers of events are the dispatchers. Their principal role is to transport goods, not to ensure safety. The latter concern is assigned to fleet safety supervisors (if companies have them) or the drivers themselves. According to dispatchers, professional driving includes awareness of safety.

Dispatchers assign loads to truckers. They demand that drivers attend to all factors for delivery of loads. Although truckers have the legal right to disobey, and in extreme cases of hazardous/illegal driving expectations, report dispatchers to the authorities, they seldom do so. It would be like ratting. With the support of management, dispatchers do whatever they can to encourage profits. To help them achieve this goal, dispatchers discipline drivers who challenge their orders or who are unable to meet their demands.

In Chapter Six we have Danny who was ordered by the dispatcher to drive six hours over the legal limit, despite the fact that he already put in a day's work. Vic, in Chapter Two, spoke about being assigned to unprofitable runs for a month for refusing to fulfill his dispatcher's demand.

Dispatchers told me that if a lucrative load had to be delivered and if either the assigned driver or vehicle were not in peak form, the cargo would be hauled regardless. A fatigued driver and/or a poorly maintained truck will be expected to haul the load. If a weigh scale needs to be missed, the dispatcher may organize it accordingly. Yet in the event of a police inspection, the driver is on his own. He becomes the victim or the fall guy for the dispatcher.

Truckers feel vulnerable in the dispatching game. They can receive more downtime because dispatchers may reassign loads to other drivers or withhold cargo previously scheduled. If truckers decide to repair their vehicles instead of making trips expected by dispatchers they lose the revenue of the immediate trip and future revenues because of dispatcher's retaliations. If truckers decide to fulfill the dispatcher's demands and drive poorly maintained vehicles, they may get caught by the police and suffer legal repercussions at the hands of the highway patrol.

For the most part, company drivers, but moreso owner operators, are subordinates in the transportation industry. They are told what to do, how to do it, and when it is to be done, regardless of legalities. Unfortunately not enough attention is paid to this side of trucking when it comes to police enforcement and legislation. As Simon, the driver in Chapter Five told me, "We're the guys who always get crapped on. When it comes to being screwed, the buck stops here."

Problem Number One: Drugs and Alcohol

Repeatedly, owner operators and company drivers told me that from their perspective there is no more pressing safety risk than the trucker's perceived or real use of illicit drugs and alcohol. Based on my research, trucker use of drugs follows a contingency model where trucker take drugs to avoid potential loss in time, money and dispatcher acceptance. They pop pills when demands are so tough that they seek artificial help in gaining alertness and road awareness. I seldom found truckers who take drugs to promote a career of use.

Dale, described in Chapter Six, typified the contingent user. He took drugs to compensate for the pressures placed upon him by his dispatcher. To keep his job he pleases his dispatcher whose demands push Dale to depend on chemical assistance. He takes drugs to delay or retard fatigue so he can drive for a longer period of time beyond the hours-of-work regulations. Pink ladies, white crosses, black beauties or other amphetamines are the drugs of choice truckers pop to retain mental and physical alertness on the road.

Fighting boredom is a second reason truckers rely on drugs. On long straight stretches of flat highways truckers often become bored. Although many listen to loud music, smoke cigarettes and engage in other mental alertness techniques such as checking mirrors, observing the countryside and using the CB, some rely on bennies or uppers. If the drugs are in short supply, they can be readily purchased at truck stops or through the CB at convenient locations on the side of the road. To combat fatigue, some truckers choose cannabis and cocaine, or the more easily accessible and legal codeine. The main point is that based on trucker interviews, taking drugs is highly dependent on economic or job related pressures.

It was not unusual for me to hear older truckers speak about their biography of drug use. Many quit before they "became wasted." As they became more experienced and roadwise, they foresaw the dangers of continued drug use and instead relied on other techniques for staying awake and for controlling unreasonable demands made by their dispatchers. They became confident enough to say no to illegal requests, confident that if the dispatcher punishes them, they can wait it out.

Although every driver with whom I spoke was aware that drug use is a problem in trucking, the problem definition was usually presented in quantitative rather than qualitative terms. Informal estimates of drug use in trucking ranged from twenty-five to seventy-five percent. Mental and physical damage arising from drug use and leading to risky driving conditions was never considered to be a major point of discussion. Truckers argued that each driver's behavior is unique, depending on his level of stress, psychological make-up and outlook on his job. Truckers questioned laboratory tests that do not account for factors such as driver fatigue, expertise, experience and motivation to deliver loads safely, yet suggest drugs have a detrimental affect on driving performance.

Although drivers generally agreed that too many truckers take drugs, they were concerned about being made the scapegoat of a broad social problem. They suggested that researchers and officials pay greater attention to overall societal use of drugs. Because estimates on truck driver use of illicit drugs are seldom compared with use in other industries, truckers rejected the claim that they are an isolated case demanding attention. They considered themselves to be convenient scapegoats for problematic behaviors shared by all members of society.

The scapegoat thesis was often mentioned when truckers were asked about mandatory urinalysis tests. Users and non-users, company drivers and owner operators agreed that regardless of whether they would participate in the tests, mandatory urinalysis tests conflict with their constitutional rights. Mandating drug testing for truckers without parallel procedures for other groups of people constitutes blatant discrimination, an assessment that offends all truckers. Why should they, as a group, alone carry society's burdens on their backs?

The truckers may feel stigmatized, but they are not the only ones forced to become involved. As of December 18, 1989, four million workers with safety related jobs were subject to random drug tests. Besides truckers, they included workers for the Federal Aviation Administration, Coast Guard, Federal Railroad Administration, Research and Special Programs Administration and Urban Mass Transit Administration besides truckers (Cushman Jr., 1989: A16).

Use of alcohol entails a different rationale. To drink liquor above the legal age in Canada and the United States is not a breach of the law. Consequently, many truckers do not define it as a problem. It becomes illegal when truckers drink alcohol above certain BAC rates (usually .05, .08 or .1 depending on the state or provincial jurisdiction) and then drive. To have a few drinks, and drive, is not necessarily an offense. However, it should be stated that the United States Bureau of Motor Carrier Safety does not allow any consumption of alcohol while driving. The effort of enforcement by the police is limited.

Because truckers are most likely to be legal when they have a few drinks and drive (e.g., below .04 BAC for Interstate Commerce), generally speaking the amount they drink reflects in large part their own judgments. It is a trucker's personal assessment as to when he believes his driving behavior will be affected by how much alcohol. BJ in Chapter Seven judged it to be three beers. Unfortunately, some drivers misjudge the alcohol's influence on their behaviors because they have confidence in their driving skills and place a great deal of faith in their experiences as truckers.

A different line of reasoning underlying drinking and driving is the prevalence of company regulations. Some companies have a policy of strict abstinence. Drivers are monitored to assure adherence to the regulation. Any violation leads to quick dismissal. Other companies acknowledge that they have driver alcohol-use policies but they are reluctant to enforce them. A third group of companies have no drinking policy, placing the responsibility entirely on the driver. Owner operators, regardless of the fleet to which they are contracted, generally have no drinking policy to which they must abide. Their only concern is the law.

Problem Number Two: Fatigue

Truckers do not hold their heads in the sand when it comes to the prevalence and dangers of fatigued drivers on the road. They are seriously concerned about driver fatigue, assigning it as the number one cause of accidents. It became apparent, however, that they mistrust the essential meaning of fatigue because of confounding variables such as boredom, monotony, time on the job, physical exertion and driver motivation.

The featured argument about fatigue is not the trucker's disclaimer of it, rather the truckers' right to determine its oncome and their response to it. Truckers feel they are in control. They are capable of driving long distances, of compensating for possible fatigue-related physical/psychological decrements. They feel confident about their judgments on how much sleep their bodies and minds need. Hence they expect full jurisdiction on determining their hours of driving.

Most drivers do not follow the ten hour regulation in the United States and the thirteen hour law in Canada. Depending on circumstances of time, location, need and dispatcher demand, they are prepared to exceed the legal limits. To help them succeed, they cheat on their log books, a practise considered normal and prudent by most truckers.

Problem Number Three: Truck Maintenance

From the perspective of safety, two vehicle maintenance issues stand out for discussion. The first is brakes and the second is lights. The major focus on the braking issue is truckers driving with brakeless front axles and operating vehicles with brakes out of adjustment.

In the United States, trucks over ten thousand pounds must have front-axle brakes. The same law is not evident in Canada. However, Canadian truckers who regularly run south must abide by the United States regulation.

Many drivers, particularly Canadian ones, cling to the belief that front-axle brakes are a greater hindrance than they are a help. They place great faith on their experiences of having successfully driven trucks for years without front-axle brakes. A driver like Karl, a sixty-three year old line driver, refused to be swayed by research studies that proved trucks with front-axle brakes more than halve stopping distances and they help prevent jackknifing and spin-outs on ice and show. Many truckers trust their experiences more than they do science, clinging faithfully to their original beliefs. In the meantime, the chance of these drivers causing rear-end collisions or hitting oncoming traffic because of a spin-out on wet road is increased.

Also concerning the issue of brakes is the art of setting them. Normally, to set the brakes the trucker usually rotates the adjusting nut in the clockwise direction. However, some brake systems operate on a counterclockwise direction. An untrained driver may, therefore, adjust the nut in the wrong direction, rendering the truck brakeless. Based on police officers' estimates, most truckers operate vehicles whose brakes are not set properly. Consequently, they become safety hazards on the road.

Headlights, or conspicuity, is the second major issue that involves truck maintenance. Research has found that daytime running lights are significant innovations that reduce head-on crashes. Truckers and fleet carrier officials, however, are reluctant to use them, citing cost factors such as bulb burnout and battery drain. Consequently, few over-the-road vehicles were observed using daytime running lights.

Recommendation for Social Policy

At the risk of sounding naive, I am convinced truckers are never satisfied. However, they do have an articulated sense of right that reflects their needs for survival. These rights are interrelated with the demands of the economic and political system. I think that they deserve serious attention from down-to-earth policy developers and trucking officials concerned about safety.

The Right to Make a Decent Living

Few truckers expect to become rich driving a rig. But they expect fair remuneration for their work that allows them to meet the basic needs of their families without having to risk breaking the law. In light of this reasonable right I recommend that:

> the state and provincial governments review the rate structure for setting an industry standard minimum rate per mile or kilometer which is fair and equitable.

We already have minimum wage laws, which on the practical side may not reflect the actual cost of a suitable living, but it sets a philosophical precedent to help overcome worker exploitation. Truck crashes caused by truckers driving at high risk to make the illusive dollar, reach hundreds of millions of dollars. It would, therefore, be reasonable to develop an accurate cost benefit formula which establishes the negative and positive sides of a minimum but fair hauling rate, to be respected by the transportation industry.

The Right to Fair Working Conditions

The right to fair working conditions impacts the entire trucking industry. To date, most, if not all, regulations are directed at the trucker. Seldom are the dispatchers and/or fleet safety supervisors implicated. Yet it is here where many of the safety problems on the road originate.

To address the dispatcher influence, I make the following two recommendations:

> that dispatchers are properly educated at a recognized institution, whereupon they are certified by the state or provincial governments,
>
> that dispatchers are held more accountable by the legal authorities for their possible implications in the trucker operations on the road.

To date, few dispatchers have been formally educated about their role in the trucking industry. Yet they are in charge of transporting billions of dollars worth of goods and ordering thousands of truckers to make trips, many of which carry safety implications. Typically their credentials for dispatching are driving experience. I believe that safety is too important an issue to be given second rate attention by dispatchers whose major role is to make a fast dollar.

The education of dispatcher should be followed by rigorous assessment strategies to assure the public that these people know important aspects of the law, psychology of the driver, nature of the cargo and the capability of the vehicle. Upon graduation the dispatchers should be compensated appropriately in title, respect and salary.

In trucking, the dispatchers are often the silent contributors to crashes. They are complicators in breaches of the law and negation of safe driving practises. To correct this situation, greater attention should be placed on monitoring dispatcher activities through government audits and on-site observation and through specific police attention to dispatchers who are suspected of having directly contributed to truck crashes.

The Right to be Like Everyone Else

Concerning Drugs

There is little doubt that truckers are aware of drug problems in the trucking industry. Most would like to see the problem solved, but not by urinalysis testing. Truckers believe that this process scapegoats them and is an infringement on their rights. Whereas the latter is being challenged in the courts, concerning the former, I offer the following recommendations:

1. that increased police vigilance be administered on the highways to detect drivers who have taken drugs and/or alcohol.
2. that urinalysis tests be considered for other industries as, for example, construction, law enforcement, education and health services.
3. that more research be undertaken on drug use and truck driving and that the research of drug use in trucking be expanded to other relevant social groups.

Drugs and alcohol do not mix with driving. The dangers of the combination are well documented. Consequently, the legal system must continue, if not increase, its vigilance. This may mean that increased training for police officers and increased funding for manpower are necessary, and truck driver inspections become a higher priority.

For the sake of consistency, objectivity and uniformity, testing workers in a variety of areas becomes increasingly important. To isolate transportation workers for urinalysis is discriminatory. There are many employment areas where taking drugs and alcohol can lead to horrendous circumstances. Serious thoughts should be given to administering urinalysis tests here.

If other employment sectors are already involved in mandatory urinalysis programs, then an awareness program should be designed to educate truckers about the breadth of the policies. This endeavor would help alleviate suspicion and help erase the trucker accusation of being scapegoated for society's ills.

The Right to Learn

Truckers are busy people. They operate huge machines at high speed often on crowded roadways. Many are unaware of the changing technological features of their trucks, risks in driving, the research on general road user profiles and accident types in which truckers are involved. To address this problem, I recommend that:

> government agencies, community education/distance education organizations, fleets, insurance companies and other relevant agencies develop information/learning sheets that periodically address information topics based on research and that are structured in appropriate instructional format.

Truckers have a right to know about the latest research in their business. Awareness is the first step towards acknowledgment of a problem or situation and a hoped-for change in attitude and behavior. To promote this series of events, I believe professionally designed lesson plans and other information handouts should be prepared for truckers so that they stay abreast on vital technological, psychological, social and epidemiological information.

The Right to be Considered on the Road

Few people enjoy following a loaded semi trailer unit. Hence, they may take chances by passing the truck, then cutting in front of it, destroying the safety cushion a trucker has left with the vehicle in front. In short, motorists cut off truckers. To counter the trend, truckers reduce the chance of a car cutting in by tailgating cars ahead. Furthermore, many motorists tailgate trucks without considering the possibility of a flat tire, jackknife or loose equipment. Because of the large number of trucks on the highways, I propose that:

> the state or provincial motor vehicle departments and insurance companies develop literature for motorists that describes truck features, and the need for motorists to respect trucks by driving in appropriate fashion. The pamphlet could be presented to a driver upon renewal of license and/or insurance premium.

Truckers expect motorists to be aware of what trucks can and cannot do, and behave accordingly. This does not mean truckers secure themselves the right to drive any way they wish while motorists are pressured to be attentive. Rather, it makes the motorists aware that a flat tire on a truck may cause swerving or that a rig's braking capacity in an emergency is limited. Such information may be the first a motorist has ever received. It would certainly be valuable.

A Final Note

How safe is safe? To the truckers, safety means to earn a fair living, take a few risks, and anticipate a favorable outcome. If a fair living is difficult to attain, severe safety risks become negotiated options. Accidents happen, statistics are assigned, public outcry is noted. Benuzzi (in Mitchell, 1983), offered a quote from World War II that is insightful for the truck driver situation:

> At the front one takes risk, but one does not suffer; in captivity one does not take risks, but one suffers (in Mitchell, 1983:194)

The latter part of Benuzzi's quote is especially relevant to owner operators. If they do not take risks on the side of safety they may suffer economically. Any definition of trucker safety necessitates a broad institutional approach that covers the socioeconomic horizon. Once the perspective is broadened out, factors surface that are vital in determining the causes underlying driver actions. By attaining a more comprehensive description of truck driver behaviors within their socioeconomic environment, we are in an advantageous position to draft intervention strategies that "hit the mark." When we do this we are swimming upstream in the research world. We arrive at new destinations, unavailable to us if we were swimming with the tide downstream.

References

Agar, M.H. 1986. **Independents Declared: The Dilemmas of Independent Trucking**. Washington, DC: Smithsonian Institute Press.

Carson, W.G. 1982. **The Other Price of Britain's Oil: Safety and Control in the North Sea**. New Brunswick, NJ: Rutgers University Press.

Cushman Jr., J.H. 1989. "More Private Workers To Face Drug Tests." **New York Times**, National. December 18, 1989.

Glendon, A.I. 1987. "Risk Cognition." In W.T. Singleton and J. Havden (Eds.), **Risks and Decisions**. New York: John Wiley and Sons.

Heimer, C. 1988. "Social Structure, Psychology, and the Estimation of Risk." Annual **Review of Sociology**. 14:491-519.

Mitchell, R.G. Jr. 1983. **Mountain Experience: The Psychology and Sociology of Adventure**. Chicago: University of Chicago Press.

Norton, W. 1978. **Convoy**. NY: Dell Paperbacks.

Kahneman, D. and Tversky, A. 1982. The Psychology of Preference. **Scientific American** 246(1): 160-173.

Thomas, J.H. 1979. **The Long Haul**. Memphis: Memphis State University Press.

ACRONYMS

BAC   –   Blood Alcohol Concentration

CCMTA –   Canadian Council of Motor Transport Administrators

CDL   –   Commercial Driver License

CVSA   –   Commercial Vehicle Safety Alliance

DOT   –   Department of Transportation

DRE   –   Drug Recognition Expert

FHA   –   Federal Highway Administration

ICC   –   Interstate Commerce Commission

IIHS   –   Insurance Institute for Highway Safety

LTL   –   Less than Truckload Carrier

NSC   –   National Safety Code

OMC   –   Office of Motor Carrier

O/O   –   Owner Operator

OOIDA –   Owner Operators Independent Drivers Association of America

RCMP   –   Royal Canadian Mounted Police

TL   –   Truck Load Carriers

UMTRI –   University of Michigan Transportation Research Insitutue

APPENDICES

APPENDIX A
NOTES ON THE METHOD

THE OVERALL APPROACH

The task of this study was to apprehend and reconstruct, as closely as possible, the perspectives of trucking and safety from two different yet converging perspectives – one everyday involvement of truckers, the other empirical reconstruction of the trucking scene. Special attention was placed on the interrelationship between the two social worlds.

Standard statistical analysis of subsocieties and first hand accounts of social/cultural events, when used separate from one another present the investigator with problems. The first lacks information on the common-sense, or contextual factors that influence or determine thinking and behavior. The latter fails to provide data on the "overall picture" on attitudes, characteristics and other identifiable variables directly related to social phenomena. However, when standard statistical measurements complement everyday life descriptions we are in a position to generate a more total portrayal of social phenomena that maintains integrity in both perspectives.

Deciphering the Truckers' Perspective

A vital purpose of the study was to ascertain how truckers conduct themselves in naturally occurring truck driving settings. I did not intend to follow a stereotype passed through the pages of cheap magazines or the frames of sensationalist media presentations. I wanted to see trucking with a fresh vision to the point that it was possible.

A general description of the methodological approach to the trucker descriptions would be: truckers, dispatchers, police officers, waitresses, fleet supervisors and other related individuals were interviewed at length about their daily events, their opinions about their peers, relevant institutions, truck safety, family and each other. They were also observed behaving in various truck driving settings.

The Trip

To interview and observe truckers and others in their natural settings I participated in a truck driving trip that took me to different points in British Columbia and to Washington, Oregon, California, Arizona, New Mexico, Colorado and Alberta.

Through the Insurance Corporation of British Columbia's Commercial Vehicle Operations Department, I drove with fifteen different truckers throughout the trip. Each leg of the trip lasted from a minimum of five to a maximum of thirty hours. I spoke with another thirty drivers at different locations. In all nine drivers were company operators and six were owner operators. Of the forty-five truckers that were interviewed, twenty-two were owner operators.

Also interviewed in depth were seven police officers, three carrier managers, ten dispatchers, two safety supervisors, two motel managers, five truck stop waitresses, three service station attendants, and three weigh scale operators. The entire trip took a month.

The Interviews

Interviews were unstructured. Truckers were asked questions around certain issues, problems or features particular to trucking. Others were asked about information, inferences, attitudes, and perspectives given by the truckers. This process had several benefits. It provided alternative points of view to the trucker, created opportunities of doubt about certain answers that may have been "put ons" or falsifications, and it allowed for greater scope of the truckers' responses.

Arising from the many lengthy interviews was a corpus, an inventory of verbal artifacts and experiences. It served as a major source out of which grew my understanding of the truck driver landscape.

The interviews with truckers ranged with the amount of time I traveled with each driver. The average interview lasted eight hours with on-and-off conversation. All interviews were recorded on tape and transcribed. Shorter times were given to other interviews.

The following list of domains and question areas served as the skeleton of trucker interviews:

DOMAIN	QUESTION FOCUS
Driver – Self	1. Self and image of freedom, contentment while driving – solitude, loneliness
	2. Myths about self a trucker
	3. Lifestyle – role of truck in it

DOMAIN	QUESTION FOCUS
	4. Expectations of driving
	5. Future goals, hopes, dreams
	6. Getting into trucking
	a) years of experience
	b) quality of experience
	c) permanence of job
	d) driver training
	i training schools
	ii testing, psychology, skills, screening
Driver – Family	1. Relationships with family members
	2. Quality and quantity of time spent at home
	3. Recreation, hobbies
	4. Sleep opportunities
	5. Influence of driving on family
	6. Examples of + and – experiences of truck and family life
	7. Preparing for a trip
	8. Welcome after a trip
	9. Sex on the road or at stops (dare we ask?) (Jim Ryan told me of an actual case where it caused a crash)
Driver – Truck Driver Culture	1. Views on alcohol and drugs – testing
	2. Use of drugs by **other** drivers – how widespread within the industry
	3. Views on important features that make up truck driver
Driver – Machine	1. Meaning of the truck
	2. Perspective on cab layout
	3. Maintenance of truck
	4. Cost of truck
	5. Preference of truck
	6. Brakes
	a) Front wheel
	7. Safety procedures of truck
	8. Vehicle configuration, ability and safety
Driver – Other Driver (Truckers)	1. Stereotypes of drivers/hierarchy
	2. Preferences of other drivers
	3. Meaning of other drivers/other drivers' perceptions of him
	4. Risks other drivers take
	5. Collegiality factors
	6. Image of others
	7. Overall business sense
Driver – Business	1. Influence of dispatcher on life and safety
	2. Influence of management on life and safety
	3. Scheduling procedures

DOMAIN		QUESTION FOCUS
	4.	Company truck maintenance
	5.	Payment and profit
	6.	Loading, cargo size, unloading
	7.	Priority lists for trips
	8.	Distance of trips/time on the road
Driver – Union	1.	Role union membership plays on driving, safety, pay, etc.
Driver – Driving Conditions	1.	Road or highway conditions – pleasant to hazardous
	2.	Roadside hazards
	3.	Preferred and depreferred weather
	4.	Risk taking in hazardous conditions
Driver – Law	1.	Trust or mistrust of police
	2.	Police stereotyping truckers
	3.	Fairness of enforcement
	4.	Contacting other drivers re speed traps, etc.
	5.	CVIP program (perhaps this is under Policy below)
	6.	U.S. "zero tolerance" program
Driver – Weigh Scales	1.	General treatment
	2.	Burden or positive features of scales
	3.	Negotiating loads
	4.	Do they sometimes avoid scales (i.e., take alternate routes if possible)
Driver – Policy	1.	Use of log books and/or other recording devices
	2.	Policy on driving hours
	3.	View on deregulation – related to image, profit
	4.	Inspection centers
	5.	Licensing and interstate registration
Driver – Personal Economics	1.	Cost of living, quality of life
	2.	Output in relation to cost and profit
	3.	Effect on number and length of trips
Driver – Accidents	1.	Definition/stories about accidents
	2.	Definitions/stories about close calls
	3.	Personal involvement
	4.	Risks
	5.	Causes, real or imagined
Driver – Truck Stops	1.	Meaning of them
	2.	Possible drug trade
	3.	Location
	4.	Maintaining friendships and contacts on road (other truckers and people at stops – C.B. and truck stops, etc.)

Processing the Interview Data

The amount of data collected was voluminous. The first step was to transcribe the interviews onto hard copy. Once they were documented in tangible form I reduced the transcripts or divided the interviews into segments. The most prominent topic for each interview transcript became the focus for the description of that leg of the trip. As other interviewees, diverse in interest and roles, discussed the focus a systematic pattern in the corpus developed. At times the focus was narrowed to fit into the trucker-safety point of view.

Validation of the Data

The intent of interviews is to gather revelation of truths about "one humanscape to the occupants of another" (Agar, 1986; 13). To help assure that the description and interpretation of the data reflect as close as possible the accounted for reality, I followed several strategies.

First, I wittingly discussed a significant point made by one trucker with other truckers and related individuals. Secondly, whenever a significant point was made within the interview I allowed it to resurface later in the interview under the guise of a related focus. By spending upwards of twenty hours with a trucker, validating specific or changing meaning of a trucker's perspective is easier than it would be in a one hour face-to-face interview.

Content Analysis

A crucial ingredient for any ethnographic portrayal of human action is the analysis of documents, statistics and popular textual writings that describe the humanscape from another perspective. Written accounts on the subjects serve as important artifacts about activities in which truckers participate.

For the purpose of this study, research reports, published manuscripts, truck magazines, learned journal articles and government publications were analyzed in relation to specific questions, issues, features and problems that arose from the interview data.

Statistical Analyses

Two basic forms of statistical manufacture were used. One consisted of the British Columbia accident data base, the second resulted from survey research.

British Columbia Accident Data Base Analyses

The accident data base employed was constructed using data from police-reported injury-producing accidents occurring in 1986, 1987 and 1988. All injury-producing accidents in British Columbia were investigated by the police and, therefore, constitute a more reliable source of data than property damage-only accidents, many of which are self-reported. The obtained sample size of about 9,066 drivers with related accident, vehicle, claim and past driver record information provides ample scope for unbiased, meaningful comparisons amongst variables.

Chi square analysis was used whenever truck driver actions or behaviors were compared to other drivers. Where appropriate a subsample of accidents involving only truckers and other drivers was formed. Appendix C outlines important findings from the data analysis.

Surveys

Two surveys were reported. The first consisted of a series of attitude surveys undertaken in British Columbia and Washington. One was a "call-in" survey to identify perceptions of motorists who had a recent reportable encounter with a truck. Motorists who had: (a) a crash with a truck; (b) been involved in a non-crash, negative encounter with a truck; or (c) experienced a positive encounter with a truck, were asked to report to researchers located at the University of Washington, Washington, and the University of British Columbia in Canada. Appendix B provides a more detailed review of the survey.

APPENDIX B
IMAGE AND TRUCKERS SURVEY
FINDINGS

Image, Graphics, and Truckers:
A Trucker Survey

In the latter part of 1988, 145 semitrailer truck drivers in Washington and British Columbia responded to a 19 item questionnaire on image, graphics and behavior. The study, undertaken at Washington and British Columbia roadside locations, was intended to provide a sketch of reality, a glimpse of how graphics and vehicle imagery reflects driver attitude and behavior.

Drivers reflect the image of a well-known company. Many people see the truck and form opinions on the truck's appearance and how it is driven. The 1982 American Trucking Association study on the visual effect of truck imagery was carefully reviewed by a team of researchers (Harle, 1987). They concluded that:

> The 1968 study showed that an over-the-road tractor-trailer combination made 66 visual impressions per mile during daylight hours. Assuming an average annual mileage of 100,000, that's 6.6 million impressions per year.
>
> In 1977, a much greater exposure was found – 101 visual impressions per mile during daylight hours. For 100,000 yearly miles; 10.1 million impressions. (pg. 1)

The concept of truck imagery, company allegiance and driver behavior became a focus for a small West Coast study. By way of survey questionnaire we queried truckers and random motorists about perceptions on image features and trucking.

Truck Graphics, Driver and Company

Of the truck drivers that completed the questionnaire 76 percent replied that they prefer pulling trailers that clearly mark a company or industry name. Furthermore, 98.6 percent of the truckers agreed with the item,

"When you operate a unit which has large company or industry graphics on it, do you feel it is important to drive in a way that creates a positive image for the business?"

The data show that truckers in the study preferred to drive trucks with graphics that personify a company or an industry. But, do they feel more accountable to a company or industry when they operate such a unit? The answer appears to be yes. Eighty-one percent of the trucker respondents felt more accountable.

It appears, however, that accountability is not equated with a change in driver operating strategy. When asked, "Do you operate a unit with large company or industry graphics differently than a unit you operate without graphics?" only 20 percent answered affirmatively. Although 82.6 percent of the drivers believe that they are more closely observed by people when they operate a tractor-trailer unit with graphics, 70 percent would not change their driving behavior while ten percent offered no opinion on the matter.

The above results equate nicely with the data received from trucker interviews on the trip. They are proud of how they drive, no matter for whom they drive or the cargo they haul. Time and time again truckers clarified that they drive in a consistent manner–regardless of whether they haul hazardous materials, gasoline or paper rolls, and regardless of whom they haul for. With little hesitation drivers invoked the professional trucker principle, namely, as a professional, the trucker always drives cautiously and gets his load to his destination in a safe, efficient manner.

Interestingly, 77 percent of the drivers agreed to the question, "When you operate a unit with a large company or industry graphics, do you feel your driving style influences people's buying habits?" Thirty-seven percent answered "definitely so." Truckers know that they are being observed, and that people's judgments are positive. Their driving style does not change, regardless of greater attention or focus. Overall 97.2 percent of the respondents expressed that people develop an impression of the company or industry on the basis of the drivers' behaviors. Similarly 97.9 percent believed that people develop an impression of a company or industry from the overall appearance of the tractor and trailer.

Truck Drivers' Views on Motorists and Truck Graphics

Conventional wisdom suggests that motorists notice trucks and behave according to the looks of the truck and the operator's style of driving. To establish the extent to which people notice truck graphics and form opinions of the company and/or industry on that basis, we included several questions on the questionnaire.

To begin the description, a general question was asked of random truckers, "Do you feel motorists think trucks are threatening?" Seventy-two percent of the drivers agreed. A follow-up question was posed to the one hundred and forty-five truckers, "Do you think motorists feel trucks with graphics are less threatening than those without graphics?" The responses varied. Table One outlines the findings.

Table One
Truck Drivers' Views on Motorist Feelings of
Threat and Truck Graphics

Variable (n = 145)	Response Categories						
	No Response	Defi- nitely So	Probably So	No Opinion	Probably Not	Defi- nitely Not	Com- bined
Trucks with graphics are less threatening than those without graphics	.7% (1)	11% (16)	27.6% (40)	20.7% (30)	31% (45)	9% (13)	100% (145)

Table One shows a broad spectrum of support for graphics. Whereas 38.6 percent of the truck drivers agreed that truck graphics reduce motorists perceptions of threat, 40 percent disagreed while 21.4 percent expressed no opinion. (No response, 7% and no opinion, 20.7%.)

A relevant question was asked of truck drivers about their roadway maneuvers and motorist displeasure. Their perceptions are reported in Table Two.

Table Two
Truck Drivers' Perspectives on Truck Driver Behavior and
Motorist Displeasure

Variable (n = 145)	Response Rate
Truck driving maneuvers that upset motorists:	Percent
Slow Moving	33.8
Following Too Close	27.6
Passing a Motorist	12.4
Cutting off a Motorist	11.7
Left/Right Turn Squeeze	4.8
Speed/Driving Too Fast for Conditions	4.1
Lane Change	2.1
Missing Data	3.5
TOTAL	100.0

The most announced driving maneuver that truckers think upsets motorists is driving slow. In itself, slow moving is an inconvenience, especially on winding two lane highways with little opportunity to pass. It may become a cause for concern when motorists take risks to pass a slow moving truck.

Following too close or tailgating on the other hand is definitely unsafe, as can be a semitrailer truck passing a motorist and/or cutting off the latter. They can directly cause accidents or motivate motorists to overdrive their capabilities to stay ahead of a truck. The result may also be misfortune.

To see how the truck drivers' version of reality generally interfaces with motorists, a survey of the latter was also undertaken. The more relevant findings are herewith reported.

Image, Graphics and Truckers: A Motorist Survey

Like the truck driver survey, 186 motorists in Washington state and British Columbia were asked a series of questions at roadside stops. The items followed the conceptual trend established in the truck driver survey.

Truck Graphics, Driver and Company

Whereas 97.9 percent of the truck drivers answered that people develop impressions of a company or industry from the overall appearance of a tractor trailer, the percentage of motorists that agreed with the statement was 81.3 percent. Furthermore, 77.5 percent of the random motorists answered that people's impressions of companies/industries are also based on the truckers' driving styles.

Eighty-one percent of the truckers responded that they feel more accountable when driving a rig with company graphics. This enthusiasm for accountability or responsibility is not readily shared by motorists. In the survey only 56.4 percent of the motorists felt that truck drivers drive more responsibly when pulling a trailer with large company or industry graphic. Nearly 54 percent (53.8 percent) said they nearly always notice graphics on trucks while another 39.8 percent answered that they noticed graphics on trucks occasionally.

Threats

Are trucks a threat to motorists? The indication is yes but . . . . Although 72 percent of the truck drivers answered affirmatively, the number of motorists answering "yes" was 59.1 percent. The threat factor appears to be less relevant to motorists than truck drivers perceive. Of all the motorist respondents, 7.5 percent had crashes with trucks and 57 percent had negative experiences with truckers such as, for example, tailgating, lane jumping or driving too fast in rain/snow.

Consistent with motherhood and apple pie, 89 percent of the motorists felt that truckers should strive to create a positive image for the industry. Of course the majority of truckers agreed (96.5 percent).

Truck Driver Behavior

A parallel question for random motorists to that asked of truck drivers was, "What truck driving maneuver do you think upsets motorists the most?" The findings are reported in Table Three. For comparison, the truck driver percentages to the same question are also recorded.

Table Three
Motorist and Truck Driver Perspectives on
Truck Driving Behavior that Upsets the Motorists

Variable	Response Rates (%)	
	Motorists (n = 186)	Truck Drivers (n = 145)
Truck Driving Maneuvers that Upset Motorists:		
Following Too Close	34.9	27.6
Slow Moving	15.1	33.8
Cutting off a Motorist	13.4	11.7
Speeding/Driving Too Fast for Conditions	11.3	4.1
Passing a Motorist	7.5	12.4
Lane Change	5.4	2.1
Left/Right Turn Squeeze	4.3	4.8
Missing Data	8.1	3.5
TOTAL	100.0	100.0

There are some visual differences in answers provided by truck drivers and motorists. The latter stressed unsafe behavior such as "following too close," while the truckers stressed convenience such as "slow moving." Motorists did not judge slow moving to be an exemplary problem. The issue of speeding was more announced for motorists (11.3 percent) than it was for truckers (4.1 percent), whereas passing a motorist received more emphasis from truckers (12.4 percent) than it did from motorists (7.5 percent).

When motorists were asked about truck driving maneuvers which truckers fail to undertake, two categories were emphasized: "Pulling aside to let traffic by" and "keeping proper distance behind vehicles." Each item received a 30.6 percent response. Not driving according to conditions was the third behavior a group of motorists (26.9 percent) outlined as a trucker weakness.

Economic Follow-Up and Graphics

On the survey questionnaire motorists were asked two probing questions. What would they do if . . . ? The questions and results are tabulated in Tables Four and Five.

Table Four
Motorist and Truck Driver Perspectives on
Truck Driving Behavior that Upsets the Motorists

RESPONSES	ITEMS	
	Question 1	Question 2
	Action Motorist Should Take if Hit by a Driver of a Supermarket Truck with Graphics:	Action Motorist Should Take if Endangered by a Driver of a Supermarket Truck with Graphics:
	(%)	(%)
Complain to Store	43.5	69.9
Don't Know	33.3	8.6
Take no Further Action	6.5	3.2
Complain to Other Group(s)	4.3	11.3
Family Boycott Store	1.6	.5
Friends Boycott Store	0.0	.5
Other	10.8	5.9
TOTAL	100.0	100.0

A reading of Tables Four and Five brings several interesting possibilities to mind. First, based on motorist responses, the place of business is the focus for follow-up action. This is most announced in the event of a threat or danger posed to a motorist by a truck driver (69.9 percent) and not in the event of having been in an accident with a truck driver (43.5 percent). It appears that motorists either do not believe in the effectiveness of a boycott or they are doubtful of the concept. Only 1.6 percent of those surveyed suggested that motorists should encourage family members to boycott a store whose driver hit a motorist, while one percent proposed that family and friends boycott a store if a motorist was endangered by a trucker. Yet, when respondents were asked about possible follow-up strategies for positive encounters with truckers, eight percent answered that family and friends should be encouraged to continue or begin to do business with the driver's sponsoring business.

Table Five
Motorist Follow-Up Action After Positive
Encounter with Truck

RESPONSES	ITEM Action Motorist Should Take if Well Treated by Driver of a Supermarket Truck with Graphics: (%)
Complimentary Letter to Store	54.8
Take no Further Action	17.7
Don't Know	10.2
Complimentary Letter to Groups (e.g., Union, Truck Assoc.)	5.4
Family Begin/Continue doing Business with Store	4.8
Influence Friends to do Business with Store	3.2
Other	3.8
TOTAL	100.0

Motorists Speak About Negative Encounters
with Trucks, Image and Graphics

To broaden the field of enquiry we asked two hundred and sixteen (216) people who had negative encounters with trucks to discuss issues of importance to them, circumstances about their encounters, and whether they noticed graphics on the trucks in question. Through advertisement in Washington and British Columbia newspapers, we invited motorists to share their experiences by telephoning a hotline at the University of British Columbia, and the University of Western Washington.

Of the two hundred and sixteen motorists who telephoned to discuss their encounter with trucks, 36.6 percent represented crash involvement while the remaining 63.4 percent involved a negative incident such as tailgating or being cut off by the truck. Most often the crashes or incidents occurred in the summer months, most likely as the result of work responsibilities (20.4 percent), business (19.4 percent), entertainment (14.4 percent) or holiday travel (14.4 percent). Table Six illustrates the month of crash/incident happenings.

Table Six
Crash or Negative Incidents with Trucks
by Month

(n = 216) MONTHS	FREQUENCY (%)
July	17.6
August	17.6
September	9.3
October	9.3
November	7.9
June	6.0
May	5.6
March	5.6
December	4.2
January	3.2
February	2.8
April	2.8
Missing Data	8.3
TOTAL	100.0

Seventy-nine percent (79.2 percent) of the time the negative event occurred during daylight hours. Furthermore, most often the weather conditions were sunny (70.8 percent) and the road conditions dry (82.9 percent), and the visibility was good (86.6 percent).

Of the motorists who had been at odds with trucks 44.9 percent stated that they were aware of the products affiliated with the truck and 57.9 percent answered that they "generally notice graphics on trucks." An additional 29.2 percent responded that they "sometimes notice graphics on trucks."

Nearly 38 percent (37.5 percent) of the troubled motorists identified the graphics of the truck in question. Fifteen percent saw it at the side/back of a trailer while 22.2 percent spotted it on the side of a tractor door. Based on the truck drivers' behaviors towards motorists 35.2 percent thought negatively of the industry or company, and 31.5 percent did not change their point of view about the industry or company. Thirty-one percent (31.5 percent) failed to answer. Furthermore, 48.6 percent of the motorists did not nor do not plan follow-up action against the industry represented by the truck driver.

Two hypothetical questions were asked of motorists reporting a mishap, (a) "What action do you think motorists should take if they were **hit** by a supermarket truck with highly visible graphics and it was the truck driver's fault" and (b) "What action do you think motorists should take if they were endangered by a driver operating a supermarket truck with highly visible graphics?" The responses to the two questions are included in Table Seven.

Table Seven
What Would Motorists Do if Hit or Endangered by
Truck Drivers Operating Supermarket Trucks

Responses	If Motorist Hit by Truck Driver (%)	If Motorist Endangered by Truck Driver (%)
No Action	5.6	3.7
Have Family Boycott Store	1.9	1.4
Influence Friends to Boycott Store	.5	–
Complain to Store	47.7	56.9
Complain to Other Groups	7.9	
Complain to Authorities	12.0	16.7
Take Court Action	13.4	.5
Lay a Formal Charge	1.4	
Nothing/No Response	9.7	9.3
TOTAL	100.0	100.0

At first glance it seems that complaining to the store represented by the truck graphics is more relevant for motorists endangered by truck drivers (56.9 percent) than those hit by them (47.7 percent). Furthermore, more court related action is evident for crashes than dangerous situations.

How do these people generally feel about large trucks after having experienced negative encounters? Fifty-two percent (51.8 percent) are still negative, 18.1 percent are value neutral, and 25.9 percent feel positive. As a result of the mishap 53.2 percent of the motorists reported that they have changed their driving pattern around trucks. More specifically they now drive more cautiously (40.7 percent) and they are more aware (12.5 percent) of what the truck driver is doing.

APPENDIX C
TRUCK ACCIDENTS: A
STATISTICAL FORMULATION

Findings

Accident Time

Combination trucks operating in British Columbia were involved in 9066 distinguishable accidents through the years 1986 to 1988. Broken down by year and percent, of the 9066 crashes, 30.6 occurred in 1986, 30.9 in 1987 and 38.5 in 1988. When broken down in six hour time periods, the data group accordingly.

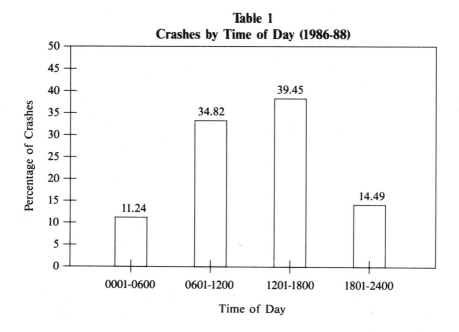

Table 1
Crashes by Time of Day (1986-88)

A further breakdown of time of day by year showed virtually no difference in percentage breakdown. The number of accidents by time proportional to the total number of crashes during the year was virtually identical for the three years in question.

To analyze further the significance of the number of crashes by time period, we require exposure data on truck traffic during different hours. This is especially relevant for the 12:00 Midnight to 6:00 a.m. time slot. The 11.2% of the total crashes happening during this time may be over represented because the traffic flow during these hours is extremely low.

The truck accident data breakdown by day of week is illustrated in Table 2.

Table 2
Crashes by Day of Week (1986-88)

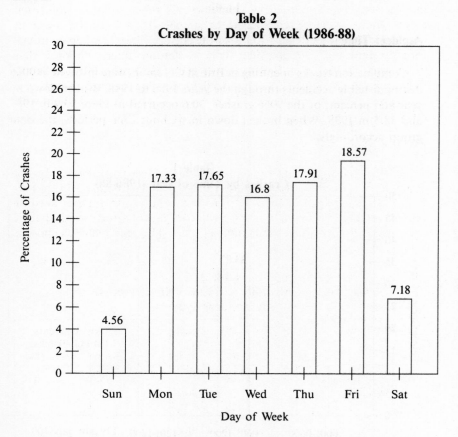

As we can see, the traditional work days, Monday to Friday have the bulk of truck accidents (88.26%) as do the traditional work hours 6:00 A.M. to 6:00 P.M. (74.27%).

Environment

One of the first questions anyone asks about crashes is, "where did it happen?" The analysis of the accident data base identified that from 1986 to the end of 1988, 47.9% of the truck-involved crashes occurred between intersections. Nearly thirty-four percent (33.8%) happened at intersections. A large number of crashes (16.8%) were not identified by location, leaving the remaining 1.5% of the truck recorded crashes for highway/freeway entrance acceleration lanes and/or ramps and at exit deceleration lanes/ramps.

For 10.9% of the total number of truck related accidents, the intersections were governed by traffic signals which were, for the truck driver, green (5.5%), red (4.2%) or amber (1.2%). Traffic signs at intersections were evident in 10.1% of the crashes. They breakdown to 8% for stop signs and 2.1% for yield signs. A cautious interpretation is that the colour of the signal light relates to the vehicle probability at fault.

During the time of the crashes, 58.5% of the time the roadway was dry, 22.2% wet, 9.7% snow/slush and 7.6% ice. Most often it was daylight with good visibility (70.5%).

Accident Types

Of the 9066 accidents documented, 6887 (76%) involved property damage only in excess of $400, 2016 (22%) produced bodily injuries and 163 (2%) resulted in fatalities. To provide a comparison without need of exposure data, we compared truck-involved accident severity with that of the overall number of accidents minus trucks. The year 1988 was chosen. Table 3 shows the findings.

Table 3
Truck vs All 1988 Accidents (Minus Trucks)
by Accident Type

Accident Types	Truck Accidents		All Accidents (Minus Trucks)	
	n	(%)	n	(%)
Property Damage Only	2729	78	98,458	76.2
Bodily Injury	710	20.3	30,225	23.4
Fatal	59	1.7	476	.4
Total	3498	100	129,249	100

A chi square analysis (goodness of fit test) of the data shows that the difference between the distribution of accident types for trucks and all other crashes minus trucks is 178.47. This is highly significant. Visually, we see that although there is less bodily injury reported for truck accidents than for all accidents minus trucks, more deaths result in truck accidents. The deaths are usually to the other driver.

Pre-Collision Truck Driver Action

The majority (51.5%) of truck drivers were categorized by the police as proceeding straight ahead at the time of, or immediately preceding, the collision. Turning right (9.7%) or left (7.6%) when combined, produced another important driver action contributing to crashes.

Somewhat unique, when compared to the overall accident statistics, is the prominence of actions under the title of "slow moving – stopping action." When we add variables as "starting," "slowing/stopping," "stopped," "parking/parked" and "backing," we compile a pre-collision rate of 18.3%. On the other end of the scale are actions that could be labeled "fast moving-overtaking." It was defined as the major pre-collision action 5.5% of the time.

When we take into account all of the recorded accidents in which trucks were involved, 15% of the truck drivers were judged to have probably caused the accident. This is definitely misleading because of collisions involving two or more trucks or single truck accidents and because much of the time the police do not include causal variables in the accident report forms. To compensate, we extracted truck-passenger car collisions to identify police charges.

Of special importance is to analyze the collision data according to truck driver and other driver, in light of constant trucker complaints that four wheelers (passenger car drivers) are poor drivers and they are impervious to truck driver's rights and problems.

In terms of official police charges against truck drivers compared to the charges against other drivers in collision with trucks, a percentage breakdown is featured in Table 4.

Table 4 indicates that truck driver and other driver perceptions are substantiated. First, truckers in the same collisions as other drivers were charged 13.4% on site versus 21.3% for other drivers. In relation to the number of charges truckers and other drivers received, truckers scored substantially higher on lane violations (trucks, 16.2%; cars, 9.7%), following too close (trucks, 16.2%; cars, 3.1%) and backing up (trucks, 10.7%; cars, .6%). If we recall in chapter six, it was tailgating and overtaking that people thought were the two primary driving evils in which truckers participate. According to the accident data, the perceptions are not without fact.

The major difference lies in the catchall category "other" where 70% of the automobile drivers who were charged were located compared to 50% of truck drivers. Speeding and driving without care (the latter of which is going through redefinition of the British Columbia Motor Vehicle Department) were charged more often to automobile drivers than they were to truck drivers.

Table 4
Truck Driver/Other Driver Charges in
Truck-Passenger Car Collisions 1986-88

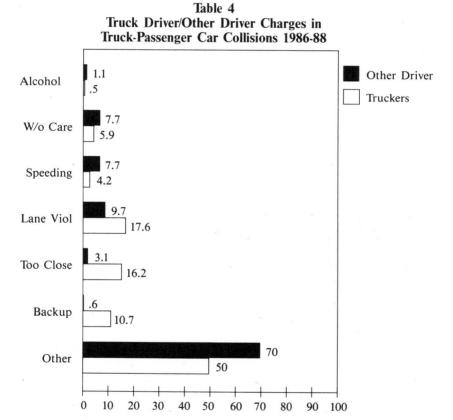

Percentage

Age

For the years, 1986 to 1988, by age the 25 to 34 year olds (31.6%) and 35 to 44 (26.9%) were the most heavily represented in the data. We do not know, however, the total number of British Columbia and visiting truck drivers that fall into the age groupings. Consequently, for descriptive purposes, the age breakdowns for accidents are given in Table 5.

Table 5
Truck Driver Age and Crash Involvement

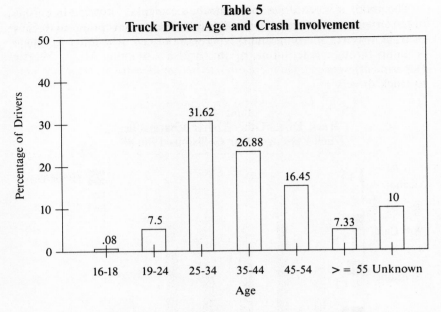

Of interest is that in British Columbia the minimum age for receiving a class 1 license (combination vehicle plus air brakes) is 19. Consequently, young driver accidents 16 to 18, prevalent in the general accident data is not evident in the truck accident data.

Let us return to the truck-passenger vehicle collisions to gain a more precise picture of age and crash involvement.

Of the 2991 accidents (1986-88) the breakdown of truck driver and other driver ages is recorded in Table 6.

The breakdown of age of truck drivers and other drivers in the same two-vehicle collisions is as might be expected. About sixty-three percent (62.7%) of the truckers were within the 25 to 54 year old range, compared to 57.2% of other drivers.

The big surprise is in the unknown. There is more missing data about truck driver ages (12.5%) than there is about other drivers (2.2%).

Proportionate to their involvement in crashes, a breakdown of truck driver and other driver being allocated possible offender by age are illustrated in Table 7.

The ratios in Table 7 show that the possibility of being the offender in a crash is little different by age between truck drivers and other drivers. The only age category worth reporting is for other drivers 16 to 18 years old of whom .42% were classified as possible offender in the crashes with trucks. For the truck driver population, the number involved in crashes, 16 to 18 years old was zero. As previously stated, this was primarily because of age restriction for receiving a license 1 with air brakes in British Columbia. The minimum age is 19.

Table 6
Ages/Truckers and Other Drivers in Same
Collisions 1986-88

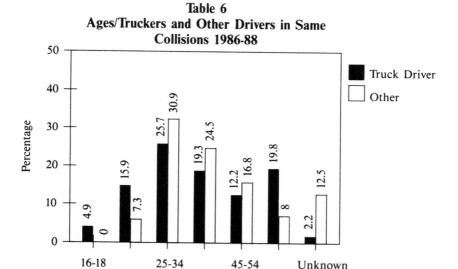

Table 7
Truck Drivers and Other Driver Charges by Age
in the Same Collisions 1986-88

Ages	Truck Drivers In Accidents	Truck Driver Poss. Off.	Ratio	Other Driver In Accident	Other Driver Poss. Off.	Ratio
16-18	0	0	0	147	62	.42
19-24	219	65	.30	477	140	.29
25-34	924	232	.25	767	211	.28
35-40	735	182	.25	579	154	.27
45-54	501	142	.28	361	82	.23
> 55	239	73	.31	594	179	.30